The Smart Investor's Guide to Real Estate

The Smart Investor's Guide to Real Estate

*Big Profits
From Small Investments*

Robert Bruss

Crown Publishers, Inc.   New York

Library of Congress Cataloging in Publication Data
Bruss, Robert.
The smart investor's guide to real estate.
Revised and updated.
Includes index.
1. Real estate investment. I. Title.
HD1382.5.B78 1982   332.63'24   82-1514
ISBN: 0-517-542323   AACR2
Design by Camilla Filancia
10 9 8 7 6 5 4
Revised and Updated Edition

Contents

Introduction

Why invest in real estate? That is a question which is often asked but rarely answered. In a nutshell, the answer is, there is no better long-run investment.

But real estate is cyclical. Whether you are buying your first home or investing in a multimillion dollar commercial property, the value and resalability will fluctuate with economic conditions. In the long run, however, virtually every sound, well-located property goes up in value. Most of this appreciation in value is due to inflation. But it is also due partly to real estate's unique characteristic of rising demand (from increasing population) and scarcity of supply in good locations.

This book is about "insider's secrets" of buying property wisely, how to hold it for maximum tax and income advantages, and how to sell it for the biggest profits. Along the way, many topics are explained.

Practical "nuts and bolts" information about real estate is the theme of this book. Tips on the right and wrong ways to handle real estate transactions are explained, especially in the question and answer section of each chapter. These questions and answers, edited from my syndicated "Real Estate Mailbag" newspaper columns, add to the basic content of each chapter.

The field of real estate attracts some of the finest investors, sales agents, and others that you will ever meet. But because real estate offers opportunities unmatched elsewhere, it attracts a few of the worst people too.

Fortunately, these "crooks" are a tiny minority in the real estate industry, but it is essential to protect against becoming their victim. This book explains how to avoid being swindled in real estate, as well as how to gain maximum benefits from real estate without taking unfair advantage of anyone. It is known as the "win-win" strategy.

That is what this book is all about—how to profit from real estate by using insider knowledge.

The Smart Investor's Guide to Real Estate

1.

Why Real Estate Is the Best Investment in the World

Real property, when properly bought, managed, and sold, offers the greatest economic return of any form of investment in the United States. That may sound like a broad, oversimplified statement, but it is true.

Whether you are buying your first home or your umteenth investment property, always look at your realty purchase as an investment. If the property gives extra "pride of ownership" benefits, that is great. But never, never, never buy just for emotional benefits. If you follow this strategy, you will never buy a bad property.

Homes purchased for personal use, unfortunately, often are bought with the heart instead of the head. Emotional decisions have no place in real estate, even in home purchases. If a home is not purchased as an investment first, and as a place to live second, it can easily turn into a losing proposition.

Consider all the overpriced, unique one-of-a-kind homes that have been bought or built for prices far above what rational buyers will pay for homes. Many owners of these "white elephant" homes find they can get their money out only by waiting many years for inflation to bail them out. It is known in real estate as the "greater fool" or "latest sucker" strategy. Avoid being its victim by purchasing wisely according to the insider principles spelled out, for the first time, in this book.

Andrew Carnegie said, "Ninety percent of all millionaires become so through owning real estate. More money has been made in real estate than in all industrial investments combined." The reason Carnegie was right is real estate values do not depend upon emotions but upon the hard facts of supply and demand.

Unlike the stock or commodities markets, which are a form of legalized gambling, real estate market value is under the owner's control. If he thinks a particular property is worth a certain amount, he waits until he can get his price from a buyer. But buyers and sellers of common stocks and commodities are at the mercy of the "marketplace" which may or

1

may not reflect the owner's opinion of the asset's value. If you do not believe this, check the per share book value of stocks selling on the New York Stock Exchange.

Many stocks are selling for less than their corporation's per share book value. Why? Because the marketplace is not placing as high a value on that stock as do the shareholders.

In other words, the real estate owner sets the value for his property. If buyers do not agree, no sale takes place. The result is the realty owner controls what happens to his property. He can let it run down, hence it loses value. Or he can improve it, thus increasing its market value if he makes the right improvements.

INCREASING DEMAND FOR REAL ESTATE

"Every person who invests in well-selected real estate in a growing section of a prosperous community adopts the surest and safest method of becoming independent, for real estate is the basis of wealth." When Teddy Roosevelt made that statement, our nation's real property was worth far less than it is today. Before Roosevelt's time, and certainly after, real estate has appreciated in value—far beyond the expectations of even the most optimistic, knowledgeable real estate experts.

Much of this market value appreciation, of course, is due to inflation. But part is also due to the increasing demand for well-located property, brought about by shifting and increasing population pressures. The best realty usually increases in market value at a rate either equal to or greater than the inflation rate. Good times or bad, real estate continues to be a safe, consistent hedge against inflation.

REAL ESTATE BETTER
THAN BUSINESS INVESTING

Of course, not all real estate goes up in market value. The secret is to anticipate which property will increase in worth. This is done by selecting only well-located realty. That means buying real estate where people want to live and work, even though that property costs more than poorly located property.

One of the great retailing empires of this century was built by Marshall Field of Chicago. Although he was an extremely successful businessman, he recognized the importance of real estate when he said "Buying real estate is not only the best way, the quickest way, and the safest way, but the only way to become wealthy." Unfortunately, after Marshall Field passed away, his successors in the department store business, which he built by selecting good locations and offering merchandise people wanted, forgot this principle. They made some serious errors which have hurt the profitability of the Marshall Field department store chain.

In the short run, business profits can be excitingly large. But for the long term, real estate profits can be not only large, but also consistent. Real estate values do not change overnight, as can the fortunes of a business operation. Witness the formerly financially sound W. T. Grant chain which became bankrupt a few years ago. Even though that firm was insolvent, in the bankruptcy proceedings its major assets turned out to be its real estate leases and owned property. Another example is the Penn Central Railroad. Its vast real estate holdings turned out to be the only profitable part of the business.

While there is nothing wrong with business profits, and no investor should give up a going business or a good job to switch into full-time realty investing until he can safely afford to do so, real estate profits are, over the long term, far more assured than are unpredictable business profits.

THE INGREDIENTS FOR SUCCESSFUL REAL ESTATE INVESTING

There are two key factors in successful real estate investing: (1) understand the inherent value of land and the added value of improvements constructed on that land and (2) understand how the dynamic tax consequences of real estate ownership lead to profit. Land plus tax benefits are the first secrets to unlocking the door of real estate profits.

Contrary to what a few people think, profit is not a dirty word. Without profit our nation would not have the highest standard of living in the world. Capitalistic profits benefit everyone. Those who become rich benefit from the incentives offered by our profit-motivated system. And the poor benefit too by having the availability of profit opportunities and jobs if they want to improve their lives.

Unfortunately, many of the poor have little or no desire to improve themselves. So they remain poor. But in our nation even the poor are pretty well off, compared to the "have nots" in more socialistic nations.

Profits from real estate have made more people wealthy than has any other source. Contrary to popular myth, it does not take money to make money in real estate. Many ways to acquire realty with little or no cash will be discussed later.

How are real estate profits earned? One way is from the inflationary increase in property values which have done better than most other investments in keeping ahead of inflation. Many realty investments, especially single-family homes, have appreciated in market value faster than the inflation rate. As a result, most home owners realize their residence is their best investment. If one house is a good investment, two, three, or more would be better.

THE SECRET OF CREATING REAL ESTATE WEALTH

Creating wealth by owning real estate is simple. Realty wealth is created by increasing the property's market value. Although inflation helps increase market value of most real estate, smart property investors do not rely on inflation alone. A real estate wealth creator is a person who improves real property at a cost that is less than the marketplace will pay for the increased value of those improvements.

"Improvements" mean not only new construction but also renovation of existing structures and creating a new use for underutilized buildings or underused land.

For example, if a person spends one dollar to improve his or her home and, as a result, that home's market value goes up by two dollars or more, real estate wealth has been created. Thousands of real estate investors are creating realty wealth this way in virtually every town in the United States. The person who spends $10,000 adding a bedroom to his home may be adding $20,000 to its market value if there is a demand in that community for larger homes.

WHY LOSSES OCCUR IN REAL ESTATE

No one should get the idea that losses never occur in real estate. They do. Some of the most successful real estate developers have lost everything by making foolish realty investments. The famous William Zeckendorf is the best known example of a highly successful real estate investor who lost virtually everything. Why?

Because he was in the riskiest part of the real estate business—development. He underestimated costs of developing his properties, including construction and financing, and he overestimated market demand for what he was constructing. Further, he was a victim of real estate cycles because he needed financing money when it was not available or was prohibitively costly.

When a real estate developer, sometimes called a promoter, loses money in real estate, it is usually because he went wrong in his estimates, as William Zeckendorf did. Property development is the riskiest way to make real estate profits. The potential for both high profits and high losses is great. Novice investors should stay away from development, especially since there are so many better and easier ways to earn profits in real estate. The secret is stay away from real estate development unless you can afford to lose everything.

Most real estate profits do not come without work and careful planning. Even buying vacant land, sitting back, and waiting for population pressures to increase its value takes time, money, and work (to earn the money elsewhere to pay the carrying costs for property taxes and mortgage payments while awaiting possible land resale profits).

WHY RAW LAND IS USUALLY NOT A GOOD INVESTMENT

Although many property profits have been made investing in vacant, raw land, chances of earning high profits are slim. The reasons are inflation and carrying costs.

Just to break even, vacant land must appreciate in market value at least 30 percent per year. The reason is the owner must pay property taxes (usually 1 to 3 percent of value), mortgage interest (perhaps 12 percent, usually financed by the seller because banks and other mortgage lenders regard land mortgages as too risky), real estate sales commission upon resale (5 to 10 percent of the sales price), lost income on the down payment cash investment (10 to 15 percent per year), and inflation (pick your own figure for this).

Land ownership is so risky that even home builders (the biggest real estate risk takers of all) try to avoid buying land until just before they start construction of a new housing development. Instead, home builders buy options to purchase land, a neat financing trick which gives the builder control of the land with only a minimal cash investment until construction is ready to begin.

But if raw, vacant land is not a good investment, what is a sound realty investment? The answer to that question will have to wait until the four key variables of any investment are discussed. As you read the following section, apply these variables to any investment you wish, including real estate. Consider land, homes, apartments, shopping centers, warehouses, or whatever interests you.

THE FOUR VARIABLE FACTORS IN ANY INVESTMENT

Any monetary investment involves four key variables that are related to each other. They are (1) safety, (2) potential for change in market value, (3) yield, and (4) liquidity.

SAFETY

The primary factor most people consider when making any investment is safety. The investments considered safest by most people are U. S. Savings Bonds, bills, notes, and other federal government obligations. These securities offer virtually 100 percent safety of principal because the chances of the U. S. government failing to repay these debts when due is practically nil. But such obligations rarely show any increase in value, other than accumulated interest (which is never as high as the inflation rate).

Although the safety of U. S. government obligations is excellent, there are discounts and fees charged for early redemption before maturity. Many U. S. obligations now owned by banks, if the banks had to sell them today, could only be sold at deep discounts from their book value. The reason is the low interest rate on these government obligations reduces their value.

After considering the loss of purchasing power on the invested dollars (due to inflation) and federal income taxes (but not state income taxes) on the interest income, U. S. government instruments in recent years have consistently shown losses to investors. Their only redeeming factor is high safety of the principal, even if that principal has lost value due to inflation.

Next in order of safe investments are the various types of insured savings accounts and certificates of deposit offered by savings and loan associations and banks. These accounts are now insured by federal government agencies up to $100,000. If there were a serious run on these depositories, the government printing presses would work overtime to pay off the investors (in inflated dollars, however). The U. S. treasury would probably come to the rescue, but it is not now legally obligated to do so.

THE BIG DRAWBACK OF SAVINGS ACCOUNTS

Even though it is considered admirable to save money in savings accounts and similar savings instruments, the big drawback for savers is these accounts offer no appreciation in value. In fact, the dollars in those accounts depreciate in value after considering the lost purchasing power of the dollars sitting idly in savings accounts losing value because of inflation.

Since the interest rates paid on savings accounts and certificates are usually below the inflation rate, savings instruments can be very expensive investments for the investor. Most people cannot afford the luxury of losing money on their savings. But they do not realize it. The banks and savings associations, of course, do not want people to know what foolish investments savings can be in times of high inflation rates.

For example, suppose you earn 12 percent interest on a savings certificate. If you are in a 20 percent tax bracket, income taxes will eat up about 2.4 percent of the interest earnings, reducing the yield to about 9.6 percent. If the inflation rate exceeds this after-tax yield, the saver loses purchasing power on his dollars kept in savings.

In fairness, however, the big liquidity advantage of savings accounts should be emphasized. Or at least that is what savers think. Although savings account withdrawals are customarily paid upon demand, if you read the fine print it says up to thirty-days advance notice can be required by the bank or savings association before your withdrawal request is honored.

Some eastern savings banks have refused to allow early withdrawals on savings certificates even though the saver is willing to pay the interest penalty for early withdrawal. So savings account liquidity really is not what the banks and savings associations lead their customers to believe.

THE SAFETY OF REAL ESTATE INVESTMENTS

Since this book is about real estate, the safety of realty investments should be discussed. Because each property is unique, unlike any other, the safety of real estate investments varies with each specific property.

Well-located, sound real estate is the safest investment in the world. It is not going to disappear, as can the value of dollars put into savings accounts. Neither will real estate values be lost because of inflation. In fact, property values tend to increase at a pace at least equal to the inflation rate. Most homes have appreciated at a rate greater than the inflation rate (due mainly to strong buyer demand and insufficient supply of newly constructed homes).

When was the last time you heard of a real estate investor selling his property for less than he paid for it? Exclude developers who have more in common with Las Vegas gamblers than with investors. Would you sell your home today for the price you paid for it? Probably not, if you are like most homeowners who have large profits in their homes.

Most real estate owners know their property is increasing in market value year by year. They feel perfectly safe continuing to hold on to it. Real estate holds its value and increases in market worth far faster than most other investment alternatives and with much less downside risk.

The reason real estate holds its value and is not subject to wild value fluctuations is it is a scarce commodity in limited supply. To be more precise, well-located real estate is limited. There will never be any more of it. As population increases, value of well-located land increases too. This result is not true for most other investments, such as common stocks, bonds, or savings accounts.

Unless a real estate owner must sell his or her property very soon after purchasing it, assuming the owner did not pay more than its fair market value, it is a very rare situation where money is lost on realty investments.

Because of all the safety factors in real estate, mortgage lenders will loan a higher percentage of value on real property (usually 70 percent to 90 percent of market value, sometimes more) than on most other investment security.

The federal government will even go so far as to guarantee GI home loans for qualified veterans for 100 percent of the purchase price. And real estate lenders will loan money secured by real property for a longer term, usually twenty-five to thirty years, sometimes forty years, than on any other security. Since these lenders are notoriously conservative, real estate must be a safe investment.

POTENTIAL FOR CHANGE IN MARKET VALUE

If you offer to sell me your passbook savings account, if I am in a good mood, I will probably pay you the amount of your account's balance. I would be a fool to pay any more. The reason is a savings account is worth only its value in dollars, never any more.

But real estate is different. It offers both upside and downside potential for change in market value. Fortunately, most good real estate goes up in value. But there are a few exceptions, such as poorly located property that is away from growing areas or located in high-crime areas where buyers are few and far between. Another way realty can lose value is by neglect. It must be properly maintained to avoid a loss in market value.

The market value of every specific real estate parcel depends on the demand for such property as well as the available supply of similar parcels. Since well-located land is in limited supply, values go up as demand increases. The better the location, the greater the potential for appreciation in a property's market value.

Of course, the safety of real estate investments is a factor in market value changes, usually upward, but other considerations also apply. The two major factors tending to force property values up are (1) increasing demand from an increasing population for a limited supply of well-located land and improvements, and (2) inflationary cost increases for new construction that make existing properties more valuable than their original construction cost.

The availability of mortgage financing also enters into the picture. If mortgage money is easily available, this tends to allow property values to rise rapidly. But if mortgage money is tight and expensive, property values do not rise rapidly. However, when hard money lenders (such as banks and savings associations) cut off mortgage money, a new source develops. It is the seller. Property sellers often finance their buyer's purchases if the buyer is willing to pay the seller's price for the property. This financing development, especially during times of tight mortgage money, tends to keep property values rising even when normal mortgage lenders are out of the market.

Real estate values traditionally rise at least 3 percent per year, good times or bad. But in recent years of runaway hyperinflation, property value increases of 20 percent to 30 percent per year, especially for well-located homes, have become commonplace.

Unimproved land values, however, usually increase at a much slower pace unless the land is located on the very fringe of development. That is why it is essential for real estate land investors to check market value trends for the immediate area before any vacant property is bought. Real estate agents usually have ready access to statistics on recent sales prices in the local vicinity.

But watch out. Just a block or two in distance can make a big difference in the rate of market value appreciation. Do not be fooled by statistics. Location is the key to successful realty investing. If a property is offered at what looks like an especially cheap price, there is probably a very good reason. Find out why before, rather than after, you buy.

YIELD

The third factor of any investment, yield, means the annual return from the purchased asset. For example, a passbook savings account might earn 5½ percent annual interest. This is that investment's yield.

Sound real estate investments far surpass any other type of equity investment for consistent total yield, commensurate with safety and liquidity. However, the yield in real estate is not a fixed amount. Rather it is the sum of at least two components.

These components of real estate yield are (1) the net income (or loss) produced by the property and (2) the income tax dollar savings resulting from the tax deductions for the property. Income tax dollar savings often increase the investor's annual real estate yield by 3 percent to 20 percent, sometimes more, depending on the owner's income tax bracket.

Most professional real estate investors will not even consider making a property purchase that will not yield at least 20 percent to 30 percent total annual yield. Some investors include market value appreciation as part of their annual yield. But most do not because it is an uncertain amount until reduced to possession at the time of reselling the property. Probably the safest and most conservative approach is to consider market value appreciation as "bonus yield" that will most likely be realized upon sale of the property.

LIQUIDITY

The fourth factor to consider when making any investment is liquidity. It is defined as the time delay required to convert an asset into cash.

For example, common stocks listed on the New York Stock Exchange are considered relatively liquid since they can be sold and converted into cash within three or four days at most. But the "cost" of that liquidity is that the stock is sold at its market price on the day of the sale, and the investor has no control over what that price will be. Other examples of highly liquid investments are savings accounts and U. S. Savings Bonds, which can usually be converted quickly into cash. However, the dollars received from the sale of such highly liquid assets are usually worth less than when they were invested. This is due to the dollar's constantly declining purchasing power caused by inflation. Most highly liquid investments, such as savings accounts and common stocks, offer little or no inflation hedge.

Many people think real estate's biggest drawback is its lack of easy liquidity. Real estate certainly is not as liquid as a savings account. But most good property can be sold within thirty to ninety days for its true market value. However, due to unrealistic pricing by many sellers who often take longer to try (and sometimes succeed) in getting top dollar for their property, realty sales often take a long time. This inflationary property price squeeze to wring the last dollar of profit from properties contributes to rising property sales prices in a neighborhood.

But there is another aspect to real estate liquidity. It is the refinance bonus. Except in times of extremely tight mortgage money, which real estate experiences cyclically, most good property can be refinanced to produce liquid cash. A major advantage of refinancing a mortgage, instead of selling the property, is this refinancing cash is tax-free to the property owner. Since it is a loan, there is no tax due on the cash produced from mortgage refinancing.

Mortgage refinance liquidity is an advantage most other investments lack. For example, it is possible to borrow on the security of common stocks, bonds, and personal property such as autos. But the loan-to-value ratio is usually not as high as for real estate. And the payback term, normally thirty years for real estate mortgages, is much shorter for other investments.

So real estate is really more liquid than most people think. But there are times when real estate liquidity suffers, such as during mortgage crunches when mortgage money is either very expensive or unavailable. This slight disadvantage, however, is more than compensated by the bonus advantages of real estate, such as refinancing and the special income tax savings benefits.

ADDITIONAL ADVANTAGES OF REAL ESTATE INVESTING

So far we have discussed the four variable factors to consider when making any investment. Real estate came out pretty good, but not perfect.

No investment will ever come out perfect when applying these four variables, so do not waste time looking for the "perfect investment." It just does not exist. But real estate comes pretty close.

There are additional advantages offered by real estate investment that most alternative investments lack. Real estate offers these bonus advantages that many potential investors do not completely understand. It is important to comprehend at least the concept, if not the details, because property evaluation can be intelligently made only after considering all its advantages and disadvantages.

1. HIGH LEVERAGE OPPORTUNITIES IN REAL ESTATE

Leverage means investing the least possible amount of the owner's cash when buying investment assets in order to earn the maximum percentage return on those invested dollars. In other words, leveraging means borrowing money. Real estate investors call those borrowed dollars OPM (other people's money).

In real estate, thanks to leverage, the property owner controls his entire property even though his own cash dollars invested may be only 10 percent to 25 percent of the purchase price. The ultimate leverage of all, of course, is no cash down payment at all.

The balance of the purchase price is usually financed with a first mortgage and possibly also with a second mortgage. Maybe even a third or fourth mortgage is used too.

No alternative investment asset allows such a low down payment percentage without corresponding disadvantages. Real estate leverage lets the investor get the entire benefit from the property's appreciation in market value with only a small cash investment (the down payment).

If the property should lose value (which rarely happens in sound, well-located real estate investments), the investor's loss is limited to his dollars invested.

Especially in highly leveraged property purchases, in case the property should lose value due to some unexpected event, it is important that the investor not have personal liability on the mortgage. The property alone should be the security for the mortgage loan.

If the investor does not have personal liability on the mortgage, and a foreclosure loss results, the lender cannot sue the investor for the deficiency loss. Several states, such as California, automatically bar such deficiencies if foreclosure is at a trustee's sale (rather than a court judicial sale).

Leverage is the insider's real estate secret that maximizes the smart investor's return on his investment. For example, suppose you buy a $100,000 income property, such as a commercial store building or perhaps a small apartment house. You can pay 100 percent cash down payment or possibly as little as 5 percent or 10 percent. The variables are infinite as to the relationship between the amount of the down payment and the mortgage(s) and the investor's return on dollars invested.

There is no one best leverage alternative for all real estate investors. Variables include the amount of cash the investor has available, his or her income tax bracket, the need for tax shelter, the desire for cash flow from the property, the seller's need for cash, and the buyer's need to conserve cash for later expenses such as improvements to the property.

What is the best leverage ratio? How much cash down payment and how large a mortgage is best?

As the next chart shows, the higher the leverage (lowest cash down payment, maximum OPM borrowed funds), the higher the total percentage return on the invested dollars.

While it is not always possible to get 90 percent high leverage financing, even using first and second mortgages, this is usually a good objective to try to achieve if the property can comfortably carry itself from its rental income produced. Many professional real estate investors regularly achieve 100 percent financing by combining various financing techniques.

Even home buyers can achieve 100 percent financing by using a GI home mortgage. FHA home loans achieve about 95 percent financing. If the government encourages maximum leverage when buying a home, there is no reason properties purchased without government financing cannot be bought the same way. With the aid of a seller-financed mortgage, high leverage is usually possible.

Note that while the annual spendable cash increases as the amount of cash down payment increases, the percentage total return on invested dollars decreases. Also, the tax shelter is highest with the largest equity and tax shelter is lowest with the smallest equity. In summary, the following leverage chart says:

1. Lowest Leverage (Highest Cash Investment) = Highest Tax Shelter and Highest Cash Flow
2. Highest Leverage (Lowest Cash Investment) = Lowest Tax Shelter and Lowest Cash Flow

But the overall total return on investment is about the same, approximately 12 percent in this example, regardless of whether or not maximum leverage was used.

Using a hypothetical $100,000 income property investment, such as apartments, stores, or offices, here are some possible leverage alternatives to illustrate the dramatic results:

1.	Cash Down Payment	$100,000	$50,000	$40,000	$25,000	$10,000
	(Equity)	100%	50%	40%	25%	10%
2.	Annual Mortgage Payment					
	(30 years, 12% interest)	0	6,172	7,406	9,258	11,109
3.	Minus: Annual Interest					
	(Tax Deductible)	0	6,000	7,200	9,000	10,800
4.	Annual Equity Mortgage					
	Build-up *(First Year)*	0	172	206	258	390
5.	Annual Net Operating Income	12,000	12,000	12,000	12,000	12,000
6.	Annual Net Cash Spendable					
	Income After Loan Payments	12,000	5,828	4,594	2,742	891
7.	Depreciation *(15 Years)*					
	$80,000 Building Value,					
	175 Percent Method *First*					
	Year)	9,600	9,600	9,600	9,600	9,600
8.	Taxable Income *(or Tax Loss)*					
	(Line 5 minus 3 minus 7)	(2,400)	(3,600)	(4,800)	6,600)	8,400)
9.	Tax Sheltered Tax-Free Income*					
	(Line 7 minus 4)	9,600	9,428	9,394	9,342	8,210

RETURN ON CASH DOWN PAYMENT IN RELATION TO

Annual Net Spendable Cash	12%	11.6%	11.5%	11%	8.9%
Annual Equity Buildup as					
Percent of Down Payment					
(First Year)	0%	.4%	.5%	1%	3.1%
Total Return on Investment	12%	12%	12%	12%	12%

Plus Income Tax Dollar Savings Due to Tax Losses

*Tax shelter is the same as (1) depreciation minus equity buildup or (2) the amount by which annual net cash spendable exceeds taxable income. These amounts are always identical. The difference between the equity buildup on the mortgages and the depreciation is tax sheltered, but it does not require any cash outlay since depreciation is a noncash bookkeeping tax deduction.

$$\frac{\text{Depreciation}}{\frac{\text{Minus: Equity Buildup}}{\text{Tax-Sheltered Income}}} = \frac{\text{Cash Spendable After Payments}}{\frac{\text{Minus: Taxable Income}}{\text{Tax-Sheltered Income}}}$$

More about the "tax magic" of depreciation will be discussed later. For now, all that is important is to understand depreciation is another of the benefits of owning depreciable real estate. It contributes to the owner's total return from his or her real estate investment.

2. TAX-DEFERRED EXCHANGES

Many of the benefits of owning real estate are a creation of the tax laws written by Congress. Without the unique tax breaks given to realty owners, much of the incentive to own property would be gone. Although a real estate investment should never be made for the tax benefits alone, they are a powerful investment incentive.

Perhaps the reason real estate tax breaks are so good is so many congressmen own realty. This investment continues to be the tax-favored investment, far exceeding the tax advantage of owning oil, gas, timber, coal, common stocks, bonds, commodities, gems, and other investment alternatives.

Tax-deferred exchanges are just one of the many tax benefits of owning real estate. Although such exchanges are more fully explained later, at this point exchanges must be listed as a major tax break for real estate investors. Thanks to the tax deferral rule of Internal Revenue Code Section 1031, it is possible to pyramid one's wealth from a small beginning into millions of dollars of net equity—all without paying one dollar of profit taxes.

Such property swaps are often referred to as "Section 1031 exchanges." Some real estate agents, when discussing realty trades, erroneously refer to them as "tax-free exchanges." This gives clients the wrong impression that such property trades are a way to completely eliminate tax on their profit when disposing of one property and acquiring another. This is not true!

A qualified real estate exchange is a way to *defer* the tax on a profitable real estate trade. This tax postponement, however, can last forever because it is possible to make a continuous chain of trades, never paying profit tax as the investor goes from a small property to a multimillion dollar one.

Only if the investor makes an outright sale, will the deferred profit tax become due. And, thanks to a new technique called a "Starker exchange," it is now possible to make an outright sale and still defer the profit tax. Starker exchanges will be more fully discussed later.

Tax-deferred exchanges can be used for both owner-occupied principal residences and investment or business property. When exchanging your personal residence for another, use Internal Revenue Code Section 1034. Other exchanges come under Internal Revenue Code Section 1031.

The details of Internal Revenue Code 1034's "residence replacement rule" will be discussed later.

The term "tax-deferred exchange" primarily refers to deferring profit taxes when disposing of one investment property or business property and acquiring another. This tax rule of Internal Revenue Code 1031 cannot be used if the owner's personal residence is involved (then IRC 1034 should be used).

To qualify for an IRC 1031 tax-deferred exchange, both properties must be "held for investment or for use in a trade or business." That means just about any property can qualify, except one's personal residence.

For example, vacant land may be traded for apartments, a warehouse can be traded for a hotel, or an office building can be exchanged for industrial property, all without paying any profit tax. It is all due to the special tax-deferred exchange rule of IRC 1031.

WHY TRADE?

Frankly, most investors who want to dispose of one property and acquire another do not want to trade. But the tax law requires the myth of an exchange if the profit tax is to be deferred. However, the real result is the investor disposes of his first property and winds up with one he wants more.

The intermediate step of a trade is well worth the slight inconvenience since the investor's profit is not eroded by income tax if a trade is used. A deferred tax is always better than one paid today.

Investors have many reasons for using tax-deferred property swaps. For example, many want to use their equity in a small property, such as a two-family duplex, for trading as the down payment on a larger property such as a fourplex. Other reasons for making tax-deferred exchanges include (1) disposal of an otherwise hard-to-sell property, (2) acquisition of a larger property that is easier to manage, (3) increasing depreciation tax benefits, and (4) consolidation of several small properties into a larger one.

THREE-WAY EXCHANGES

After making a tax-deferred exchange to a larger "like-kind" property, the "up trader" has completed his part of the trade. He accomplished what he wanted, namely (a) avoidance of tax payment and (b) acquisition of a larger property. But the party disposing of the larger property in the trade usually does not want to keep the smaller property offered by the "up trader."

So the "down trader" usually sells the smaller property so that cash will be received for it. This is known as a "cash out sale." It will not disqualify the tax-deferred exchange for the up trader. Such a cash out sale accomplishes the result the owner of the larger property wants, namely to sell his property and receive cash. These are called "three-way exchanges" because there are three parties involved, the up trader, the down trader, and the cash buyer for the smaller property sold after the exchange is completed.

3. INSTALLMENT SALES DEFER PROFIT TAXES

Another major tax benefit of real estate is installment sale tax deferral. This type of tax deferral, unlike the exchange's indefinite tax postponement until the acquired property is disposed of without exchanging again, spreads out the tax over the years the buyer makes payments to the seller.

Many property sellers, especially retirees, use installment sales to minimize their profit tax by spreading it out over several years to avoid being thrown into a high tax bracket in the year of the property sale. Also, the excellent interest earnings on the buyer's unpaid debt to the seller produce extra income for the seller. Security for installment sales can be a mortgage, deed of trust, land contract of sale, long-term lease-option, or other security device.

Property installment sales often result in doubling the total amount received from a realty sale. For example, suppose you sell a property for $120,000 with $20,000 down and take back a $100,000 installment sale mortgage at 12 percent interest. That note would produce $1,000 monthly income. The principal balance could either be amortized or there could be a balloon payment due in perhaps five or ten years. If it is a ten-year mortgage note, for example, the total interest income for ten years will be $120,000, equal to the sale price.

The basic requirements for installment sales were greatly simplified by the 1980 Installment Sales Revision Act, which became effective October 20, 1980. Now any deferred payment sale profits are taxable (as long-term capital gain if the property was owned over twelve months) in the year the seller receives the profit payment from the buyer. Of course, interest earned on the unpaid balance is taxed in the year of receipt as ordinary income.

To qualify for an installment sale today simply requires that at least some part of the profit payment from the sale be deferred into a future tax year. No longer required are any 30 percent limitation on payments received in the year of the sale or that there be at least two installment payments in different tax years.

Even if a property has an existing mortgage on it, an installment sale can be used to spread out the profit tax payments. Major installment sale benefits of offering "easy financing" mean the seller can usually (a) get top dollar for the property and (b) make a quick sale without outside financing.

Each installment sale payment from buyer to seller, whether received in the year of the sale or in a future tax year, is allocated to (a) nontaxable return of the seller's capital investment, (b) profit (taxed at low, long-term capital gain rates if the property was owned over twelve months before sale), and (c) interest (taxable as ordinary income).

If the installment sale seller needs cash, either right after the sale or later on, he can usually hypothecate or collateralize his note as security for a loan to produce tax-free cash. Or the mortgage note can be sold to an investor, often at a discount, but this will involve payment of tax on the remainder of the profit.

4. SPECIAL CAPITAL GAINS TAX BENEFITS

How many investments, other than real estate, can be sold for the same price as the original purchase price and yet produce a profit? Thanks to the tax magic of depreciation, real estate has this unique advantage which permits conversion of ordinary income from rents into long-term capital gains at the time of the property's sale.

THE TAX MAGIC OF DEPRECIABLE REAL ESTATE

Suppose an income investment property is purchased for $100,000 and $20,000 is allocated to the nondepreciable land value (because land never wears out and loses value) with $80,000 allocated to the depreciable building improvements. Using a fifteen-year estimated useful life, if it is an older structure, the straight-line depreciation method gives a $5,333.33 annual depreciation deduction ($80,000 divided by fifteen years).

If the property is held for just three years, that means $16,000 of its rental income will have been received tax-free thanks to the $16,000 ($5,333 for three years) depreciation deduction which "shelters" rent income from taxation. Depreciation is a noncash bookkeeping expense, so it requires no actual cash payment to be entitled to this tax deduction.

After three years of ownership, if the property only sells for its $100,000 purchase price, since the owner's basis is depreciated down by $16,000 to $84,000, the $16,000 profit ($100,000 sales price minus $84,000 basis) is taxed as a long-term capital gain (since the property was owned over twelve months). Long-term capital gains are only 40 percent taxable and are 60 percent tax free.

The tax result is that only 40 percent of the $16,000 profit ($6,400) is added to the seller's other taxable income and the remaining $9,600 escapes tax. Thus, ordinary income (rents) are converted to long-term capital gains, which are the most lightly taxed of all profits.

That is how the "tax magic" of depreciation works. While it is very rare to not sell a depreciable property for more than its purchase price, due to appreciating property values in most areas, there is still a profit for the owner if he or she sells for only the amount that was paid to acquire the property.

Long-term capital gains profits are lightly taxed because Congress wants to encourage investment. As of this writing, only 40 percent of such profits are taxed; the remaining 60 percent are tax-free.

For example, suppose you sell a property for $100,000 long-term capital gain profit. Only $40,000 (40 percent) will be taxed. This $40,000 will then be added to your other ordinary taxable income, such as job salary. Even if you are in a 50 percent bracket, the tax on this $40,000 would be no more than $20,000. That is only 20 percent of the total $100,000 profit. Most people would gladly pay $20,000 tax to net $80,000. By contrast, if $100,000 of wages are received and the taxpayer is in a 50 percent income tax bracket, he will owe $50,000 tax and get to keep only $50,000.

But the best part of real estate capital gains taxation of income property is that it is the tenants who buy the building for the owner. Their rent pays the expenses. After making the initial down payment, the owner should not need to put any more of his own cash into the property. But if the building needs improvements, most banks and savings associations gladly make improvement loans that, again, are paid off with the tenant's rent payments.

5. SPECIAL INHERITANCE BENEFITS

The tax law gives special benefits to persons inheriting realty. Unfortunately, to take advantage of this tax break, someone has to die—a rather extreme and irreversible action!

The general rule is a person inheriting property receives it at its fair market value on the date of the decedent's death. All untaxed capital gains are forgotten.

For example, suppose you inherit some land worth $100,000. The decedent paid only $10,000 for it years ago. If he had sold it the day before he died, he would have owed capital gain tax on the $90,000 profit. But that potential capital gain is forgotten upon death. If you sell the inherited property for $100,000, you owe no profit tax since your basis is the $100,000 fair market value on the day the decedent died.

In the case of joint tenancy, property received by a surviving joint tenant, this stepped-up basis rule applies only to the portion received from the decedent.

To illustrate, suppose husband and wife own land worth $100,000 on the day the husband dies. They paid $10,000 for the land. So each joint tenant has a $5,000 basis for each half interest in the property. After the husband's death, the wife's basis for the property as surviving joint tenant will be $5,000 (for her half interest) plus $50,000 (fair market value of the half received from the decedent joint tenant), a $55,000 total. If she sells for $100,000 she has a $45,000 taxable capital gain ($100,000 minus $55,000).

If you live in a community property state, your attorney should be consulted because there are certain tax benefits of owning real estate as community property rather than as joint tenants.

6. THE BEST BENEFIT OF ALL—TAX-FREE REFINANCING CASH

The best advantage real estate has over most alternative investments is it can be refinanced to produce tax-free cash for the owner.

Real estate's acknowledged inflation hedge is universally recognized. As the market value of good property keeps pace with inflation, lenders will increase the amount of their mortgage loans secured by a property. For example, suppose you buy a home for $100,000 and obtain an $80,000 first mortgage. Most homes appreciate in market value 5 percent to 15 percent per year, sometimes more. Suppose in a few years your home has appreciated in market value to $150,000. Using the traditional lending standard, most lenders will loan up to 80 percent of its appreciated value. That is $120,000 in this example. The $40,000 cash received from the refinancing is tax free (because it is a loan, and loans are nontaxable).

Many investors live off tax-free cash received from refinancing. By doing so they legally never pay income taxes. In case of an emergency, by keeping their mortgages at maximum levels they make resale easy because properties with big assumable mortgages are generally easy to sell quickly.

SUMMARY

After considering the four factors of any investment (safety, potential for change in market value, yield, and liquidity) plus the special benefits of real estate, property ownership comes out far ahead of alternative investments. Investors planning real estate purchases, however, should analyze these benefits as applicable to the specific property under consideration for purchase.

No other investment offers the flexibility of real estate to meet each investor's specific requirements such as cash flow, tax shelter, resale profits, or just plain old pride of ownership. With the aid of qualified real estate agents, tax advisers, and attorneys, realty investors can find the right property and buy it in the right way to maximize its benefits. Now that you know real estate is the world's greatest investment, use this insider's knowledge to accomplish your investment goals.

QUESTIONS AND ANSWERS

HOW REAL ESTATE CAN PROVIDE
YOUR RETIREMENT INCOME

Q. I am forty-four and my wife is forty-six. Our children will soon graduate from college. I have a secure job with the phone company, but it doesn't pay too well. We're now starting to think about our retirement years as I realize social security and my pension won't be enough to live on if 10 percent annual inflation continues. In another seven years we'll own our home free and clear. It's worth at least $85,000 today. Our only major asset is our home. We think owning real estate is the best way to beat inflation. For retirement income, what kind of property would you recommend? —*Joseph Y.*

A. Congratulations on planning your retirement now. You will never be dependent on relatives, friends, or welfare (as are many retirees) if you invest in sound income property now.

Depending upon how much time you have available to manage property, you may wish to buy apartments (except in rent control areas), rental houses, commercial property, offices, or industrial buildings. But before you buy, spend a few months looking at investment properties to find out which type is best in your community.

By purchasing income property, the rent paid by your tenants will pay the mortgage and operating expense payments. Avoid buying vacant land as it usually produces little or no net income. The only hope of profit from vacant land is resale or development profit, both highly speculative. After considering carrying costs and inflationary loss of purchasing power for dollars invested, land must appreciate in value at least 30 percent per year just to break even. It is too risky an investment for most people.

When you become too old and feeble to manage your income property, then you can sell it on installment sales which should provide at least twenty-five or thirty years of secure retirement income. While you are young, buy income property. Refinance it every few years to create tax-free cash with which to buy more property. When you are older, then you can sell and use the installment sale earnings for safe, extra retirement income.

HOW TO GET OFF THE SALARY TREADMILL

Q. Your articles about how to make money in real estate fascinate me. As I have about $25,000 to invest, do you recommend I quit my job to buy good income property? It seems every time I get a pay raise, it's eaten up by withholding tax or social security increases. How can I best invest in real estate to get off my salary treadmill? I don't want to give up my job. —*Vickie M.*

A. You do not have to quit your job to profit from real estate. In fact, it is advisable to keep your job, as it helps you establish credit with which to buy realty.

There is no reason you cannot invest in real estate while you continue your job. Unless you buy a huge income property, such as a large apartment house or office building, real estate will not provide the cash flow your job gives you.

However, your long-range goal should be to invest so your job will be just a supplement to your real estate income. After a few years of real estate ownership, you will have built up a steady source of tax-free income.

The secret is to buy at least one income property per year for at least five years. As soon as mortgage conditions are good for refinancing, refinance the mortgage on at least one property each year. Cash received from mortgage refinancing is tax-free.

For example, suppose you buy a $100,000 income property today, and it has $90,000 of mortgages against it. In other words, you pay $10,000 cash down payment. In five years, at 10 percent average annual appreciation in market value, your property will be worth at least $160,000. If you then get a new first mortgage for 75 percent of $160,000, which is $120,000, you will pocket the $30,000 excess tax-free cash after paying off the $90,000 old financing. If you do this often enough, you can quit your job and get off the salary treadmill.

WHY HOUSING PRICES WILL KEEP GOING UP

Q. We were going to wait for six months or so to buy our first home. But I'm pretty discouraged, as I just read a magazine article which says home prices will keep going up even if we have a recession. That doesn't make sense does it?—*Bayless J.*

A. Yes, it does. Even if we have a recession, home prices in most communities will continue rising. Of course, there will be a few local exceptions, such as areas where the major employer closes a factory, thus creating a temporary oversupply of homes for sale.

Except for local situations like this, prices of new and resale homes will keep going up. Part of the reason, of course, is inflation. New construction becomes more costly every month, due to rising material and labor costs. The result is increasing prices of new homes. Sellers of used homes then find their homes in greater demand, so they can get higher prices.

Another factor is rising demand for housing due to increased number of family formations. Part of this demand comes from more people living in smaller living units, such as single people and divorced people. Another portion of this demand comes from the rising number of young, first-time home buyers who are reaching the home-buying ages of twenty-five to thirty-five.

The number of these first timers will increase about 10,000,000 in the 1980s over the number of potential first-home buyers in this age group in the 1970s. To satisfy this demand, we need about 2,000,000 new homes each year, but we are building far less than this number. The result is and will continue to be rising home prices even if we have a recession.

THE BEST INFLATION HEDGE OF ALL

Q. I am disgusted with the way our economy is being run. When I put my money in the bank, they only pay me 5.5 percent on a passbook account. If I had $10,000 I'd put it into Treasury Bills. But even those higher-yielding T-Bills are a rip-off when you consider that inflation is at about the same rate those bills pay. I used to invest in the stock market until I discovered it really is the "world's biggest casino" as you often say. As I am sixty-eight and too old to buy real estate, where should I put my money? Where is the best place for an old man like me to invest to keep ahead of inflation?—*Byron A.*

A. I could not have explained the dilemma elderly people face better than you did. Everything you said is correct. Savings accounts are losers today. It is best to keep only money for emergencies there. Keeping idle money in a savings account today is very costly. Even putting money in the higher-paying money market funds is not profitable because they usually yield about the same as T-Bills (but without tying up your cash for long time periods), and this is about the same as the inflation rate.

You knew I would suggest buying good income property, such as rental houses, apartments (in non-rent-control areas), offices, or stores. If you cannot manage such property, hire professional management. I know many active real estate investors, much older than you, who are profiting from their properties far more than they could earn any other place.

Do not ever say you are too old to invest in good real estate. If other people, older than you, can succeed in property investing, you can too.

NO INFLATION PROTECTION IF YOU DO NOT INVEST IN REAL PROPERTY

Q. I am 64, one year away from retirement, and have about $20,000 excess funds to invest. I own my home free and clear and am a widow. My son suggests I invest my $20,000 in several second mortgages. What do you think?—*Laura M.*

A. I think you should first decide what your investment goals are. Income? Inflation protection? Pride of ownership? Tax shelter? Leaving a big estate to your heirs?

All of these above can be accomplished in real estate. But usually not at the same time in just one investment. If you invest in second mortgages, for example, you will probably maximize your income yield. That is why so many retirees invest in second mortgages. But there is no inflation protection and no tax shelter for the excellent interest earnings of second mortgages.

If you buy a small income property, however, it will probably appreciate in market value at least as fast as the inflation rate. But such property will not give you immediate cash income equal to what you can earn on second mortgage investments.

To help decide which form of real estate investment is best for you, consult a real estate counselor. If you do not know such a person, you can find one through your local board of realtors. For a reasonable fee, you will be objectively counseled and guided into the best real estate investment for your circumstances.

2.
The Importance of Understanding Real Estate's Tax Benefits

Never buy real estate for the tax benefits alone. That is the first message of this chapter. The second point is: maximize the tax advantages of real estate ownership by understanding tax angles that further enhance ownership benefits.

In other words, real estate's inherent advantages are increased by the tax incentives of ownership. But if you own a lousy piece of property, its tax advantages will not make it into a great investment.

Many so-called real estate investors have gone wrong buying real estate just for its tax advantages. This is the way most limited partnership syndications are sold, often by stockbrokers who know little or nothing about real estate. The promoters of syndications know that 98 percent of the limited partner investors could care less about the property—all they want is the income tax savings resulting from ownership.

But tax savings alone are never a sound reason to buy real estate. That motivation can lead to losses if the property is not inherently good.

Truly professional realty investors buy property first for its basic benefits, such as investment safety and potential for increased market value. Secondarily, they buy for the bonus income tax savings.

An example will illustrate how to combine real estate's inherent advantages with its bonus income tax savings advantages.

About a year ago I bought a three-bedroom rental house in San Mateo, California, for $103,000. Today that house is worth at least $120,000, probably more. Why has it proven to be a sound investment? There are several reasons.

First, it is in a good neighborhood not far from a freeway, a bus line, and shopping. Second, the house is in basically sound condition, although it needed about $1,500 of painting and fixing up to get it in presentable rental condition. Third, much of that home's increase in market value is due to inflation. If inflation had not been 15 percent in 1980, that home probably would have gone up in market value only about 5 percent instead of over 17 percent.

Real estate insiders understand these concepts. But there is another one which is even more important. It is leverage. Leverage means borrowing other people's money (OPM) to make more money.

That house was purchased a year ago for $20,000 cash down payment. That is not especially high leverage, rather conservative in fact. But its $17,000 value increase is an 85 percent annual return on the $20,000 investment. The nice thing is that "profit" is not taxable until the house is eventually sold. Better yet, it will probably be traded so the profit tax can be deferred indefinitely. More about tax-deferred exchanges in Chapter 10.

To summarize, this basically good property offered not just a 17 percent increase in market value in one year, based on its $103,000 purchase price. But rather it produced an 85 percent annual return on the $20,000 invested dollars.

THE BONUS ADVANTAGE OF REAL ESTATE INVESTING

But the bonus advantage of investing in this property is its income tax savings. That is right. In addition to the 85 percent return on invested dollars from appreciation in market value, income tax savings add even more yield.

Here is a quick summary of how the income tax savings on that house work. These tax benefits will be discussed in greater detail in Chapter 4.

First, the $103,000 purchase price must be allocated between the nondepreciable land value and the depreciable building value. If a significant portion of the purchase price was for acquisition of personal property, such as furniture or appliances, a three-way allocation is necessary to include the personalty. Most owners use the local tax assessor's land-to-building ratio shown on the property tax bill for making this allocation.

Let us suppose this allocation comes out $3,000 for personal property, $20,000 for land value, and $80,000 for building value. It is up to the taxpayer to make the allocation, using any rational method such as using the tax assessor's bill. Some taxpayers hire a professional appraiser, but this usually is not necessary. Other investors use their fire insurance agent's replacement cost estimate, allocating the balance to land value.

Of course, do not use the tax assessor's land-to-building ratio if it does not fairly reflect the true valuations. For example, if the ratio was 60 percent for land value and 40 percent for building value, the owner might get an independent appraisal that, hopefully, will show a more favorable allocation.

The higher the allocation to the value of the depreciable building and to the depreciable personal property the better. Taxpayers seek to minimize the allocation to the land value because, since land never wears out, it is not depreciable and yields no income tax savings.

Second, these allocated values for the depreciable building and any personal property must be depreciated over their estimated remaining useful economic lives.

The 1981 Economic Recovery Tax Act set the useful life for depreciable buildings acquired after January 1, 1981, at fifteen years, except manufactured housing (pre-fabs), which can be depreciated over ten years. No longer will taxpayers have to argue with IRS auditors about their buildings' depreciable useful life.

WHAT IS DEPRECIATION?

Depreciation is strictly a bookkeeping or paper-entry tax deduction allowance for wear, tear, and obsolescence. It is purely an estimate. In most cases, while the building and personal property are theoretically wearing out, the land value is actually going up. The end result is the owner's market value for his property is rising while his book value for income tax purposes is dropping. Illogical as this seems, the tax laws require taxpayers to depreciate their buildings owned for investment or for use in their trade or business. Isn't Uncle Sam wonderful?

HOW DEPRECIATION DEDUCTIONS SAVE INCOME TAX DOLLARS

The 1981 Economic Recovery Tax Act really should be called the real estate investor's tax bonanza law. The reason is, it cut to just fifteen years the depreciable useful life for commercial and residential rental buildings acquired after January 1, 1981. However, the old twenty, thirty, forty and sometimes longer useful lives still apply to buildings acquired before 1981.

In addition to reducing depreciable useful life to fifteen years for most buildings, the 1981 Tax Act added a new category of 175 percent accelerated depreciation. This means that if a taxpayer elects to do so, he can take an extra 75 percent depreciation deduction beyond the normal one-fifteenth annual straight-line depreciation deduction.

For example, suppose you buy a $100,000 investment property and allocate $80,000 of its purchase price to the depreciable building. Using the straight-line depreciation method yields an annual $5,333.33 ($80,000 divided by fifteen years) depreciation deduction for the next fifteen years. But if you elect the new 175 percent rapid depreciation method instead, during the first twelve months of ownership you can deduct $9,600 depreciation. This amount is determined from the official IRS 175 percent accelerated depreciation chart found in Chapter 4 (where depreciation is explained more completely).

If the owner of the building in this example is in a 30 percent income tax bracket, the $5,333.33 straight-line depreciation deduction saves him about $1,600 of income taxes; a 50 percent tax bracket taxpayer will save about $2,666.

But if the taxpayer elects the 175 percent accelerated depreciation method (also known as "Accelerated Cost Recovery System" or ACRS), if he is in a 30 percent income tax bracket the tax dollar savings will be about $2,880. A 50 percent tax bracket investor will save approximately $4,800 of income taxes he will not have to pay to Uncle Sam.

WATCH OUT FOR NEW DEPRECIATION "RECAPTURE" RULES

Needless to say, most taxpayers will elect this new 175 percent rapid depreciation method because of the maximum income tax dollar savings. However, when a property is sold that has been depreciated using this 175 percent rapid method, special "recapture" rules apply.

This means that Uncle Sam, at the time of sale, wants to tax the accelerated depreciation deducted. The new rules are as follows:

1. If the property is used for residential rentals, at the time of sale the difference between the accelerated depreciation deducted and the straight line depreciation that could have been deducted is taxed as ordinary income. To illustrate, if you deducted $20,000 of accelerated depreciation during ownership and $15,000 would have been allowed at straight line rates, the $5,000 difference will be taxed as ordinary income at the time of sale. Since you had the use of the tax dollars saved, however, this result really is not so bad.
2. If the property is commercial or industrial, and accelerated depreciation deductions were claimed during ownership, *all* depreciation deducted is recaptured at the time of sale and taxed as ordinary income. For most taxpayers, this means they should avoid the 175 percent rapid depreciation of commercial buildings.

NEGATIVE CASH FLOW IS NOT A TAX BENEFIT

A big problem with investment properties today is that rents have not kept pace with inflation. The result is many such properties do not produce enough rent to pay the mortgage interest, property taxes, and maintenance costs.

Some owners think that negative cash flow really is not bad because it saves them from paying income taxes to Uncle Sam. These owners reason that it is better to pay out cash from their pocket to meet negative cash flow than it is to pay Uncle Sam income tax dollars which are gone forever.

But what good does it do to pay out one dollar to get a one dollar income tax deduction that may save only twenty cents, thirty cents, or even fifty cents in income tax dollars? The answer is it does not do any good *unless* the property is appreciating more in market value than the negative cash flow is costing the owner.

For example, the $103,000 house discussed in this chapter has a negative cash flow of about $200 per month. Negative cash flow, of course, does not include the paper depreciation tax deduction. Yet the house is going up in value at least $1,400 per month (about 17 percent per year). Clearly, it pays to have a $200 per month negative cash flow to earn $1,200 net monthly appreciation in market value.

Many prospective investors shy away from negative cash flow properties. Such acquisitions should be avoided only if (1) the property is not reasonably expected to appreciate in market value at least as much per month as the negative cash flow costs and/or (2) the owner absolutely cannot afford to pay out the monthly negative cash flow dollars.

Of course, the way to invest in potentially negative cash flow properties is to structure the purchase on terms which avoid any monthly deficit. This can be done with creative finance techniques. An example would be getting the seller to carry back a purchase-money second mortgage that provides for the payments to be added to the principal amount, with the total amount due in perhaps five years (when the property's first mortgage can be refinanced to pay off the second mortgage).

Negative cash flow is definitely not a tax benefit of owning a deficit property. But if that cash loss enables the taxpayer to earn more than the negative cash flow costs, assuming the owner can afford to make the negative payments, then it is an ownership benefit that permits the taxpayer to take advantage of the property's other attributes.

To summarize, do not be afraid of negative cash flow. But accept it only if you can afford the deficit and the property is appreciating in value more than the negative cash flow costs in cold, hard cash.

A simple calculation will show when this occurs. First, multiply the monthly negative cash flow by twelve. Second, estimate the annual market value appreciation for the property plus any appreciation in value that will be created by new capital improvements (such as a room addition) exceeding the cost of these improvements. If the negative cash flow is less than the annual estimated increase in the property's value, it is probably a good investment property.

A WORD ABOUT THE BENEFITS OF OWNING YOUR HOUSE OR CONDOMINIUM HOME

Recently, I sold a house to one of my tenants for nothing down. Their monthly payments to me will be about $420 per month higher than it cost them to rent that same house. They said to me that their primary reason for wanting to buy and pay these high amounts was "We're tired of paying Uncle Sam and would rather take the tax deductions instead."

They were buying for the wrong reason. Not wanting to get into an argument, I did not explain that it really does not do any good taxwise to pay out one dollar for mortgage interest or property taxes to get a one dollar itemized income tax deduction that may save twenty cents, thirty cents, or even fifty cents in income taxes, depending on the taxpayer's income tax bracket.

My tenants did not realize it, but they should be buying because that property promises to be an excellent inflation hedge. It has appreciated at least 10 percent per year, usually more, in the twelve years that I owned it. There is no reason to believe that will not continue in the future. The real reason those tenants should buy, and the reason I let them buy, is inflation protection, not income tax deductions.

In other words, never buy real estate just for the tax deductions. Buy only because you expect the property to hold its value safely and to probably appreciate in value. In a nutshell, that is why smart real estate investors buy property. The tax benefits are just an additional bonus for owning real estate.

QUESTIONS AND ANSWERS

WHAT ARE THE BEST REAL ESTATE TAX SHELTERS?

Q. Please explain how realty tax shelters work and what are the best real estate tax shelters? I heard that apartments used to be best but that now commercial buildings offer the biggest tax loopholes. Please explain. —*Meri T.*

A. A "tax shelter" means the taxpayer gets a bigger income tax deduction than what he had to pay out in cash. In other words, a tax shelter "shelters" ordinary income from being taxable.

But please do not confuse a tax shelter with an itemized income tax deduction. For example, your home mortgage interest is a dollar for dollar itemized income tax deduction. If you pay $1,000 in mortgage interest, you get a $1,000 itemized interest tax deduction. Such a deduction is *not* a "tax shelter" because you have to pay out one dollar for every one dollar of such a tax deduction.

But a tax shelter means you get more than one dollar of tax deductions for each one dollar you pay out.

Suppose you own a small rental property which earns $10,000 annual gross rents and has $4,000 of operating expenses. If annual mortgage interest is $5,000, you would have $1,000 of net income. Mortgage principal amortization payments, incidentally, are not tax deductible as is interest.

Owners of income-producing buildings get an annual bookkeeping tax deduction allowance for wear, tear, and obsolescence. This is a noncash tax deduction expense called depreciation.

For example, if your building is entitled to an annual $4,000 annual depreciation tax deduction (which, remember, requires no actual cash payment), your building would show a $3,000 "tax loss" or "paper loss" ($1,000 net income minus $4,000 depreciation deduction).

This $3,000 paper or tax loss can shelter $3,000 of your other ordinary income as job salary which would otherwise be taxable. In other words, the $3,000 tax or paper loss shelters $3,000 of your ordinary income from taxation.

Today's best real estate tax shelters are probably commercial buildings which have not been remodeled for at least thirty years. The reason is costs of renovating such buildings qualify for the 15 percent investment tax credit in addition to the normal depreciation deductions. Another good bet are historical buildings qualifying for the rapid five-year depreciation for costs of renovation. Ask your tax adviser for details.

HOW INFLATION AND TAX DEDUCTIONS MAKE HOME OWNERSHIP COST-FREE

Q. We've been putting off buying our first home for over a year now in hopes that mortgage interest rates will come down. But it seems prices continue to go up, even though we understand mortgage interest rates might drop. How soon do you think mortgage interest rates will drop? —*Corry M.*

A. I do not think we will see 10 percent interest rate home loans for a very long time, perhaps never. The reasons include inflation and the ever-rising cost of funds for mortgage lenders.

When you consider the income tax savings from home ownership, plus the likely appreciation in market value of good homes, even if you pay 12 percent or more interest on a home loan, your home will cost you little or nothing in net expense.

For example, suppose you buy a $100,000 home with $10,000 cash down payment and get a $90,000 mortgage at 12 percent interest. If you are in a 30 percent income tax bracket, after the itemized deduction for mortgage interest, that loan will cost you only about 8.4 percent (30 percent of 12 percent is 3.6 percent; 13 percent minus 3.6 percent is 8.4 percent). Since most homes appreciate in value at least 10 percent per year, that home mortgage is virtually cost-free in the long run. Buy now before home prices go higher.

HOW TO COMPUTE TAX BENEFITS OF BUYING YOUR HOME

Q. Several times you've mentioned the tax benefits of buying a home. Please explain more. I know mortgage interest and property taxes are deductible. But I would like to know how much this saves me in actual tax dollars.—*Peter M.*

A. Your question gives me an opportunity to show how to evaluate a contemplated home purchase to compute your true after-tax housing cost.

For illustration, let us assume you are buying a $100,000 home with a $20,000 cash down payment and a $80,000 mortgage at 12 percent annual interest for 30 years. I am also going to assume the annual property taxes are $1,000 and that you are in a 30 percent combined federal and state income tax bracket.

1. Your monthly mortgage payment on the $80,000 loan will be $822.90 of which about 99.6 percent or $819.61 per month will be first-year, tax-deductible interest. The monthly property tax will be $83.33 ($1,000 divided by 12 months).

   So your total monthly mortgage and property tax payments are $906.23 ($822.90 plus $83.33) of which $902.94 ($819.61 plus $83.33) are itemized income tax deductions. If you are in a 30 percent income tax bracket these deductions save about $270.88 (30 percent of $902.94) per month in income tax dollars, thus reducing your net monthly housing cost to approximately $635.35 ($906.23 minus $270.88).

2. Each month you will be paying off your mortgage balance slightly. In the first year, this payoff only averages about $3.29 per month, but the monthly principal payment gradually increases so the loan will be paid off in thirty years. This principal payoff is like a forced savings account in which you gradually build equity. $635.35 minus $3.29 is $632.06 which is your net housing cost after income tax savings and equity buildup.

3. Next, estimate your home's probable appreciation in market value.

As you know, homes are considered an outstanding inflation hedge because they usually appreciate in market value at least at the inflation rate.

Let us be conservative and presume your home will go up in market value only 5 percent per year on the average. This is far lower than the national average in recent years of over 10 percent annually.

Five percent of $100,000 is $5,000 value appreciation per year. That is $416.66 per month. Subtracting $416.66 per month from $632.06 gives an estimated net housing cost (after income tax savings, mortgage equity payoff, and market value appreciation) of $215.40. Of course, there will be nontax consequence expenses for maintenance and fire insurance to consider too, perhaps $200 or so per month.

But after calculating your income tax dollar savings, the mortgage equity buildup, market value appreciation of the home, and upkeep costs, it is usually more profitable to own your home than rent, even at today's high mortgage interest rates.

HOW TO COMPUTE TAX ON PROPERTY SALE PROFIT

Q. We just closed the sale of our home. The buyer, a veteran, got a new VA mortgage for which we had to pay the mortgage company a 4 percent loan fee. Our sale price was $93,000. We also paid a $5,500 real estate sales commission. How do we compute our sale profit? Our cost was about $22,000 for the house, but we have added about $12,000 of improvements such as landscaping, new roof, new garage, and kitchen remodeling.—*Conners M.*

A. Congratulations on your all-cash sale which is difficult to achieve in today's home sale market. Most sellers have to help finance their buyer's purchase.

That 4 percent VA loan fee of $3,720 to get a cash sale was expensive, but probably worthwhile if you have a good use for the money received.

Your profit is the difference between the "adjusted sales price" and the "adjusted cost basis" of your home.

"Adjusted sales price" means the home's gross sales price minus selling expenses. Your $5,500 real estate sales commission and the $3,720 loan fee paid for the buyer's VA mortgage appear to be your only selling expenses. So $83,780 ($93,000 minus $5,500 and $3,720) is your adjusted sales price.

"Adjusted cost basis" is your purchase price (including closing costs that were not tax deductible at the time of purchase), plus capital improvements added during ownership, minus any depreciation and casualty loss tax deductions taken during ownership. So your adjusted cost basis is $22,000 plus $12,000, a total of $34,000.

Your profit is $83,780 minus $34,000 which is $49,780. Since you owned the house over twelve months, it qualifies as a long-term capital gain. That means only 40 percent of $49,780 ($19,912) is taxable. The other 60 percent ($29,868) is tax-free. The $19,912 taxable portion is added to your other ordinary taxable income and taxed at regular income tax rates. For example, if you are in a 40 percent tax bracket, the tax on $19,912 would be $7,965. That is only about 16 percent of your total $49,780 sales profit.

Of course, if you are eligible for one of the special home sale tax rules, then you can avoid taxation on your profit. If you buy a more expensive replacement principal residence within twenty-four months before or after the sale you must defer paying your profit tax. Or, if you are fifty-five or older and qualify for the $125,000 home sale tax exemption, you may wish to use your once-in-a-lifetime tax-free benefit. Ask your tax adviser for details.

DOES UNCLE SAM REALLY SUBSIDIZE HOME BUYERS?

Q. You've said that Uncle Sam subsidizes home buyers in the form of income tax savings due to itemized deductions for mortgage interest and property taxes. This isn't entirely correct as any single person can take a $2,300 standard deduction and married couples get a $3,400 zero bracket tax deduction. So taxpayers who buy a home and pay less than $2,300 or $3,400 for their itemized deductions don't get any extra tax benefit.— *Michael M.*

A. You are partly correct. However, it is pretty hard to buy a home today and pay less than $2,300 to $3,400 per year total for property tax and mortgage interest. Since most homeowners pay more than these amounts, it pays them to itemize their income tax deductions.

For example, suppose you are in a 30 percent income tax bracket and you are buying a home with a 30-year mortgage for $50,000 at 12 percent interest. The itemized interest deduction will be about $5,976 per year, resulting in income tax dollar savings of about $1,792.

Another way to look at it is the true interest rate is only about 8.4 percent (12 percent multiplied by 30 percent is 3.6 percent; 12 percent minus 3.6 percent is 8.4 percent).

DO NOT CANCEL PROFITABLE SALE JUST TO AVOID TAX

Q. Six months ago I contracted to sell my apartment house which I've owned for many years. The sale will yield me over $200,000 profit. I wanted a long closing time, so I could find a larger property to trade up to, so I could defer my profit tax. But I haven't been able to find a suitable property to exchange up to. What is the best way to get out of this sale so I won't have to pay that big profit tax?—*Reid M.*

A. Do not cancel your profitable sale just to avoid paying a little tax to

Uncle Sam. While it would be nice to defer your profit tax by means of a "like kind" tax-deferred exchange, since you cannot find a suitable property to exchange for, paying the profit tax will not be so bad.

As you may know, on November 1, 1978, the long-term capital gains tax rates were reduced. The 1978 reduction means only 40 percent of your long-term capital gain is taxable; the other 60 percent escapes tax. The result puts the long-term capital gain tax rate in the range of 5.6 percent minimum to 20 percent maximum, depending on your income tax bracket.

Do not fear paying a little tax. It is better than being sued by the buyer if you fail to deliver the apartment house as agreed in the sales contract. P.S. Read Chapter 10 to learn about new Starker "delayed" tax-deferred exchanges.

THE INHERITANCE TAX LOOPHOLE

Q. My mother is very ill and is expected to die shortly. I am her sole heir. But it worries me if I inherit all her properties, which she has owned for many, many years. During the Great Depression she bought many properties for nothing down and now they are worth a fortune. What worries me is the tax I fear I'll owe on these properties. Is there any way to avoid the capital gain tax?—*Richard W.*

A. Your mother's estate will pay the estate tax on the value of all her estate assets, minus the generous estate tax exemptions. Estate tax is levied by the federal government on the net assets left by decedents.

When you receive the properties, however, you will not owe any estate or capital gain tax. The reason is the estate, not you, pays any federal estate tax due. If necessary, the estate's executor can sell some of your mother's properties to raise cash to pay the estate tax.

However, you may owe state inheritance tax on the value of the assets you inherit. The inheritance tax rates vary widely by state and the blood relationship of the decedent to the heir.

Thankfully, there is a big tax loophole which saves capital gain tax on inherited property. Even though your mother has a very low-cost basis for her properties, your inherited basis will be the value of the properties on the day of your mother's death. In other words, the difference between her low-cost basis and the market value on the date of death completely escapes capital gain tax. Congress made this tax rule permanent in the 1980 Oil Windfall Profits Tax Act.

DO NOT FORGET UNCLE SAM,
YOUR PARTNER, WHEN BUYING A HOME

Q. Home buying is looking more and more impossible for us, and it's getting my wife down. We live in an apartment with our two kids. But my wife is expecting our third, so we've got to find a home soon. Do you think we should wait until interest rates come down? A few weeks ago a realtor found us a home we could buy, but the monthly payment would have been $745.95 at 10 percent interest (the seller would finance the sale). Property taxes are extra. I have a good job, earning over $2,000 per month. What should we do?—*Keith Y.*

A. Buy that home. Finding a low 10 percent interest rate mortgage is not easy in today's market. You passed up a "good deal" without knowing it.

While $745.95 per month for the mortgage payment seems high, it really is not when you consider your silent partner, Uncle Sam, who wants to help you. Your interest is tax deductible, of course. So are your property taxes.

In the early years of the mortgage, most of your payments go toward tax-deductible interest. For example, if you are in a 30 percent income tax bracket, you will save about $223 per month in income tax dollars for that $745.95 monthly mortgage payment. This reduces your after-tax mortgage interest cost to about $523. The same tax savings apply to your property tax payment too.

Instead of wasting money on rent, you will be building equity in a home. And I will bet your family will be much happier with more space and the security of building equity instead of a pile of worthless rent receipts.

3.

How to Get the Greatest Income Tax Savings from Your Home

The first real estate purchase for most taxpayers is their home. A home may be a single-family house, a condominium or cooperative apartment, a mobile home, or even a houseboat. To qualify for home ownership income tax benefits, the land underneath the residence need not be owned. It can be leased. The only criteria for eligibility for the major tax savings of home ownership is that the owned residence be the taxpayer's principal residence.

This chapter is divided into two major sections. The first deals with the tax benefits of owning a home. The second discusses the tax savings available when selling a home.

PART 1 TAX BENEFITS WHILE YOU OWN YOUR HOME

Home ownership can be a source of major income tax benefits. Some of these deductions are well-known to most taxpayers. Others are known only to a few tax-wise homeowners. Smart homeowners take advantage of these tax benefits if circumstances qualify. Some tax deductions, such as the casualty loss deduction, apply only in very special situations. But wise homeowners need to know about such conditions so they can recognize a tax-saving opportunity if and when it occurs.

TAX SAVINGS FOR LOAN INTEREST PAID

The general rule for itemized deductions is it is tax deductible if the interest was paid in connection with an indebtedness or forbearance. Of course, interest paid on your home's mortgage (or other obligation secured by the residence, such as a deed of trust, contract for deed, installment sale contract, land contract, or long-term lease-option) is a major income tax deduction if the taxpayer itemizes personal deductions on Schedule A of IRS Form 1040.

36

These rules apply to all loans secured by real property, such as first and second mortgages, improvement loans, deeds of trust, and land contracts. Of course, the taxpayer cannot itemize the interest deductions if he or she uses the standard deduction available to all taxpayers ($2,300 for single taxpayers and $3,400 for married taxpayers filing joint returns for tax years ending in 1979 and thereafter).

With the high cost of interest, few homeowners come out better using the standard deduction. Therefore, most homeowners elect to itemize their deductions if their total itemized deductions exceed the $2,300 or $3,400 standard nonitemized deductions.

However, some taxpayers who use part of their home for business purposes (discussed later) elect to take the standard nonitemized deduction, but they can still deduct the business use allocation of their home interest expenses as a business cost on Schedule C or E of their income tax returns.

A word of caution is in order if the purpose of the borrowing, secured by your residence, is for business purposes. Examples would include refinancing your home mortgage to use the cash to buy or start a business. Then the mortgage interest, even though the security for the loan is your personal residence, qualifies as a business expense rather than a personal itemized tax deduction. Such a business expense interest deduction should be listed on Schedule C or E and subtracted from the gross income of the business.

In such a situation, the interest is fully deductible as a business expense even if you elect to not itemize your personal income tax deductions and take the standard $2,300 or $3,400 deduction instead. It is the *use* of the borrowed money, not the specific property which secures the debt, that determines whether the interest is a personal itemized deduction or a business expense deduction.

MORTGAGE LOAN INTEREST DEDUCTIBILITY

If you are on the cash basis of reporting your taxable income, as most taxpayers are, mortgage loan interest is deductible in the tax year paid. Repayments of the loan's principal amount, of course, are not tax deductions. Most mortgage lenders provide their borrowers with an annual allocation of payments to nondeductible principal and to deductible interest.

PREPAID INTEREST

Until 1967, a cash-basis taxpayer could deduct, in the year of payment, all interest paid in advance of its due date. But in 1968, in response to growing abuse of the prepaid interest deductions, IRS Revenue Ruling 68–643 said prepaid interest deductions greater than for the current tax year, plus up to twelve months in advance, would be disallowed as "material distortions of income."

In 1976, the Tax Reform Act eliminated even this twelve-month advance prepaid interest allowance. Now only interest paid during the current year, and earned by the lender for the current tax year, is deductible. In other words, *no more prepaid interest deductions are allowed.* Of course, interest can be paid in advance, but such a prepayment is not allowed as an income tax deduction until the tax year when the lender earns the interest (even if the lender received the interest in the year before it was earned).

TAX DEDUCTIONS FOR "LOAN FEES," "POINTS," AND "LOAN-PROCESSING FEES"

Most savings and loan associations, banks, and mortgage brokers making home loans charge "points" or a "loan fee" for granting a mortgage. No matter what the name, if the charge is for use or forbearance of money, it is interest and is tax deductible. If the loan is secured by your personal residence, and the purpose is to buy or improve the home, such a loan fee is fully tax deductible as interest in the year paid.

But loan fees paid to obtain a loan on any other property, such as land, apartments, or commercial property, must now be amortized (deducted) over the life of the loan. The 1976 Tax Reform Act made this important law change. This means, for example, if you pay a $1,000 loan fee to obtain a 30-year mortgage on your commercial building, for the next 30 years you will have a $33.33 annual interest expense deduction for that loan fee. If the property is sold before the loan fee is fully amortized, the unamortized portion is capitalized and added to the book value basis of the property. Remember, however, the amortization of loan fees only applies to property other than your personal residence.

However, FHA and VA loan points or processing fees, whether paid by the home buyer or seller, are "service charges" and are *not* tax deductible as interest (Revenue Rulings 67–297 and 68–650). Such fees, which are paid by the home seller, are a selling cost that should be subtracted from the home's gross sales price. By law, the buyer is limited to paying a maximum one point FHA or VA "loan-processing fee" (which is *not* tax deductible as interest). Of course, the buyer can deduct the interest portion of his monthly payments on his FHA or VA mortgage.

To summarize, loan fees or points (one point equals one percent of the amount borrowed) are tax deductible as interest in full in the year paid if the purpose of the loan was to buy or improve your personal residence and if it is not a VA or FHA home mortgage. Loan fees paid to obtain a loan secured by any other type of property, or by your personal residence if the purpose was not to buy or improve it, must be amortized (deducted) over the life of the loan, even though the entire loan fee was paid in the year the loan was obtained. FHA and VA loan fees paid by the seller qualify as sales costs to be subtracted from the home's gross sales price. Such fees are never deductible as interest by either seller or buyer.

TAX SAVINGS FOR LOAN PREPAYMENT FEES AND PENALTIES

If you prepay your mortgage, whether secured by your home or other property, any prepayment fee or penalty is tax deductible in full in the tax year in which it is paid to the lender.

HOME IMPROVEMENT LOAN INTEREST

The cost of home repairs and maintenance, of course, is not tax deductible for your personal residence (unless it qualifies as a business expense if you use part of your home for an office or shop or for rental to tenants). The cost of capital improvements, such as room additions and remodeling, should be added to your home's purchase cost book value. Save the receipts forever.

But interest paid on a loan used to pay for home improvements is tax deductible in the year the interest is paid. If the improvement loan is of the discount type (rather than simple interest), the next paragraph on discount loan interest explains how to compute your interest deduction.

DISCOUNT LOAN INTEREST

FHA loans, home improvement loans, and some bank mortgages are of the discount type. This means interest is charged in advance at the time the loan is granted. Such interest is "discounted" or subtracted from the amount of funds actually given to the borrower.

> EXAMPLE: Jim took out a three-year, $5,000 home improvement loan at 5 percent discounted interest (the true annual interest rate is about 10 percent) to pay for kitchen remodeling in his home. He signed a promissory note for $5,750 payable in 36 monthly payments. He receives $5,000 cash to pay for the improvements. $750 is his total interest cost, discounted in advance. The interest is 1/36 or $20.83 each payment. If Jim made seven loan payments in this year, he would deduct on his Schedule A $145.81 or 7 times $20.83 as itemized interest.

GROUND RENT

A little-known income tax deduction is ground rent for homes located on leased land. Annual or periodic payments on redeemable ground rents may be deductible as interest. To qualify, the lessee-homeowner must have a lease of at least fifteen years with the right to eventually buy the lessor's ownership interest in the land by paying an agreed sum.

The lessor's ground lease is a security interest to secure the rental payments due to him, much like a mortgage is security for future payments. For more details, see Internal Revenue Code Sections 763C and 1055.

If the ground rent is for the mere use of the land, such as farm land rented to a farmer, with no eventual right to buy the land, such a lease does *not* include a redeemable ground rent. There is no interest deduction in such a situation (although there may be a business expense deduction if the land is used for business purposes). Of course, principal payments to buy redeemable ground rent property for a home are not tax deductible.

PENALTIES AND INTEREST ON
LATE PROPERTY TAX PAYMENTS

Penalties for late payment of property taxes are *not* tax deductible. However, interest paid on late property tax payments qualify as itemized interest deductions.

TAX SAVINGS FOR REAL ESTATE
PROPERTY TAX PAYMENTS

As a general rule, state and local real estate taxes paid on your personal residence are deductible as itemized income tax deductions. Property taxes are deductible in the year they are actually paid to the local tax collector. The date the tax accrues is immaterial to cash basis taxpayers.

The date of the actual payment determines the tax year of the deduction. Payments to a collection agent, such as a bank impound escrow account, are *not* deductible until the tax year such property taxes are remitted to the tax collector.

NO LIMIT ON PROPERTY TAX PREPAYMENTS

Property taxes may be prepaid to the tax collector without limit and fully deducted on your income tax returns in the year paid. However, most tax collectors will not accept advance property tax payments beyond the current property tax fiscal year.

PROPERTY TAX BUSINESS DEDUCTIONS

If part of your residence is used for business purposes, such as an office or shop, or for rental to tenants, then a proportionate share of the real estate taxes paid are deductible as personal itemized deductions on Schedule A. The balance qualifies as a business expense.

Although the entire amount of the property tax is deductible, it must be apportioned between the personal and business use. Such a taxpayer can use the standard deduction (and not itemize his personal tax deductions) and still deduct the business portion of his real estate taxes.

EXAMPLE: Martin paid $600 for 1980 property taxes on his home. He used ⅓ of his home for his insurance sales business. So he can deduct $200 of his property tax on his business tax return (Schedule C), even if he elects not to itemize his personal income tax deductions on Schedule A and uses the standard deduction instead.

REAL ESTATE TAXES PAID
IN THE YEAR OF PROPERTY SALE

When real estate is sold, unless the parties agree to the contrary, the property taxes must be prorated between buyer and seller according to the number of days in the property tax fiscal year each owned the property.

EXAMPLE: Albert bought a house from Victor. The transfer was on April 1. Victor had already paid the property tax of $800 which, under local law, pays the property tax for the fiscal year which ends on June 30. The $800 property tax is apportioned $254/365$ to Victor because he owned the property 254 out of 365 days of the property tax fiscal year which runs from July 1 to June 30 in that state. So Victor can deduct $254/365$ (69.6 percent) or $556.80, providing he actually paid all the tax. If he paid part in the previous year, only the part he paid this year is deductible on this year's income tax returns. Albert, the buyer, can deduct the other $243.20 or $91/365$ of the total property tax paid, even though Victor actually paid the money to the tax collector. Tax bills are usually prorated as part of the closing settlement for most property transfers.

Even if the property tax has not yet been paid to the tax collector before title transfers to the buyer, the property tax must be apportioned between buyer and seller at the closing settlement so the seller can deduct his share. IRS Regulation 1.164.6 gives the details.

EXAMPLE: Jane sold her home to Mary on December 1. The property tax in their state is due on January 10. It covers the fiscal tax year from July 1 to June 30. Although the Internal Revenue Code says a cash-basis taxpayer can deduct taxes only for his income tax year in which the property taxes are actually paid to the local tax collector, this is the *only exception* to the rule. Here, Jane can deduct $185/365$ of the property tax (July 1 to December 1), even though the tax was not paid this year. The theory is that Jane "paid" her tax share to Mary, the buyer, at the title transfer closing, and Mary paid the tax collector on January 10.

SPECIAL ASSESSMENT OR BENEFIT TAXES

Taxes assessed against your home for local benefits which will increase the value of your home are *not* tax deductible.

> EXAMPLE: Sidewalk or street paving assessment taxes are capital improvements (nondeductible) and should be added to the cost basis book value of your home. But if all or part of such a special assessment tax is for maintenance of civic improvements, then the tax *is* deductible as a property tax. Or if part of such a special assessment tax is for interest, the interest portion is tax deductible as an interest expense.

TRANSFER AND RECORDING FEES AND TAXES

Many local and state governments impose transfer or recording taxes and fees on the sale of a home or upon the recording of a new mortgage loan against a property. Such taxes are tax deductible only if connected with operation of a trade, business, or income property. So if part of your home is used for business or rented to tenants, then part of your transfer and recording taxes or fees will be deductible.

All transfer taxes and recording fees or taxes should be added to the purchase cost basis or book value of your home. Then, if you are entitled to a depreciation deduction for business use or rental of your home, you will automatically deduct a proportionate share of such transfer and recording taxes and fees. If you are not entitled to such a depreciation deduction, the transfer fees and taxes will remain part of the cost basis of your home.

If the home seller paid the transfer tax, he or she should subtract that tax as a sales expense from the gross sales price of the home. But transfer taxes paid by home buyers must be capitalized and added to the cost basis of the home.

EFFECT OF LIEN DATES OR PERSONAL
LIABILITY PROPERTY TAX DATES

In some states, property taxes become a lien against real estate on a certain date (usually called the lien date) each year. In other states, realty taxes become a personal liability against the property owner as of a specified date.

For cash-basis taxpayers, unless the property tax is actually paid on the lien date, *these lien dates are irrelevant* and have no effect on the income tax deductibility of the property tax.

The important rule is to deduct the property tax in the income tax year when it is actually paid to the tax collector. This rule applies even if the property tax is paid after it became due. No payment, no income tax deduction!

The *one exception* to this rule, discussed earlier, occurs when the property is sold during the year but before the property tax is paid to the tax collector. Of course, accrual-basis taxpayers deduct property tax in the year the liability accrues even if it has not yet been remitted to the tax collector.

TAX SAVINGS FOR BUSINESS USE OF YOUR HOME

To qualify for income tax deduction of normally nondeductible home operating expenses, such as repairs, fire insurance premium, heating, garbage, and other expenses, part of the residence must be used for business purposes. Qualified renters can deduct part of their rent if they use a portion of their apartment for business use. There are several strict tests that must be met to qualify for the business-at-home tax-saving deductions.

THE EXCLUSIVE BUSINESS USE TEST

If you use part of your residence for an office or shop, or if you rent part of your home to tenants, you are entitled to tax deductions for the expenses of operating that business use portion of your residence. This is a legitimate income tax deduction, which, unfortunately, has been abused by some taxpayers. So in recent years the IRS has become overly tough about allowing such deductions. But if you are qualified, use this deduction to maximize your income tax savings from your home business use.

The "exclusive use test" requires that the business portion of your residence be used *only* for business purposes. Part-time use of the same area for business and personal use disqualifies entitlement.

A separate room used only for business, full or part time, clearly qualifies. Use of part of a room for business, however, probably does not qualify. Clearly, use of a chair in your living room in the evenings to read business reports or magazines will not qualify.

EXAMPLE: Margaret has a desk in one corner of her living room from where she makes stock market investments. Such investments produce a major portion of her income. Margaret uses the desk to keep records of dividends, purchases, and sales as well as to make business phone calls. The rest of the living room is used for television viewing, pleasure reading, and entertaining guests. Since Margaret's "business area" is not used exclusively for business purposes, she cannot qualify for the home business use tax savings deductions.

EXAMPLE: Susan is an outside sales representative for a cosmetics company. She uses a spare bedroom in her home for storing supplies, writing orders, arranging deliveries, and contacting clients by phone.

She uses the bedroom-office exclusively for an office. Susan concludes this business space occupies one-fifth of her home's square footage. So she deducts one-fifth of household expenses for utilities, insurance, maintenance, mortgage interest, and property taxes as business expenses.

If part of your home is used for both personal (nondeductible) and business (deductible) uses, then allocation of business expenses on the ratio of time used for each purpose is no longer acceptable, according to the 1976 Tax Reform Act.

EXAMPLE: George manages apartment houses. He spends about two hours each morning doing bookkeeping, calling managers, etc., from a desk in his den. The rest of the day the den is used by George and his family for television viewing and reading. Since this area is used for both business and pleasure, George gets no business deduction for it. Of course, George can deduct his business telephone cost and any other direct business expenses.

THE BUSINESS LOCATION TEST

If you meet the "exclusive use test," in addition, your residence must be either (1) your principal place of business or (2) a place of business used to meet patients, clients, or customers.

EXAMPLE: Tom is a salesman for ABC Supply Company that furnishes him with a desk at its offices. But Tom frequently entertains customers at his home and sometimes writes up their orders in his home. If Tom meets the exclusive business area test, he can also meet the test of using his home to meet customers there. But he cannot qualify on the basis of his home being his principal place of business since his employer furnishes his desk space.

THE EMPLOYER'S CONVENIENCE TEST

While the two previous tests apply to all taxpayers desiring to claim deductions for home business expenses, an additional test applies to persons who are not self-employed, such as Tom in the example above. If an employee is to claim business deductions for home use, such use must be "for the convenience of the employer."

Frankly, this is a gray area of tax law. In the earlier example involving Susan, the cosmetics sales representative, although she is an employee she can easily meet the home use test if her employer does not furnish her with any desk space or is located in a distant city. But Tom, in the example above, would have a hard time meeting the "employer's convenience test" since the employer furnishes desk space for Tom.

However, there have been several tax court decisions involving school teachers allowing them to claim office at home deductions. These occurred where the teachers were ordered to leave the school after classes because of security problems. In such a situation, the teacher has little alternative to taking student papers and other classroom work home. Of course, such a teacher would have to meet the "exclusive business area test" and the "business location test" too.

WHAT OFFICE-AT-HOME EXPENSES ARE DEDUCTIBLE?

Self-employed persons should report their expenses for a qualified home office or shop on Schedule C of IRS Form 1040. Employees using part of their residence for their employer's convenience use IRS Form 2106 for Employee Business Expenses.

Part of all ordinary residence expenses affecting the "business area" are tax deductible. Examples include a portion of home utilities, insurance, mortgage interest, repairs, and property taxes. In addition, the "business area" can be depreciated.

Depreciation is a noncash bookkeeping estimate of wear, tear, and obsolescence of the "business area." To arrive at a depreciation estimate, your home's cost basis (the lower of original purchase price plus capital improvements added during ownership or market value on the date business use began) must be allocated between nondepreciable land value and building value (partly depreciable). Use the new fifteen-year, 175-percent rapid depreciation for home business use begun in 1981 or later.

EXAMPLE: Dave paid $40,000 for his house which is now worth $100,000. The $40,000 cost is Dave's basis for depreciation. He estimates the land value cost was $10,000. So he allocates $30,000 to the value of the house and uses a fifteen-year useful life. Dividing $30,000 by 15 years is $2,000 per year. If Dave uses one fourth of his home for business, $500 is his annual depreciation deduction.

The IRS constantly revises its rules in the field of home business use because this tax area has, in the past, been abused by taxpayers. Recent IRS proposals, for example, would ban home business deductions if the taxpayer has a full-time job and seeks to deduct expenses for a part-time home business. Congressional opposition to such IRS regulations is strong so watch for new clarifications by Congress in this tax area.

MOVING EXPENSE TAX DEDUCTIONS SAVINGS

If you bought or sold your personal residence during the tax year, or if you moved from and/or to an apartment, you may be eligible for the generous moving expense tax deduction. Both renters and homeowners are eligible for this often overlooked tax break.

But this tax-saving benefit applies only when the taxpayer changes his job location. If the move is for personal reasons, unconnected with a job site change, the moving expense deduction is not available.

If qualified, taxpayers can claim the moving expense deductions even if their other income tax deductions are not itemized. IRS Form 3903 is the place to claim your eligible moving cost deductions.

ELIGIBILITY FOR MOVING COST DEDUCTIONS

To qualify for moving cost tax savings, both the distance and time tests must be met.

A. The Distance Test

Moving expenses are tax deductible if your new job site is over thirty-five miles further away from your old home than was your former job location.

EXAMPLE: If your old job location was ten miles from your home, your new job location must be at least forty-five miles (ten plus thirty-five) away to qualify.

B. The Time Test

If the distance test is met, the taxpayer must continue employment in the vicinity of the new job site at least thirty-nine weeks during the twelve months after the move. Self-employed persons must work at their new location at least seventy-eight weeks during the twenty-four months following the move to the new location.

Either husband or wife can qualify for these two tests. If, at the time your tax return is due, you have not met these thirty-nine or seventy-eight week tests, you can either (a) take the moving expense deduction and amend your tax return in the future if you fail to qualify, or (b) file an amended tax return after you meet the test and claim a tax refund at that time.

NO LIMIT ON DIRECT MOVING COSTS

No dollar deduction limit applies to direct moving expenses for (a) transporting the taxpayer and household members from the old home to the new one, (b) moving household goods, and (c) meals and lodging en route. Careful records of these expenses should be kept to document the deductions. Deduction for auto transport costs can be either actual expenses or nine cents per mile en route, plus actual tolls and parking during the move.

A LIMIT ON INDIRECT MOVING COST DEDUCTIONS

Although there is no limit to the amount of direct, actual moving costs which can be tax deductible, there is a $3,000 limit on some indirect moving costs. Examples of expenses in this category include (a) up to thirty days temporary housing at the new job site location, (b) cost of house-hunting trips from the old home to find a new one, and (c) expenses for sale, purchase, or lease of a residence (including attorney fee, title fee, real estate sales commission, and other sales costs). Not over $1,500 is deductible for temporary housing and house-hunting travel.

Even if you defer paying your profit tax on the sale of your old residence (using the "residence replacement rule" of Internal Revenue Code Section 1034, described later in this book) or if you use the "over-55 rule" $125,000 home sale tax exemption of Internal Revenue Code Section 121 (described later in this book), it usually pays to deduct home sale and purchase costs up to the $3,000 limit for indirect moving costs.

The reason is moving expense deductions offset income that is otherwise taxable. But merely subtracting home sale costs, such as real estate sales commission, from the old home's gross sales price will probably not produce as big a tax saving, if any. It is always better to take a tax deduction today rather than one in the future. The reason is that a future tax deduction will be worth less than one today, due to inflation.

EMPLOYER REIMBURSEMENTS FOR MOVING COSTS

Many employees obtain moving cost reimbursements from their employers. Such payments are additions to the employee's gross income, just like wages, and are subject to withholding tax unless corresponding moving expense deductions can be shown. However, active duty United States armed forces personnel do not have their moving expenses, which are paid by the federal government, included in their gross income.

HOW TO CLAIM MOVING COST TAX DEDUCTIONS

Eligible moving costs, both direct and indirect expenses, are subtracted from the taxpayer's gross income, rather than being a less desirable itemized deduction. Full details are available in IRS Publication 521, available free at your local IRS office.

TAX SAVINGS FOR CASUALTY AND THEFT LOSSES

If you itemize your personal tax deductions on Schedule A of IRS Form 1040, you can deduct any property casualty loss (over $100 for nonbusiness casualty losses), minus any insurance recovery. Without itemizing your personal tax deductions, the casualty loss tax saving is not available.

As mentioned earlier, insurance premiums for home casualty insurance are *not* tax deductible. They are personal living expenses without any income tax significance. However, if part of your insurance premium is allocable to a portion of your residence used for business or rented to tenants, then that portion is of tax significance as a business expense deduction.

WHAT IS A CASUALTY LOSS?

A casualty loss income tax deduction, *not* incurred in your business or involving your tenants (which would be fully tax deductible as a business expense), can be deducted from your taxable income if the event was *sudden, unexpected,* or *unusual.* Those three key words are vital to eligibility for the casualty loss deduction. Losses due to steady deterioration of your property are *not* casualty loss tax deductions.

> EXAMPLES OF DEDUCTIBLE CASUALTY LOSSES: Fire, flood, storm, theft, sonic boom, smoke, land sinking, broken pipes, blast, vandalism, accidents, and freezing.
>
> EXAMPLES OF NONDEDUCTIBLE LOSSES: Rust, well contamination, termite damage, moth damage, dry rot, carpet beetles, rat infestation, and tree disease damage. The reason these causes are not tax deductible as casualty losses is they are not sudden, unexpected, or unusual.

THE SUDDEN, UNEXPECTED, OR UNUSUAL TEST

To be tax deductible as a casualty loss, the event must be rapid and not normally to be anticipated. The difficulty is usually one of proving the speed of the loss. For example, a sudden attack on trees by insects might be allowed as a casualty loss, but not one that took many months to produce any noticeable damage. An accident, such as an uninsured car hitting your house, would usually be considered a sudden and unexpected event, and thus, it would qualify for the tax deduction.

Termite damage generally is too slow to qualify for casualty loss status. However, there are several tax court decisions approving casualty loss deductions. But in those cases, the facts presented by the taxpayers showed their termites were especially fast working. For example, if you bought your home and got a termite inspection report clearance at that time, and three months later noticed termite damage, that might qualify. But most termites work too slowly to qualify for the casualty loss tax deduction.

HOW TO COMPUTE THE CASUALTY LOSS DEDUCTION

Although most taxpayers will not have a casualty loss each year, when one occurs it pays to know how this tax deduction is calculated. In these days of unexpected events, such as a burglary of your home, the casualty loss tax deduction can at least partially compensate for your loss of any uninsured items. Or if insurance pays for only part of your loss, the other portion can be deducted as a casualty loss.

IRS Form 4684, Casualties and Thefts, should be used to report your casualty loss. This is a favorite audit topic of the IRS, so be prepared to document the casualty loss claims if your tax return is picked for audit.

The deductible casualty loss is computed as follows:

1. The lesser of (a) decrease in value or (b) adjusted cost basis
   of the property $___
2. Minus: Any insurance recovery award $___
3. Minus: $100 per destructive nonbusiness event $___
4. Your tax-deductible casualty loss deduction $___

"Decrease in value of the property," real or personal, means the difference in its fair market value just before the casualty and just after the event. An appraisal may be necessary. Deduct the cost of the appraisal under miscellaneous deductions.

"Adjusted cost basis" means the cost of the property to the taxpayer, plus capital improvements added since purchase, minus any previously deducted casualty losses.

If the damaged property is used partly for business and partly for personal use, the $100 floor per event only applies to the personal loss portion. The $100 casualty loss floor does not apply to the business loss allocation since it is fully deductible as a business expense.

EXAMPLE: Suppose your house was damaged by a fire. You paid $20,000 for your home several years ago. A year ago you spent $1,000 on remodeling. Just before the fire, your home's appreciated fair market value was $50,000. After the fire it is worth $14,000, as determined by your appraiser. All the furniture, worth $4,000, was destroyed. Insurance paid only $6,000 of the loss to the house since you failed to increase your fire insurance coverage as inflation drove up the replacement cost of your home. The insurance company refused to pay for loss to your furniture which was very old and practically worthless. Your tax-deductible casualty loss is computed as follows:

1. Value before the fire $50,000
2. Value after the fire   14,000
3. Decrease in fair market value   36,000
4. Adjusted cost basis ($20,000 cost + $1,000 improvements)   21,000
5. Loss: (the lesser of line 3 or 4)   21,000
6. Minus: Insurance payment received   6,000
7. Casualty loss on the house (net)   15,000
8. Plus: Loss on furniture   4,000

    9. Minus: Insurance payment received   0
10. Casualty loss on the furniture (net)   4,000
11. Total casualty loss (lines 7 + 10)   19,000
12. Minus: $100 per nonbusiness destructive event   100
13. Casualty loss deduction on Schedule A of IRS Form 1040 $18,900

YEAR OF THE CASUALTY LOSS DEDUCTION

Casualty losses should be deducted in the tax year when the loss occurs, minus any expected insurance or other payment to be received in the future. If the exact loss amount is unknown at the time of filing your tax returns, the casualty loss deduction can be amended anytime within the three-year statute of limitations.

Should the insurance or other payment later received turn out to be more or less than the expected amount, an adjustment can be made on the next year's income tax return rather than amending the previous year's return.

THEFT LOSS CASUALTY LOSS DEDUCTIONS

Net losses due to theft are deductible as casualty losses whether the theft occurs on or off your residence premises. Theft losses are deductible in the year of the loss discovery, not necessarily the same year as the actual theft (which may never be exactly known).

Larceny, embezzlement, and robbery are included in this theft loss category. However, losses due to misplacing or losing articles or money are not tax deductible. The $100 per event floor applies to each theft loss event. The amount of the loss is the property's actual value on the date of loss. That means its depreciated value. This is usually the original cost minus decline in value due to wear, tear, and obsolescence (depreciation). The amount of loss is *not* what it would cost to replace the stolen item (except cash would not be subject to depreciation, of course).

THE TAX CREDIT FOR SAVING ENERGY

A little-known part of the 1978 federal tax legislation was the Energy Tax Act. It enables homeowners, renters, and business owners to take a credit against federal income taxes owed if they installed energy-saving devices after April 19, 1977. Tax credits are better than tax deductions because a tax credit results in dollar for dollar income tax savings.

TWO TYPES OF ENERGY TAX CREDITS

Most home energy tax credits involve installation of conservation devices. But a more generous tax credit applies to costs of "renewable energy sources," such as devices using or transmitting (1) solar energy, (2) geothermal energy, or (3) wind energy.

TAX SAVINGS FOR HOME ENERGY CONSERVATION

A 15 percent tax credit against income tax due applies for up to $2,000 of energy conservation costs. $300 is the maximum tax credit for this category.

Examples of qualifying conservation items at your principal residence include (a) insulation for walls, floors, and ceilings, (b) new energy-efficient furnace burners, (c) storm or thermal windows and doors, (d) automatic clock thermostats, (e) exterior door and window caulking or weatherstripping, and (f) electrical or mechanical devices replacing gas pilot lights. Qualifying equipment must be new and have at least a three-year expected life.

Examples of nonqualifying devices include heat pumps, airtight wood stoves, and replacement of oil, gas, or coal furnaces. More nonqualifying items include carpets, drapes, fluorescent lights, swimming pool conservation devices, wood paneling, and exterior house siding.

BIGGER TAX CREDITS FOR RENEWABLE ENERGY DEVICES

A bigger credit of 40 percent of the first $10,000, up to a $4,000 maximum tax credit, is available for devices to transmit solar, geothermal, or wind energy. But swimming pool connected devices cannot qualify.

WHO GETS THE ENERGY TAX CREDIT?

These energy tax credits apply to both renters and owners of houses, condominiums, cooperatives, or rental apartments who install conservation devices between April 19, 1977, and the end of 1985.

The energy credits up to $300 for conservation devices and up to $4,000 for renewable energy devices are available to the taxpayer each time he moves to a new principal residence. They are allowed even if the previous owner or renter used these tax credits.

HOW TO CLAIM THE ENERGY TAX CREDIT

Use IRS Form 5695 filed with your income tax returns to claim the energy tax credit. These credits apply only to your principal residence, not to your vacation or second home or to investment property. However, special energy tax credits for business property are allowed for devices such as heat exchangers, recycling equipment, solar or wind energy devices, and heating equipment modifications which save at least 25 percent oil or gas fuel.

SUMMARY OF HOMEOWNER TAX BENEFITS

This survey of tax deductions and credits for homeowners is not intended to make anyone an expert. But its purpose is to alert homeowners to the opportunities to save income tax dollars for the tax advantages offered by home ownership. Consultation with a tax adviser or attorney is suggested to apply this tax knowledge to the specific facts of your circumstances.

The next section, one of the most profitable in this book, explains the tax angles of selling your principal residence. Taken together, the tax benefits of home ownership and at the time of sale, all these tax breaks add up to additional reasons why your home is probably the best investment you will ever make.

PART 2   TAX BENEFITS
WHEN YOU SELL YOUR HOME

In the first part of this important chapter, we looked at the major tax-savings sources during home ownership. Now the focus shifts to the time of residence sale and how to avoid paying tax on the sale profit.

Selling your principal residence, whether it is a single-family house, condominium, cooperative apartment, mobile home, or even a houseboat can be an emotional experience. To compound the trauma of moving and selling, Uncle Sam is waiting patiently for his tax on the profit. Smart home sellers keep Uncle Sam waiting forever.

There are right ways and wrong ways to sell your primary residence if you wish to avoid paying tax on your profit. On the next few pages will be found the simple and perfectly legal techniques for tax avoidance when selling your home. Few real estate agents and attorneys fully understand these methods for avoiding, deferring, and even cancelling the home sale profit tax.

Since this is just an outline of the tax angles of selling your home, consultation with a local tax adviser or attorney who thoroughly under-stands real estate is advised *before you sell,* so these methods can be applied to your specific situation.

HOW ARE HOME SALE PROFITS TAXED?

Before finding out how to avoid profit taxes, smart home sellers compute the amount of their gross sales price that is potentially taxable. They then can figure how to avoid paying tax on that amount. Remember, tax avoidance is perfectly legal and admirable. But tax evasion is illegal!

LONG-TERM CAPITAL GAIN TAX

Most home sale profits qualify for the long-term, capital gain tax rates, the lowest available. To be eligible for this low tax category, the capital asset (such as your residence) must have been owned for over twelve months. If it was not owned this minimum time period before you sell, the profit is fully taxed as ordinary income. The profit is then short-term, rather than long-term, capital gain. This twelve-month, minimum holding period for long-term capital gains took effect for sales of capital assets made in 1978 and after.

HOW TO COMPUTE THE LONG-TERM CAPITAL GAIN

The 1978 Tax Act reduced the portion of long-term capital gains which are taxable. Only 40 percent of long-term capital gain profits are taxable. The other 60 percent is untaxed (except for the alternative minimum tax which affects only a few wealthy taxpayers).

The 40:60 taxable-untaxed ratio applies to long-term capital gains received after October 31, 1978. Even if you sold property before this date, if you received the payment after October 31, 1978, the new, lower tax ratio applies. Thus, if you sold property in 1975 on an installment sale and are still receiving installment payments, the 40:60 ratio applies, even though at the time of the sale the former law taxed 50 percent of long-term capital gains.

EXAMPLE: On December 1, Larry and Stella sold their home for $75,000. Their adjusted cost basis (discussed later) was $25,000. They paid a $4,500 real estate sales commission but had no other sales costs. So $70,500 ($75,000 minus $4,500) is their adjusted sales price. Their long-term capital gain is therefore $45,500 ($70,500 minus $25,000). Larry and Stella report this amount on IRS Form 1040, Schedule D, if they are not eligible for any of the tax avoidance rules discussed later. Of their $45,500 long-term capital gain, however, only 40 percent ($18,200) is taxable. The $18,200 would be added to other taxable income received by Larry and Stella. The remaining 60 percent ($27,300) profit escapes tax. If Larry and Stella are in a 30 percent income tax bracket, they would pay about $5,460 extra income tax (30 percent of $18,200). On their overall profit of $45,500, this tax of about 12 percent is quite reasonable.

Long-term capital gains are taxed within a range of 5.6 percent minimum to 20 percent maximum, depending on the taxpayer's overall income tax bracket as determined by his ordinary income.

For example, the highest tax which could be paid by a high tax bracket taxpayer on a $100,000 long-term capital gain would be $20,000 (20 percent of the $100,000 profit). For comparison, tax rates on earned income (such as job salaries) range from 14 percent to 50 percent.

The 1978 Tax Act eliminated the so-called 15 percent "minimum tax" as it applied to long-term capital gains. However, a new "alternative minimum tax" may apply to a few wealthy taxpayers who have long-term capital gains from capital asset sales. But long-term capital gains on the sale of one's principal residence are exempt from this new alternative minimum tax.

HOW TO CALCULATE YOUR HOME SALE PROFIT

Now that you understand long-term capital gains taxation, it is important to become knowledgeable on calculating the profit on the sale of your home. Then we will show how to avoid tax payment on this profit.

To compute your potentially taxable profit, subtract the "adjusted cost basis" of your principal residence from its "adjusted sales price."

ADJUSTED SALES PRICE

The adjusted sales price is simply the gross sales price of the residence, minus sales expenses such as the real estate sales commission, transfer fees, advertising costs, escrow fee, attorney fee, title fee, FHA or VA loan points paid by the seller, and other sales expenses.

ADJUSTED COST BASIS

The adjusted cost basis is the purchase price of the residence, plus purchase or closing costs which were not tax deductible at the time of the purchase. Examples of such nondeductible purchase closing costs include legal fees, title fees, and escrow charges. Added to this basis are costs of any capital improvements added during ownership, such as cost of a room addition or new swimming pool. Subtracted from this total amount are any tax deductions claimed during ownership for casualty losses or depreciation for business use or rental of the residence to tenants.

EXAMPLE: Carla bought a house for $100,000. At the time of purchase she paid a $250 attorney fee, $300 escrow charge, $350 title fee, $400 prorated interest on the mortgage she assumed and $450 prorated share of the annual property taxes. During ownership Carla paid $4,000 for a room addition, deducted $1,000 for an uninsured casualty loss, and depreciated $2,000 for rental of a spare bedroom to a college student. Carla's adjusted cost basis is $100,000 plus $250, plus $300, plus $350, plus $4,000, minus $1,000, minus $2,000, which is $101,900. Notice that Carla's down payment and mortgage are irrelevant to calculating her adjusted cost basis. Interest and property tax do not affect basis either.

EXAMPLE: After several years of ownership Carla's house appreciated in market value to $140,000. She sold it for this amount, paying a $8,400 real estate sales commission to her realty agent. In addition she had the following sales closing costs: $450 prorated property tax, $1,000 local transfer fee, $3,000 VA loan fee paid for the buyer's new VA mortgage, and $300 attorney fee. Her adjusted sales price was $140,000 minus $8,400 minus $1,000, minus $3,000, minus $300, which is $127,300.

EXAMPLE: Carla's long-term capital gain (since she owned the house over twelve months) is the adjusted sales price of $127,300 minus the adjusted cost basis of $101,900 which is $25,400. Please notice that the prorated mortgage interest and property taxes did not enter into the profit computation because mortgage interest and property taxes are itemized tax deductions that do not affect the adjusted cost basis or the adjusted sales price.

HOW TO AVOID TAX ON THE SALE OF YOUR HOME

Internal Revenue Code section 1034 contains a very important tax rule for persons who sell their principal residences. This rule does not apply to any other type of property, just the taxpayer's primary residence.

THE RESIDENCE REPLACEMENT RULE

This tax rule, called the "residence replacement rule" applies to home sellers of any age who sell their principal residence and buy a qualifying replacement principal residence. Vacation or part-time second homes and other types of property, such as land, office buildings, or warehouses, cannot qualify.

Determination of your principal residence, however, is not always easy. Factors such as time spent living in the dwelling, voter registration location, length of ownership, business and community involvement, and other considerations can enter into the determination if there is question whether or not the residence sold was the taxpayer's principal residence.

HOW TO AVOID TAX AND PUT TAX-FREE CASH
IN YOUR POCKET WHEN SELLING YOUR RESIDENCE

To qualify for total profit tax deferral, the taxpayer must sell his old principal residence and (1) buy and occupy within twenty-four months before or after the sale another principal residence (2) that has an adjusted cost basis higher than the adjusted sales price of the former principal residence.

EXAMPLE: Emily sold her condominium for a $100,000 adjusted sales price. Her adjusted cost basis was $60,000 so she had a $40,000 long-term capital gain. Within twenty-four months before or after the sale, Emily bought a single-family house for $125,000. Since the adjusted cost basis exceeds the adjusted sales price, and Emily met the twenty-four-month time limit, she must defer paying tax on her sale profit.

A LOOK AT THE TIME LIMITS

As shown by the following illustration, the qualifying replacement principal residence can be bought anytime within a thirty-six month time period starting eighteen months before the sale of the old home and ending eighteen months after the sale of the old home. If a new home is constructed, an extra six months is allowed for completion and move in.

|← 24 months before sale →|← 24 months after sale →|

SALE
DATE

If the replacement residence costs less than the sales price of the former principal residence, then the seller's profit is taxable, but only on the difference between the two prices.

EXAMPLE: Jack sold his house for $80,000 and bought a $50,000 condominium. Jack's adjusted cost basis was $45,000. So his profit on the sale was $35,000 ($80,000 minus $45,000). Since Jack's replacement principal residence cost less than the $80,000 adjusted sales price of Jack's old house, his profit is taxable (as a long-term capital gain if he owned the house over twelve months), up to the difference in the two prices. $80,000 minus $50,000 is $30,000, so $30,000 of the $35,000 profit is taxable now. Tax on the remaining $5,000 of profit must be deferred until Jack sells his replacement principal residence without buying another qualifying replacement.

The residence replacement rule can be used over and over again without limit as to the number of times. For example, it is possible to start out with a modest $50,000 home, sell it and buy a $75,000 residence, sell it and buy a $100,000 home, and so on, and defer all the profit tax along the way. In fact, Internal Revenue Code 1034 is a mandatory law requiring tax deferral in qualifying situations. Isn't Uncle Sam nice?

Use IRS Form 2119 to report the sale and replacement, even if the tax is deferred. This form shows how to establish the adjusted cost basis on the replacement principal residence.

LIMIT ON FREQUENT USE

Although there is no limit to the number of times the residence replacement rule can be used, there is a limit on frequency of use. The rule cannot be used more often than once every twenty-four months. However, one exception exists. If the sale and replacement is part of a job location change that qualifies for the moving expense tax deduction, discussed earlier, then the rule can be used more often than once every twenty-four months.

> EXAMPLE: On January 1, 1980, Tom bought a $75,000 condominium. On April 1, 1980, Tom sold his condo for a $79,000 adjusted sales price and bought a $100,000 replacement principal residence. This situation qualifies for tax deferral using the residence replacement rule. On September 1, 1980, Tom's job location was moved 200 miles away, so he sold his house for a $125,000 adjusted sales price and bought a replacement principal residence costing $130,000. Even though Tom had just used the residence replacement rule tax deferral in April, he can use it again in September since his move qualified for the moving expense tax deduction, explained in Part 1 of this chapter.

BASIS FOR THE REPLACEMENT PRINCIPAL RESIDENCE

One difficulty that arises with the replacement residence rule is computing the adjusted cost basis of the replacement principal residence.

In the example above, Tom sold his first principal residence and bought a qualifying replacement costing more than the sales price. Although Tom paid $100,000 for the first replacement, this is *not* his adjusted cost basis for it.

Rather, it is the price he paid minus his deferred profit from his previous sale on which tax is deferred. His first-sale profit was only $4,000 ($79,000 minus $75,000). To determine his adjusted cost basis for the first replacement, he subtracts this $4,000 deferred profit ($100,000 minus $4,000) to arrive at a $96,000 adjusted cost basis.

When Tom sold that house for $125,000 his gain was $29,000 ($125,000 minus $96,000). Although his second replacement principal residence cost $130,000, Tom's adjusted cost basis is determined by subtracting his $29,000 deferred profit ($130,000 minus $29,000) to arrive at a $101,000 adjusted cost basis for the house which cost Tom $130,000. If Tom eventually sells this house, his profit will be his adjusted sales price minus $101,000.

WHAT HAPPENS TO DEFERRED PROFIT UPON DEATH?

Suppose further that in the above example Tom dies while owning that second replacement house for which his adjusted cost basis is $101,000. At the time of death, perhaps it is worth $140,000. If Tom sells one day before he dies, he will owe tax on $140,000 minus the home's $101,000 adjusted cost basis, a $39,000 taxable profit. But if he instead dies, his heirs receive that house with a basis of its $140,000 market value on the date of death. The potential $39,000 profit is forgotten by Uncle Sam.

Of course, the $140,000 market value of the house will be included in Tom's estate for federal estate tax purposes (subject to the generous exemptions). But no capital gains tax will be due. If Tom's heirs decide to sell the house at its $140,000 market value, they will not owe any profit tax. This is called "stepped-up basis."

HOW TO POCKET TAX-FREE CASH WHEN SELLING YOUR HOME

Several pages ago reference was made to deferring tax and putting tax-free cash in your pocket. Although the residence replacement rule tax deferral has been thoroughly explored, the tax-free cash angle has not.

Please notice that the residence replacement rule says nothing about mortgages or having to reinvest any or all of the cash received from the sale of the old residence into the replacement principal residence.

Smart residence sellers therefore make a minimal cash down payment on their replacement residence and use the rest of their sale cash to pay other expenses or, better yet, to buy more property as a further hedge against inflation.

EXAMPLE: Jim and Joan sell their old home for $75,000 cash. They buy a $100,000 replacement principal residence, using a new VA home loan (100 percent financing, no down payment). The result is total tax deferral plus Jim and Joan have $75,000 cash to spend as they please. Of course, they must pay off any old, existing mortgage on their former residence which was not assumed or bought "subject to" by their buyer.

THE REPLACEMENT RESIDENCE LOCATION LOOPHOLE

A special loophole in the residence replacement rule is worth attention. It involves the location of the replacement principal residence. The law does not require the replacement to be located in the United States. So if your replacement residence otherwise qualifies for tax deferral, its location outside U.S. borders will not stop the taxpayer from deferring his profit tax, even if he never returns to the U.S.

EXAMPLE: Cora sold her modest $75,000 home and bought a luxurious $100,000 qualifying replacement principal residence in Mexico. If Cora sells her Mexican home at a profit in the future, she owes tax on that profit back in the U.S. But if Cora never returns to the U.S., chances of the IRS collecting tax are not too great.

THE MYTH OF HOME SALE FIX-UP COST TAX DEDUCTIONS

There is a popular tax myth, perpetuated from one generation to the younger one (probably by real estate agents), that if you spend money to fix up your home for sale those costs are tax deductible. This is incorrect.

The only situation where tax is saved by home fix-up payments is when the principal residence seller buys a less expensive replacement.

It is true that fix-up costs to prepare your home for sale take on tax significance if certain requirements are met. Those requirements are that sale preparation costs must be incurred within ninety days before the signing of the sales contract and paid for within thirty days after the close of the sale.

Examples of home sale fix-up costs include painting, repairing, and cleaning. But items of a major capital improvement nature, such as a new furnace, new built-in appliances, or a new roof, should be capitalized and added to the cost basis of the residence.

Whether your expenditures are for major capital improvements or for just getting the house in shape for sale, save the receipts because they may save tax later on.

Qualifying fix-up costs, which normally have no tax consequence because they are normal home maintenance, become subtractions from the home's gross sales price when arriving at the adjusted sales price. But the only time such fix-up costs save tax dollars is if a less-expensive replacement principal residence is purchased.

> EXAMPLE: Dave sold his home for $110,000. He had $6,000 of sales expenses and $4,000 of qualified fix-up costs. Thus his adjusted sales price becomes $100,000. If he buys a replacement principal residence costing more than $100,000, his total profit tax must be deferred. But if he buys a less-expensive replacement, he pays profit tax only on his profit up to the difference in the two prices. So if he had a $30,000 sale profit and buys a $90,000 replacement, $10,000 ($100,000 minus $90,000) of his profit is taxed. Tax on the remaining $20,000 of Dave's profit is deferred. Without the $4,000 of fix-up costs, the difference in prices would be $14,000 ($104,000 minus $90,000) so Dave's fix-up costs saved him from paying tax on $4,000. But he spent $4,000 to do so.

SUMMARY

The residence replacement rule allows total profit tax deferral when selling one principal residence and buying a qualifying replacement. Partial tax is due if the replacement costs less than the adjusted sales price of the former principal residence.

This tax deferral rule can be used over and over again to build a tax-deferred estate. But it is only a tax deferral rule. Tax must be paid if the final home in the chain of tax-deferred sales is sold without buying another qualifying replacement. But there is a way to avoid all that deferred tax when selling the final principal residence on the deferral chain. It is called the "over 55 rule" and is the subject of the next section.

THE BIG "OVER-55 RULE" $125,000 HOME SALE PROFIT TAX EXEMPTION

If a taxpayer cannot qualify for the residence replacement rule of Internal Revenue Code section 1034, usually because he is not buying a qualified replacement principal residence, his next best tax break is the "over-55 rule" contained in Internal Revenue Code Section 121.

This tax bonanza is available to qualified principal residence sellers who are at least age fifty-five on the day they transfer title.

WHO QUALIFIES?

To qualify for the $125,000 home sale profit tax exemption, the principal residence seller must be fifty-five or older on the day title to the residence is transferred to the new owner. It is immaterial what day the sales agreement was signed. It is not sufficient if the seller became fifty-five in the year of the sale. He or she must actually be fifty-five or older on the day of title transfer.

EXAMPLE: Norman, on September 1, sold his principal residence. On December 15, he became fifty-five. He does *not* qualify and cannot use the over-55 rule $125,000 tax exemption on this sale. But if Norman is married and his wife is fifty-five or older on the title transfer date, then they can qualify if both spouses file a joint income tax return for the sale year *and* if the spouse who is fifty-five or older (the wife, here) is a title holder of the property in joint tenancy, community property, or tenancy by the entireties. It will not disqualify eligibility if title is held with a spouse who is not yet fifty-five if one spouse co-owner is fifty-five or older.

WHAT IS THE $125,000 EXEMPTION?

The $125,000 home sale tax exemption is elective, not mandatory as is the residence replacement rule. It applies to post-July 20, 1981, sales of the taxpayer's principal residence.

(For sales closed on or before July 21, 1981, the old, less generous "over-55 rule" allowed only a tax exemption on up to $100,000 profit from the principal residence's sale.

By the way, if a taxpayer used the old, now repealed "over-65 rule" before the July 27, 1978, effective date of the $100,000 "over-55 rule," he or she can use the "over-55 rule" on any post-July 26, 1978, principal residence sale.

The $125,000 exemption applies to both profits on the sale of the qualified taxpayer's current principal residence and deferred profits from sales of earlier residence sales where the "residence replacement rule" was used to defer profit tax.

THE OWNERSHIP AND OCCUPANCY TEST

In addition to the age requirement, the $125,000 home sale profit tax exemption requires the seller to have owned and lived in his principal residence at least three of the five years before the sale. Any three years will do. They need not be consecutive. Nor must they be the last three years before sale.

> EXAMPLE: Florence bought her condominium on December 1, 1977. She sold it on December 2, 1980. Florence has met the three out of five year ownership and occupancy requirement. She need not have owned her principal residence for five years before the sale, just the last three years are sufficient if she also occupied the condo as her primary residence during those three years.

> EXAMPLE: Ken and Mary have owned and occupied their house for many years. They are considering moving to a retirement community but they are not certain they will like it. The three out of five year rule allows Ken and Mary to move to the retirement community to try out living there for up to two years without losing their $125,000 home sale tax exemption if they decide to sell their former principal residence.

> EXAMPLE: Jane, age seventy-five, is in poor health. Her family insisted she move to a convalescent hospital where she could receive proper care. If Jane has owned her principal residence for at least five years, she could remain away from her home for up to two years without losing her $125,000 home sale tax exemption. But if she does not live in her principal residence at least three of the five years before she sells it, she loses the $125,000 tax-free profit exemption.

Of course this "over-55 rule," like the residence replacement rule, only applies to the sale of the taxpayer's principal residence. Such a home can be a single-family house, condominium, cooperative apartment, mobile home, or even a houseboat. The land need not be owned; it can be leased.

But the rule can be used by sellers of investment property if the seller resides in one apartment as his principal residence. To illustrate, suppose you own a four-unit apartment house and reside in one apartment. You could use the "over-55 rule" to exempt you from profit tax up to $125,000 profit on the sale of the apartment where you reside. Profit on the sale of the other three apartments will not qualify. In other words, selling such a building is like selling two separate properties. One is your personal residence. The other is the three rental apartments.

The purpose of this "over-55 rule" (Internal Revenue Code Section 121) is to enable taxpayers aged fifty-five or older to sell their primary residence without having to buy a replacement principal residence (as younger home sellers must do to defer their profit tax payment). But sellers aged fifty-five or older who buy a principal ersidence replacement should use the residence replacement rule of Internal Revenue Code section 1034 to defer their profit tax. Also, it is possible to combine the "over-55 rule" and the residence replacement rule in one sale, as will be illustrated later.

THE ONCE-PER-LIFETIME TEST

This "over-55 rule" can be used only once per lifetime. Any unused portion cannot be saved for future use.

> EXAMPLE: Grace sold her house for a $75,000 net profit. If she is eligible and elects to use her "over-55 rule" $125,000 home sale tax exemption, she cannot save the unused $50,000 for future use.

Even though each person can use this rule once, if a married couple elect to use this tax break, they get only one $125,000 exemption per marriage.

> EXAMPLE: Henry age sixty-six, and his wife Dora, age sixty-four, sell their home for a $150,000 profit. They get only one $125,000 exemption so they will owe tax on the extra $25,000 of profit (a long-term capital gain if the home was owned over twelve months).

> EXAMPLE: Frank, age fifty-five, and his wife Margo, age fifty-four, sell their home which they own in joint tenancy. Since Frank meets the age requirement, this is sufficient. ONLY ONE OWNER-SPOUSE NEED BE FIFTY-FIVE OR OLDER. No additional tax savings are available if both spouses are fifty-five or older. There is no extra tax saving for waiting to sell until Margo becomes age fifty-five because there is only one $125,000 exemption per married couple.

But if two qualified co-owners, not married to each other, sell their principal residence, then each can receive up to $125,000 of tax-free profits.

EXAMPLE: Mabel, age seventy, and Emily, age sixty-seven, are joint owners of the house where they have each resided for three of the five years before the sale. When they sell their home, *each* can take a tax exemption for up to $125,000 of her share of the sale profit. This means each co-owner who meets the age, ownership, and occupancy requirements can qualify for up to $125,000 of tax-free profits. In this example, if the sale profit is $250,000 and Mabel and Emily split it equally, the entire $250,000 profit is tax exempt. It may seem unfair to give a married husband and wife only one $125,000 exemption while unmarried joint co-owners each get a $125,000 tax exemption, but who said tax law is fair?

However, if a husband and wife *each* meet the age and time requirements, but are divorced before the transfer date of their principal residence, they can each take one "over-55 rule" $125,000 home sale tax exemption.

EXAMPLE: Bill, age fifty-six, and his wife Carole, age fifty-five, lived in their jointly owned house at least three of the five years before its sale. They decide to get a divorce. After receiving their final divorce decree, they sell their home and split the sales proceeds. In such a situation, Bill and Carole *each* can get up to $125,000 tax-free profits, just as Mabel and Emily did in the previous example. This means no profit tax will be due if the home sells for under $250,000 profit in this situation.

Of course, if a married couple get a divorce, sell their former principal residence, each claim their "over-55 rule" $125,000 tax exemption, and then remarry, the IRS will probably attack the proceedings as a sham.

This once-per-lifetime rule can be especially important to persons who remarry. If a taxpayer who has used his $125,000 exemption marries someone who has not used their examption, this bars future use of the rule for both persons.

EXAMPLE: Clara and John used their $125,000 exemption when they sold their home. John died a few years later. Clara married Victor. They lived in Victor's house which he owned before the marriage. When Victor sells that house, the $125,000 exemption is not available since Clara used up her once-per-lifetime exemption previously. This prohibits Victor from using this tax break even though the house is his separate property in his name alone. If Victor planned to sell the house, he should have done so before marrying Clara.

HOW TO CALCULATE YOUR TAX-FREE EXCLUSION AMOUNT

To calculate the tax-exempt "over-55 rule" profit which is excluded from federal income tax, subtract the principal residence's adjusted cost basis from its adjusted sales price. The first $125,000 of this amount is tax-free. IRS Form 2119 must be filed with your federal income tax return to claim this exemption. Of course, any profit over $125,000 is taxable, and any unused part of the $125,000 exemption is lost forever.

EXAMPLE: Jerry, age sixty, and otherwise qualified for the "over-55 rule" sells his condominium for a $95,000 adjusted sales price. His adjusted cost basis is $25,000. Jerry's $70,000 long-term capital gain ($95,000 minus $25,000) is tax-free since it is below $125,000. But the unused $55,000 portion of his exemption is wasted.

HOW TO COMBINE THE "OVER-55 RULE" WITH OTHER TAX-SAVING METHODS

The "over-55 rule" can be combined with other tax deferral rules if the $125,000 exemption is insufficient to shelter all the sale profit from tax.

THE RESIDENCE REPLACEMENT RULE

This rule, discussed earlier, is available to home sellers of any age who sell one principal residence and buy a replacement within twenty-four months before or after the sale. Combining this rule with the $125,000 exemption can result in both tax exemption and tax deferral. Of course, if you buy a more expensive replacement residence, you will not be using the $125,000 exemption, so the $125,000 exemption and the residence replacement rule are only used if a less-expensive replacement residence is purchased.

EXAMPLE: Larry, age fifty-five, and his wife Mary, age fifty-three, sell their primary residence, which has an adjusted cost basis of $35,000, for an adjusted sales price of $175,000. They buy a $45,000 condominium replacement principal residence. Using the "over-55 rule" $125,000 home sale profit tax exemption, $125,000 of their $140,000 profit ($175,000 minus $35,000) is tax-free.

Larry and Mary then subtract this $125,000 exemption from their $175,000 adjusted sales price to get their $50,000 "revised adjusted sales price." If they buy a replacement principal residence costing more than this $50,000 revised adjusted sales price, then tax is deferred on the remaining $15,000 of their sale profit (using the residence replacement rule) until they sell that replacement home without buying another qualifying replacement. But Larry and Mary cannot ever again use the $125,000 home sale tax exemption.

However, Larry and Mary are buying a *less-expensive* replacement principal residence, the $45,000 condo. So their remaining $15,000 profit will be taxed up to the difference in the two prices ($50,000 minus $45,000), which is $5,000. Tax on the remaining $10,000 must be deferred. This $10,000 is subtracted from the $45,000 purchase price to give Larry and Mary a $35,000 adjusted cost basis for their condo. This adjusted cost basis is the same as the adjusted cost basis on their former principal residence which they sold.

THE INSTALLMENT SALE RULE

Many home sellers use installment sales to minimize their profit tax and to provide excellent interest earnings from the mortgage, trust deed, or land contract they take back to finance their buyer's purchase. By spreading out the buyer's payments over future years, sellers of any property can avoid being boosted into a high tax bracket in the year of sale.

An installment sale (discussed further in Chapter 8) can be combined with the $125,000 exemption and/or the residence replacement rule to hold the capital gains tax down or defer it entirely. At the same time, secure installment sale interest earnings are provided by the buyer's installment obligation to the seller.

In late 1980, Congress passed major installment sale rule changes. Most are retroactive to property sales made after January 1, 1980. For installment sales made after that date, there is no minimum or maximum down payment required in the year of sale (the old installment sale law allowed the seller to receive only a maximum of 30 percent of the gross sales price in the year of sale).

Another major installment sale rule change eliminated the requirement of installment payments in two or more tax years. Now it is possible to sell a property on an installment sale with no down payment in the year of sale.

For installment sales made after October 20, 1980, the installment sale election is automatic. If the taxpayer wants to pay his tax in the year of sale and not spread it out over the years of the buyer's payments, he must "unelect" the installment sale tax deferral.

To combine the installment sale tax deferral with the $125,000 home sale tax exemption is easy. It is best illustrated by an example.

EXAMPLE: Betty, age sixty-five, sold her home and qualified for the $125,000 exemption. The adjusted sales price was $200,000 and her adjusted cost basis was $50,000, giving her a $150,000 sale profit. Her $125,000 exemption reduced the taxable profit to $25,000. Betty carried back an installment sale second mortgage to spread out her tax on this

$25,000 over the future years the buyer will make payments to her. In addition, the interest on the buyer's unpaid balance to Betty gives her safe, high-interest income.

INCOME AVERAGING

Any taxable profit on a real estate sale is eligible for income averaging. This includes long-term capital gains. If your taxable income, including capital gains, exceeds by 20 percent your average income over the past four tax years, income averaging will probably save you income tax dollars.

SUMMARY

Tax savings opportunities for principal residence sellers can be substantial. But the law's requirements must be met exactly because no exceptions are allowed. Consult an experienced tax adviser *before* selling your principal residence to take advantage of all the tax exemptions and deferrals available.

QUESTIONS AND ANSWERS

HOW TO GET MORE THAN $125,000
HOME SALE PROFIT WITHOUT PAYING TAX

Q. We have been very fortunate as we only paid about $24,000 for our home years ago. It is worth at least $160,000 today. I will retire soon. We are thinking of selling and moving to Florida. But as I read your explanations of that new $125,000 "over-55 rule" tax break, we would owe tax on about $11,000 of our $136,000 profit. Is that correct?—*Joel M.*

A. Not necessarily. You may be able to exempt from tax all $136,000 of your profit.

To qualify for the "over-55 rule" of Internal Revenue Code Section 121, I will assume you or your spouse will be fifty-five or older on the day you transfer title to your home to the buyer. In addition, you must have owned and occupied it at least three of the five years before sale and never have used this $125,000 tax exemption before. If qualified, up to $125,000 of your profit is tax-free using this law.

Subtracting the $125,000 exemption from the $160,000 sale price (which I assume is net after paying sales costs), gives a $35,000 "revised adjusted sales price." If, within twenty-four months before or after the sale, you buy a principal residence replacement costing at least this $35,000 amount, you must defer paying tax on the remaining $11,000 of your profit.

This tax rule, called the "residence replacement rule" of Internal

Revenue Code Section 1034, is available to home sellers of any age who sell their principal residence and buy a more expensive replacement. If you buy a Florida condominium, for example, costing over $35,000 (your "revised adjusted sales price"), you can qualify. For details, see your tax adviser.

WHEN A HOME BECOMES A HOUSE FOR TAX PURPOSES

Q. We just bought a run-down house, as you suggested. Frankly, it was all we could afford. Since it is in a pretty good neighborhood, with some fix-up I think it will turn out to be a profitable investment. I'm interested in the tax angles. Will the money we spend on new plumbing, wiring, and repairs be tax deductible?—*Bettina McG.*

A. Congratulations on buying a house in need of repairs. I think such properties, if in basically sound condition and in good locations, are the best buys in today's market.

If you are going to occupy the structure as your principal residence, then all your fix-up costs are additions to your original purchase price basis. Those improvements are not tax deductible.

But if you do not plan to occupy the dwelling as your home, and you plan to rent it to tenants, then the tax picture changes. Costs of capital improvements, such as the new plumbing and wiring, are added to the purchase price cost basis and are depreciable on your tax returns along with the value of the house. Repair costs, however, can be deducted as expenses if the house is rented to tenants. In addition, you can deduct costs of maintenance, fire insurance, and operating expenses. Your tax adviser can further explain the tax benefits of owning rental property.

NO TAX BREAK FOR SALE
AND REPLACEMENT OF SECONDARY HOME

Q. We just sold our Florida house for $47,500. Our primary home is near Washington, D.C. The profit on our sale was about $13,000. Next spring we plan to buy a Florida condominium for $67,000. Will we have to pay any tax? I heard it's possible to sell one property and reinvest the money in another property, thereby avoiding any profit tax.—*Goldie M.*

A. Sorry, but your situation will not qualify for profit tax deferral.

The only type of property sale on which profit tax can be deferred when a more expensive replacement is purchased is your principal residence. To qualify, both properties must be your principal residences, and the replacement must be bought within eighteen months before or after the sale. No other type of property can qualify for this tax break. Your tax adviser has further details.

THE KEY QUESTION ELDERLY SHOULD ASK BEFORE MARRIAGE

Q. I am sixty-six, and I just married a beautiful young lady of fifty-six. Before we got married last September, she sold her home and used that $125,000 profit tax exemption since her sale profit was almost $88,000. Now I want to sell my condominium so we can buy a house together. My profit will be about $75,000. My CPA told me my profit will be taxed, even though I've never used that $125,000 tax break because my new wife has already used up her once-in-a-lifetime exemption. Please tell me this bad news isn't true.—*Charlie K.*

A. I am sorry to report that your CPA's bad news is correct. Your new wife's use of the $125,000 exemption "over-55 rule" stops you from also using this tax benefit because the law allows only one such exemption per lifetime. This may seem harsh, since your condo is your separate property, but Congress apparently did not think of this bad result when the law was written.

If you each had sold your homes before you married, then you each could have taken up to $125,000 of tax-free profits from your home sales. But since your wife already used her exemption, that stops you from doing so. The key question elderly people should ask their new mate, before they march down the aisle to get married, is "Honey, have you used your $125,000 home sale tax exemption yet?"

HOME TAX DEDUCTIONS ONLY FOR OWNERS

Q. We own our home, but our son pays our mortgage payments and property taxes as we are disabled. Can he deduct these costs on his income tax returns?—*Josie H.*

A. No. To be entitled to deduct property taxes and mortgage interest on a personal residence, the person paying those costs must be the owner. You might wish to make your son a co-owner so he can deduct future property tax and mortgage interest payments.

NO LIMIT FOR MULTIPLE HOME SALE TAX DEFERRALS

Q. Several years ago when we sold our home in New York and bought our present one, we deferred paying our profit tax. Now we will be selling our present home and buying a larger one. Will we owe tax on our deferred profit as well as on the profit from our current home's sale? —*Harold L.*

A. Maybe. It depends on the purchase cost of the replacement principal residence you buy.

There is no limit to the number of times you can use the residence replacement rule of Internal Revenue Code Section 1034 to defer profit tax when selling one principal residence and buying a more expensive replacement.

But you cannot use this tax deferral rule more often than once every twenty-four months unless you change job locations and qualify for the moving expense deduction.

To qualify for the residence replacement rule tax deferral you must buy a replacement principal residence costing more than the adjusted sales price (that is gross sales price minus sales costs) of your former principal residence. If the replacement costs less, your profit is taxed up to the difference in the two prices. The replacement must be bought within twenty-four months before or after the sale.

HOW TO GET MAXIMUM INCOME TAX SAVINGS FROM YOUR HOME

Q. You often explain tax breaks for people who are selling their homes. But what about the rest of us who aren't selling? Are there any ways we can squeeze some extra income tax savings from our homes? —*Homer S.*

A. Yes, there are many tax savings breaks for homeowners. Some are well-known, such as tax deductions for mortgage interest and property taxes. Others are often overlooked, such as deductions for mortgage loan fees and prepayment penalties, business use of part of your home, moving expense deductions, casualty losses for thefts, fires, floods, broken pipes, roof leak damage, and even ground rent if your house is on leased land with an option to buy.

Of course, not every homeowner qualifies for all these tax breaks. While you may not be eligible this year, it is important to be aware of these benefits so that if you qualify, or you have a friend who does, you will know of the income tax dollars you can save.

INHERITED REAL ESTATE IS A TAX BONANZA

Q. My aunt died last September, leaving me most of her property. The two major assets are her home, worth at least $75,000, and a twelve-unit apartment house worth at least $300,000. Both are free and clear. She inherited these properties from my late uncle. As I live about 450 miles away from the house and apartments, I am considering selling them. (1) If I sell, will I owe a big capital gains tax? (2) Do you think I should sell or keep these buildings?—*Kurt R.*

A. (1) No. You will owe little or no tax if you sell the buildings after inheriting them. The 1978 Tax Act restored the old tax rule that inherited property is valued at its market value on the date of the decedent's death.

Your profit will only be any appreciation in market value between the date of your aunt's death and the day you close the sale. Of course, the estate pays the federal estate tax, and there may be a state inheritance tax too.

But no tax is due on the difference between your aunt's low basis for the properties and their market value on the date of her death. This is a big tax bonanza for you.

(2) The general rule is the more property you own, the better off you will be. But it can be difficult managing small properties from 450 miles away. If you sell, reinvest the money in good investment property closer to home.

USE $125,000 TAX EXEMPTION FOR DEFERRED PROFIT TAXES TOO

Q. In 1972, we sold our home and purchased a more expensive one, so we deferred our profit tax. If we sell the second home, can we use that $125,000 tax break to avoid tax on both profits?—*Harold P.*

A. Yes. To qualify for the $125,000 home sale tax break, you or your co-owner spouse must be fifty-five or older on the title transfer date. You must also have owned and lived in your principal residence three of the five years before its sale.

This tax benefit can be used to exempt from tax not only the profit on the sale of your current home, but also any deferred profits from previous home sales when you used the "residence replacement rule" of Internal Revenue Code Section 1034.

THE THREE-YEAR RESIDENCY FOR $125,000 HOME SALE TAX BREAK

Q. Does the three-year residency requirement for the $125,000 home sale tax exemption mean three continuous years?—*Evan F.*

A. No. Any three of the five years before sale is sufficient.

CAN UNUSED HOME SALE TAX EXEMPTION BE SAVED?

Q. If we sell our present home, we will have about $40,000 profit. When we use that $125,000 tax exemption, can we save the other $85,000 of our exemption for future use?—*Conwright M.*

A. No. You can use the $125,000 home sale tax benefit only once per lifetime. Any unused portion is wasted.

CAN MARRIED COUPLE GET TWO $125,000 HOME SALE TAX EXEMPTIONS?

Q. I am fifty-seven, my wife is fifty-four. If we wait to sell our home until my wife is fifty-five, will up to $250,000 of our profit be tax-free? —*Paul T.*

A. No. It will not pay to wait until your wife becomes fifty-five to sell your home, since only one $125,000 home sale tax exemption is allowed per married couple.

ARE HOME IMPROVEMENTS TAX DEDUCTIBLE?

Q. We recently installed new air conditioning and a new furnace in our home. We're considering installing new copper pipes. Are these expenses tax deductible?—*Robert W.*

A. No. The cost of capital improvements should be added to the purchase price cost basis of your home. Neither repairs nor capital improvements to your principal residence qualify as itemized income tax deductions. But save the receipts forever for those capital improvements.

CAPITAL IMPROVEMENT COSTS SAVE TAX AT HOME SALE TIME

Q. We recently sold our home for $89,750. The realty sales commission was $5,385 and various closing costs totaled $1,250. We bought the house many years ago for only $27,500. Since then we've spent about $6,000 for a room addition, about $550 for a new roof, $55 for a water heater, about $200 for landscaping, and around $350 for a fence. Also, we replaced the old wood windows with new aluminum ones which cost about $700. I don't have the receipts for any of these costs. How do I compute my home sale profit?—*Mr. W. W.*

A. Your home sale profit is the difference between the "adjusted sales price" (gross sales price minus selling costs) and the "adjusted cost basis" (original purchase price, plus closing costs which were not tax deductible at the time of purchase, plus costs of capital improvements, minus any casualty loss or depreciation deductions taken during ownership).

Computing your adjusted sales price is easy. That is $89,750 minus the $5,385 and $1,250 costs, or $83,115. But computing your adjusted cost basis is more difficult. Since you do not have receipts for the capital improvement, the IRS will often accept reasonable cost estimates. But repair costs are personal expenses and are not additions to your cost basis, nor are they itemized tax deductions.

A repair maintains the property, but a capital improvement improves, adds value, or extends the property's useful life. Sometimes it is hard to tell the difference between a repair and a capital improvement.

After consulting your tax adviser, you might calculate your cost basis by adding the $27,500 purchase price, plus the $6,000 room addition, plus the $550 roof, plus the $200 landscaping, plus the $350 fence, and the new

$700 windows. But the $55 water heater was probably a repair cost rather than a capital improvement addition to your home's cost basis.

Your sale profit would be the $83,115 adjusted sales price minus the $35,300 adjusted cost basis. The result is $47,815 profit.

YOU HAVE TWENTY-FOUR MONTHS TO DECIDE ABOUT HOME SALE TAX DEFERRAL

Q. Last month we closed the sale of our home at a profit of almost $52,000. We moved into a luxury apartment house that we like very much. But then I read your article about the "residence replacement rule" that says a home seller can defer paying his profit tax if he buys a more expensive replacement house or condo. We have just learned the apartment house where we are renting will soon be converted to condominiums. Would this qualify, and how long do we have if we want to defer our tax?—*Sheri T.*

A. The "residence replacement rule" gives you up to twenty-four months before or after the sale of your principal residence to buy a more expensive replacement and defer paying the profit tax.

When a less-expensive replacement principal residence is bought, then your sale profit is taxed up to the difference in the two prices.

If you buy your condominium apartment, and it costs more than the sale price of your old home, and if the sale closes within twenty-four months of the sale of your old home, you must defer paying profit tax.

PROFIT TAX DEFERRAL NOT LOST BY TEMPORARY RENTAL

Q. We used that "residence replacement rule" you often write about to defer profit tax on the sale of our old home. We've lived in our current house about eleven months. I am being transferred to New Mexico on a one-year assignment. If we rent our home during our absence, will we have to pay the deferred profit tax?—*Walter M.*

A. No. Since you have not sold your replacement principal residence, no taxable event has occurred. Conversion from personal residence to rental status is not a taxable event.

But if you fail to return to your house as your principal residence, it thereby is permanently converted to rental status and you would lose the opportunity to again use the residence replacement rule if you decide to sell it.

TAX DEDUCTIONS FOR SOME HOME LOAN FEES

Q. Please clarify for me when loan fees paid to get a home mortgage are tax deductible. As a real estate agent, I'm often asked if loan fees are tax deductible. Also, what about FHA and VA home loan fees?—*Dan F.*

A. Loan fees paid to obtain a home mortgage on your personal residence, to either purchase or improve it, are tax deductible as itemized interest deductions. But FHA and VA home loan fees are never tax deductible.

Loan fees paid to get a mortgage on any property other than your personal residence must be amortized (deducted) over the life of the mortgage.

VA and FHA loan fees are special. Lenders usually charge VA and FHA loan discount points to raise the low, government-set interest rate up to market levels. Each one point loan fee raises the lender's yield about ⅛ percent. By law, the VA or FHA home buyer cannot pay such fees. So if the seller pays, the loan fee is a sales cost subtracted from the home's gross sales price.

But the VA or FHA home buyer can pay a one point "loan processing fee" to the lender. However, this processing fee is not tax deductible as interest for the buyer.

WHAT IF BUYER AND SELLER CANNOT AGREE ON INSTALLMENT SALE?

Q. We want an installment sale of our home, but the buyer wants to pay all cash. The realty agent suggests putting the money in escrow trust which would pay us over twenty years. Will this work?—*Robert A.*

A. No. Nice try, but IRS Revenue Ruling 77–294 rejects the idea of a seller getting installment sale benefits when the buyer deposits installment sale money into a trust account for payment to the buyer.

4.

Why Income Property
Is Your Second Best Investment

The previous chapter explained the tax benefits of owning your principal residence. Smart real estate investors make their first realty purchase a home for their personal use. The pride of ownership, inflation hedge, and tax benefits of owning one's home are unequalled. Of course, such a home may be a single-family house, condominium, cooperative apartment, mobile home, or even a houseboat. But the important thing is to make your home purchase your first real estate investment.

After buying your own home, your next investment should be income-producing real estate. Just as your home can take many different forms, income property comes in lots of shapes and sizes too. Some investors prefer apartments. Others like shopping centers. A large number specialize in industrial income property such as warehouses and industrial parks. Still others buy single-family investment houses, as I do.

Each type of income property offers special advantages and disadvantages. Professional realty investors often argue the merits of each type of income property. But it is vital, before deciding which type of income property is best for you, to understand the all-important tax aspects of income property ownership.

NEVER BUY FOR TAX GIMMICKS ALONE

One basic rule of investing in income property is never, never, never buy for tax benefits alone. If a property is not inherently sound without the tax gimmicks, it probably is not a wise investment.

The tax breaks of owning income property should be viewed only as a "bonus advantage." However, these bonus tax benefits are a major reason for buying income property rather than vacant land. Raw land offers practically no tax benefits. And, since most raw land produces little or no income, the costs of holding such property almost always outweigh the possible future advantage of resale profit.

74

Even farmers have come to realize, in many areas, that their major source of profits now comes not from crops which can be raised on their land but from probable future resale profits. Unfortunately, having to sell raw land to make a profit is not as advantageous as making a profit while owning it, as income property investors do.

PROFIT DURING OWNERSHIP AS WELL AS AT RESALE TIME

Smart real estate investors count resale profits as another bonus of investing in real estate, just as the tax benefits are an ownership bonus. Why invest if you cannot make a profit while owning a property? If a property does not produce an overall profit during ownership, maybe it should not be bought (unless you can afford the risk of making your only profit dependent on resale profits).

Property investors who admit their only hope of profit will come at the time of resale are not investors. They are speculators. Speculators count on some fortuitous event, such as continued runaway inflation, for profits. But true investors create their own profits, both during ownership and at the time of eventual resale.

INVESTORS VS. SPECULATORS

In the next chapter we will look at how to find the best properties. That chapter discusses what smart investors want in a property that offers the best profit opportunities during ownership and at resale time. But before that discussion, it is vital to understand the tax benefits of property investing because the tax angles are important to understanding why it pays to buy income property rather than raw land.

An investor is a property owner who contributes something to the property, such as good management, physical improvements, or cash so someone else can use the property for their benefit. But a speculator is a quick-buck artist who contributes little or nothing to the property and is betting he can resell the property relatively quickly for more than he paid.

Characteristics of investors are (1) reasonable property management policies which are fair to tenants as well as to themselves, (2) expert financing techniques to use other people's money to purchase and improve the property (discussed in Chapter 6), (3) savvy use of ownership tax aspects to maximize their return from the property, (4) improvement and good management of the property to increase its market value (discussed in Chapter 8), and (5) creation of value by combining all these characteristics.

Indications of speculators include (1) shrewd management techniques that take advantage of the weaknesses of other people, such as property sellers and tenants, (2) little or no contribution of increased value due to physical improvements or efficient management of the property, (3) quick purchase and resale, (4) lack of concern for the long-run aspects of the property and its effect on the neighboring community, and (5) desire to maximize operating and resale profits (greed) without considering the long-term effect on the property itself.

An example of the latter is allowing deferred maintenance to accumulate and then selling the property just before major work becomes necessary. However, this can create profit opportunities for the next owner, who will hopefully be an investor rather than a speculator. A property that has two speculator owners in a row is easily recognizeable—usually with minimal cosmetic improvements such as cheap paint, least expensive carpets, and poor grade materials used throughout.

HOW TO UNDERSTAND THE MAJOR ADVANTAGES OF OWNING INCOME PROPERTY

How many times have you heard someone say "If only I had bought that property years ago I'd be wealthy today," or something similar? Today is yesterday's tomorrow. If you do not get busy investing in good real estate, you will be saying "If only I had bought" too.

While most investors believe real estate investing is the best way to keep up with and get ahead of inflation, too many potential realty buyers just talk about investing and do not take the first step of buying an investment property. Perhaps, if you are one of those lazy investors as I once was, you need a little friendly pushing. Please consider me your friendly realty "pusher"!

START BY SETTING YOUR INVESTMENT GOALS

Real estate can help investors realize many goals. Some are increased after-tax cash income, a hedge against inflation, providing a job from owning or managing property, opening up profit opportunities to upgrade property for profitable holding or resale, and many others.

But some types of properties meet investment goals better than others. For example, if you want maximum cash flow, buying vacant rural land obviously is not very smart. Investing in second mortgages would provide a higher cash flow (10 percent to 30 percent returns are not unusual for buyers of discounted second mortgages). Similarly, if you need to shelter your job earnings from income taxes, buying vacant land is not wise because it offers no tax savings from depreciation.

UNDERSTANDING REAL ESTATE OWNERSHIP BENEFITS

In Chapter 1 we looked at the four variables of any investment: (1) safety, (2) yield, (3) liquidity, and (4) potential for market value change. Although real estate did not come out perfect, overall it topped just about every other possible alternative investment.

This chapter takes a closer look at the advantages of owning real estate, specifically income properties. The term "income property," of course, refers to property which produces net, overall income for its owner. Examples include apartments, stores, and office buildings. "Nonincome property" includes vacant land, farmland, motels, boarding houses, and other property that requires personal labor to produce income from the property. As many investors in motels have found out, for example, some properties are merely real estate oriented businesses which offer the owner a full-time job. If you want to buy such property, and a full-time job, go ahead but do not think you are investing in income property because you are not. You are buying yourself a business first and a real estate investment second.

HOW INCOME PROPERTY GIVES
TAX SHELTER TO THE OWNER

In addition to all its inherent advantages, one of real estate's major attractions is its ability to shelter the owner's ordinary income, such as job salary, from income taxes. For example, an apartment house produces rents from its tenants. The owner uses that rent money to pay operating expenses (such as property taxes, repairs, utilities, and insurance) for the property. After paying all these costs, plus mortgage interest, he is left with either a positive or a negative cash flow from the property into his pocket.

EXAMPLE:

$ 20,000—Annual gross rental income from apartment rents
  −8,000—Annual operating costs *(40 percent of gross for most apts.)*
$ 12,000—Annual net operating income
  −10,000—Annual interest on mortgage
$ 2,000—Annual net income cash flow into owner's pocket

But a major expense has been left out! That is the noncash tax deduction for the building's depreciation. Income tax depreciation is a bookkeeping estimate for wear, tear, and obsolescence. It requires no cash payment to be entitled to this deduction.

Let us suppose our hypothetical building (not including the non-depreciable land value which never wears out) cost $80,000, and we elect to use a 15-year estimated remaining useful life with straight-line depreciation (these terms will be explained later in great detail).

> EXAMPLE:
> $ 2,000—Annual net income cash flow into owner's pocket
> − 5,333—Annual depreciation *($80,000 divided by 15 years)*
> $ (3,333)—Annual tax or paper loss from this income property

In this example, mortgage payments were considered to be mostly tax-deductible interest expense. In the early years of most mortgages, this is correct because only about 1 percent of the mortgage payments go toward equity buildup (loan principal payoff). The other 99 percent is tax-deductible interest.

But as the years go by, the deductible interest portion of the mortgage payment decreases and nondeductible principal amortization payoff increases. When the amortization becomes so great that a tax loss no longer results, that is the time to refinance to increase the mortgage interest tax deduction. Contrary to the thinking of most homeowners, income property owners rarely want to own their property free and clear, due to the tax disadvantages.

A tax or paper loss from income property is good. The owner of the property in the example above can subtract his $3,333 loss from his other taxable income, such as job salary.

If the owner of the building above has $20,000 taxable income, thanks to his building he will pay tax only on $16,667 (due to the $3,333 tax loss), thus saving about $666 in income taxes if he is in a 20 percent tax bracket. Yet he still can receive that $3,333 cash in the example and put it in his pocket tax-free. If this owner owns enough depreciable income properties, they can shelter all his otherwise taxable income from taxation.

HOW THE "TAX MAGIC" OF DEPRECIATION CAN SAVE YOU TAX DOLLARS

To understand how depreciation works and how it can save you income tax dollars requires some work. You may want to reread the next few pages several times because they are so important for real estate investors to fully comprehend.

Smart investors do their own income tax returns. Then they take them to their tax adviser to see if any tax deductions were missed. But without an understanding of important tax concepts, such as depreciation, you cannot do your own income tax returns for review by a specialist.

NO ONE HAS AS GREAT AN INTEREST IN SAVING YOUR TAX DOLLARS AS YOU DO.

The reason depreciation works "tax magic" is that it requires no cash payment to be entitled to this tax deduction. Other tax deductions, such as interest and property taxes, require the payment of hard, cold cash. But not depreciation.

That is why depreciation is the best tax deduction of all! It is even better than a tax credit (which is a subtraction from the income tax you owe). Although it is said "There's no such thing as a free lunch," the income tax deduction for depreciation comes pretty close.

INTRODUCTION TO DEPRECIATION

Any owner of business or rental real estate must deduct an allowance on his income tax returns for the theoretical loss in value of the improvements on his land due to the passage of time. Depreciation is a mandatory income tax deduction to compensate the owner for loss in value caused by wear, tear, and obsolescence of the improvements' value.

The value of the land on which the improvements rest, however, is *not* depreciable. That is because land is theoretically indestructible and never wears out. After the building becomes obsolete and is demolished, the land will still be there without any decline in its value due to wear, tear, or obsolescence.

WHAT IS AND IS NOT DEPRECIABLE PROPERTY?

There are three major classes of real estate that are *not* entitled to any tax deduction for depreciation.

A. Land Value

The value of land, whether it is raw, vacant land, improved farmland, or land with buildings resting on it, cannot be depreciated. While it is arguable that some land loses value, such as farm cropland which loses minerals each year, that argument is not recognized for income tax purposes.

Some land is subject to a depletion allowance, however, such as for oil or mineral removal. But depletion is not the same as depreciation and is beyond the scope of this book.

B. Personal Residences

Owners of single-family houses, cooperative apartments, or condominiums who reside in those structures are not entitled to any depreciation of those buildings. One exception exists, however, if the personal residence is used for rental to tenants or if part is used for a home office or shop. Then the personal residence qualifies for business use depreciation, as discussed in Chapter 3.

The reason personal residences are not depreciable is they are not held for investment or for use in a trade or business. This is the basic test for depreciable real estate.

However, an owner who resides in one apartment of a multi-unit apartment house can depreciate all of the building except his personal residence unit.

C. Property Held for Sale (Dealer Inventory)

Property which would otherwise be depreciable cannot be depreciated if it is held solely for sale to others. Such property is usually owned by a real estate dealer whose business is selling his inventory to others. Examples include homes constructed by a home builder for sale to customers or a new shopping center constructed by a developer for sale to investors.

WHAT IS DEPRECIABLE PROPERTY?

Just about any building, structure, or personal property used in the owner's trade or business or held for investment is depreciable. This includes buildings, sidewalks, fences, parking lot improvements, and other installations involving a "profit-inspired use." Depreciation is allowed even if the investment operation produces a loss, if there is a long-term profit intention. Even vacant buildings must be depreciated if they are held for investment or for use in a trade or business.

Orchards, orange trees, lemon groves, and other fruit and nut bearing trees are depreciable too. The *key test* for the depreciation deduction is DOES THE ASSET HAVE A DETERMINABLE LIMITED ECONOMIC USEFUL LIFE? If it does, it is depreciable!

HOW TO APPLY THE DEPRECIATION TEST

Using this test, land is not depreciable because it has no determinable limited economic useful life. For example, unless replenished by fertilizers, farmland will eventually lose its ability to produce crops. But this time period cannot be determined with any accuracy.

However, a fruit tree on nondepreciable land has a determinable useful life beyond which it will not produce a worthwhile crop. Similarly, land under a building is not depreciating due to wear, tear, or obsolescence. It just sits there, unaffected by what happens to the building that is resting upon it.

Interestingly, Revenue Ruling 74–265 held that landscaping adjoining a depreciable building can be depreciated if the owner can show the landscaping will most likely be destroyed at the end of the useful life of the building. In such a case, trees and landscaping shrubbery have the same useful life as adjoining building. The cost of planting annual flowers, of course, would be deductible as a current expense and would not qualify for depreciation.

HOW TO APPORTION THE COST BASIS

Upon acquisition of a depreciable property, the owner is required to allocate his cost basis among the (1) nondepreciable land value, (2) the improvement value, and (3) the value of any personal property.

THE CONSERVATIVE, NONCHALLENGEABLE METHOD

Allocating the cost basis of a property among its components is, at best, guesswork. It is far from a scientific procedure. Most owners start the process by looking at their local tax assessor's ratio among the depreciable assets such as building, personal property, and nondepreciable land value, as shown on the annual property tax bill. In most states, the tax assessor's bill shows his assessed value for the land, improvements, and, sometimes, the personal property. Owners who consider the assessor's ratio to be reasonable then apply that ratio to their purchase price of the property. The IRS will not challenge an allocation made by this method.

> EXAMPLE: Curt bought an apartment house for $200,000 (the amount of his cash down payment and mortgage(s) have nothing to do with depreciation deductions). The tax assessor's bill, although the assessed value is usually lower than the price paid for the property, shows 70 percent of assessed value is for the building, 20 percent for the land, and 10 percent for the personal property (refrigerators, stoves, and furniture). Curt feels this ratio is reasonable. So he allocates 70 percent of his $200,000 cost, or $140,000, to the depreciable building value, 20 percent or $40,000, to the nondepreciable land value, and 10 percent, or $20,000, to the depreciable personal property value.

Cost basis (purchase price) of the property acquisition of a depreciable property should be apportioned among land, buildings, and any personal property in proportion to their market value on the acquisition date. If the owner feels the local tax assessor's ratios are not realistic, he should use some other objective method for apportionment of the purchase price.

One way is to get a professional appraisal. Another is to obtain evidence of sale prices of nearby vacant land and then apply that square foot value to the land under the building purchased by the taxpayer, with the remainder allocated to improvements.

As will be explained later, the second safest method after using the tax assessor's ratio, is probably the professional appraiser's valuation. The third safest method is to use your insurance agent's estimate of the building's replacement cost.

ACQUISITION WITH INTENT TO DEMOLISH THE STRUCTURE

If property is bought with intent to demolish the building within a short time, then the owner cannot make any allocation of his purchase price to the building value. The entire purchase price must then be allocated to the nondepreciable land value. The cost of razing the structure must also be added to the land value, less any salvage collected. Demolition costs are not tax deductible in such a case.

Even if the owner intends to eventually demolish his building, if he rents it or uses it in his trade or business temporarily, he is then entitled to deduct depreciation for the limited use period. The depreciation basis of the building would be its present value at the time of acquisition (less land value, of course).

But if the building is not promptly demolished, any initial intent to destroy it must be ignored. When the building is later demolished before it is fully depreciated, a loss deduction is allowed for the undepreciated basis of the structure. This big depreciation-demolition deduction is deducted in the tax year of the building's destruction.

This same depreciation-demolition deduction applies if there was no intent to demolish the building when it was acquired.

BASIS ALLOCATION BY CONTRACT IS WORTHLESS

Sometimes a buyer and seller of depreciable real estate, in an arm's-length contractual negotiation, will allocate the purchase price among land, improvements, and personal property. If such an allocation makes no real difference to the seller—that is, all his profit is taxed as capital gain—the IRS will usually disregard any such allocation.

But if the seller has part of the gain taxed as ordinary income instead of as long-term capital gain due to the allocation, then the IRS will usually accept such an allocation of the purchase price. Since it is very rare to have a real estate sales profit taxed as ordinary income (property held over twelve months qualifies for profit taxation as long-term capital gain), this limited exception does not apply very often.

HOW TO MAXIMIZE DEPRECIATION BENEFITS UNDER THE 1981 TAX ACT

The 1981 Tax Act, also known as the 1981 Economic Recovery Tax Act (ERTA), greatly simplified the depreciation rules for real and personal property acquired after December 31, 1980. The old depreciation rules apply to property acquired before this date. These old, now outdated depreciation methods are fully explained in the 1981 first edition of this book (available from public libraries or local bookstores).

The new law's Accelerated Cost Recovery System (ACRS) must be used for all depreciable real and personal property "placed in service" after December 31, 1980. Please note that a property should qualify if it was bought before 1981 (such as your personal residence) but not "placed in service" for business or investment use as depreciable property until 1981 or later.

ACRS DEPRECIATION PERIODS

Depending on the type of depreciable real or personal property, you have a choice of useful life "recovery periods" as follows:

PROPERTY	USEFUL LIFE
Vehicles	3, 5, or 12 years
Other personal property	5, 12, or 25 years
Manufactured housing (mobile homes)	10, 25, or 35 years
Real property	15, 35, or 45 years

Investors desiring to maximize their depreciation benefits will select the shortest possible useful life in each category. It does not matter whether the real or personal property acquired is new or used; the same useful life applies.

These new depreciation useful-life time periods will stop the hassles taxpayers often encountered with IRS audit agents. Now the taxpayer can select the fifteen-, thirty-five-, or forty-five-year useful life for his depreciable buildings and the IRS auditor cannot challenge the selection. However, these rules only apply to federal income tax returns, not state tax returns. Unless the states conform their depreciation tax rules, a taxpayer might need two depreciation schedules—one federal and one state.

END OF COMPONENT DEPRECIATION

However, in return for establishing shorter useful lives for assets, the 1981 Tax Act removes the taxpayer's election to use the component method of depreciation. This technique permitted the property owner to depreciate separately the costs of various components such as plumbing, wiring, roof, and building shell.

Since these components usually had shorter useful lives than the composite whole, the owner maximized his depreciation deduction by using component depreciation. However, the 1981 Tax Act eliminates use of component depreciation except for depreciable property acquired before 1981.

HOW MUCH DEPRECIATION IS ALLOWABLE?

The depreciation deduction for depreciable real and personal property is limited by its cost to the owner. If the property was inherited, the owner's basis is the property's market value on the date of the decedent's death. However, if the property was a gift, the donee's basis is the lower of (1) the property's adjusted cost basis to the donor or (2) the property's fair market value on the date of the gift.

The cost of any capital improvements added after acquiring the property should be added to its basis. Salvage value need not be considered for property acquired in 1981 or later years.

The basis of depreciable real or personal property must be reduced by its allowable depreciation deduction each year under the schedule the owner adopts during the first year of ownership. Even if such depreciation reduces the owner's book value and gives him no income tax savings benefit in a particular tax year, he must reduce his book value by the allowable depreciation amount. In other words, he cannot make up in a future tax year for his loss of tax benefit in a previous tax year when the depreciation deduction gave him no tax dollar savings.

EXAMPLE: Laura's annual depreciation deduction for her three-family triplex resulted in a $2,500 tax loss on that property last year. Unfortunately, Laura's income from her other businesses also showed a loss last year. Since Laura had no other taxable income from which to deduct her $2,500 paper or tax loss from her triplex, she must reduce her book value "adjusted cost basis" on the triplex for the required depreciation even though no income tax shelter saving resulted.

USEFUL LIFE OF THE DEPRECIABLE ASSET

Two factors determine how much income tax depreciation is allowed: (1) the estimated useful life of the depreciable asset and (2) the depreciation method selected by the property owner.

For depreciation purposes, "useful life" of an asset means how long its economic life will be in the owner's trade or business or how long it will produce investment income. *Useful life does not mean physical life* unless that time is the same as useful economic life.

Under the pre-1981 law, Revenue Ruling 62-21 established "guideline" useful lives for average quality brand-new construction of various types of buildings. For example, these old guidelines suggested useful lives of forty years for new apartments, fifty years for bank buildings, forty-five years for factories, forty years for hotels, and sixty years for warehouses.

The new law abolishes these categories for buildings "placed in service" in 1981 or later years. The owner can now select a fifteen-, thirty-five-, or forty-five-year useful life for his structures regardless of the building's use or its current age.

To maximize depreciation tax deductions, 99 percent of all building owners will probably select the fifteen-year useful life. Owners selecting the thirty-five- or forty-five-year useful life would be those taxpayers who have no use for maximum depreciation deductions.

DEPRECIATION METHODS

The 1981 Tax Act allows only two depreciation methods: straight line and 175 percent accelerated.

THE CONSERVATIVE STRAIGHT-LINE DEPRECIATION METHOD

Most taxpayers use the straight-line depreciation method because (1) it is the easiest to use, (2) it eliminates any "recapture" problems (discussed later) when the property is sold, and (3) it gives easily predictable results rather than annually changing results of accelerated methods.

To use the straight-line depreciation method, the asset's basis is divided by its estimated useful life in years. The result is its annual depreciation deduction. But if the asset was not owned for the full tax year, it can be depreciated only for the number of months it was owned. In other words, prorations must be made for less than a full year of ownership.

The straight-line depreciation method can be used for all new and used depreciable real and personal property.

> EXAMPLE: Warren allocates the $400,000 purchase price of his shopping center to $300,000 for the depreciable building and $100,000 for the nondepreciable land value. He selects a fifteen-year useful life for depreciation. Dividing $300,000 by fifteen gives an annual $20,000 straight-line depreciation deduction. However, since Warren bought the shopping center in November 1981, he only deducts $2/12$ or $3,333 depreciation for the building on his 1981 federal income tax returns.

THE NEW 175-PERCENT ACCELERATED DEPRECIATION METHOD

The only other depreciation method now available for depreciable real property "placed in service" after December 31, 1980, is the new 175 percent accelerated depreciation method. This method uses the fifteen-year useful life but allows an additional 75 percent of the straight-line depreciation deduction. It can be elected whether the building is brand-new or used. However, before selecting this depreciation method, consider the "recapture" consequences at the time the building is sold (discussed later). Accelerated depreciation recapture can be very disadvantageous for commercial property owners but not so bad for residential rental property investors.

The following chart gives the annual depreciation deduction as a percent of the taxpayer's cost basis for the property. Please notice that the amount of deduction depends upon the month in which the depreciable real estate is purchased.

ACRS Cost Recovery Tables for Real Estate

All Real Estate (Except Low-Income Housing)

If the recovery year is:	The applicable percentage is: *(Use the Column for the Month in the First Year the Property is Placed in Service)*										
	J	F	M	A	M	J	J	A	S	O	N	D
1	12	11	10	9	8	7	6	5	4	3	2	1
2	10	10	11	11	11	11	11	11	11	11	11	12
3	9	9	9	9	10	10	10	10	10	10	10	10
4	8	8	8	8	8	8	9	9	9	9	9	9
5	7	7	7	7	7	7	8	8	8	8	8	8
6	6	6	6	6	7	7	7	7	7	7	7	7
7	6	6	6	6	6	6	6	6	6	6	6	6
8	6	6	6	6	6	6	5	6	6	6	6	6
9	6	6	6	6	5	6	5	5	5	6	6	6
10	5	6	5	6	5	5	5	5	5	5	6	5
11	5	5	5	5	5	5	5	5	5	5	5	5
12	5	5	5	5	5	5	5	5	5	5	5	5
13	5	5	5	5	5	5	5	5	5	5	5	5
14	5	5	5	5	5	5	5	5	5	5	5	5
15	5	5	5	5	5	5	5	5	5	5	5	5
16	—	—	1	1	2	2	3	3	4	4	4	5

EXAMPLE: Suppose you buy a small apartment house for $125,000, allocating $100,000 to the depreciable building's value and $25,000 to the nondepreciable land value. Using the chart, if you bought in January you can deduct 12 percent of the $100,000 building's cost ($12,000) the first year, 10 percent ($10,000) the second year, 9 percent ($9,000) the third year, etc.

But, again using the chart, if you buy this same building in May (the fifth month of the year), you can only depreciate 8 percent of the building's cost ($8,000) in the year of purchase, 11 percent ($11,000) the second year, 10 percent ($10,000) the third year, etc.

Whether you acquire the depreciable real property early or late in the year, however, using this 175 percent accelerated depreciation method will still result in full depreciation of the building within fifteen years. But the big advantage of using this new 175 percent accelerated depreciation method is maximization of tax shelter from the depreciation tax deduction in the early years of ownership. This depreciation method helps implement the smart real estate investor's motto: A tax deduction this year is better than a tax deduction in the future.

HOW "DEPRECIATION RECAPTURE" WORKS
AND WHY IT CAN BE EXPENSIVE

Depending on when a depreciable property was bought and when it is sold, all or part of the new fifteen-year, 175 percent accelerated depreciation deducted may be "recaptured." Recapture, in tax language, means taxed as ordinary income.

Here are the new recapture rules for fifteen-year, 175 percent rapid depreciation:

1. If the property is used as a residential rental, at the time of the property's sale, the difference between the 175 percent accelerated depreciation deducted and the allowable fifteen-year straight-line depreciation is taxed as ordinary income.

EXAMPLE: Suppose you deducted $20,000 of fifteen-year, 175 percent accelerated depreciation before you sold the property. If the fifteen-year straight-line method would have allowed only a $15,000 depreciation deduction, the $5,000 difference will be "recaptured" and taxed as ordinary income upon resale.

2. If the property is used for any purpose other than residential rental, at the time of its sale the *entire amount* of 175 percent accelerated depreciation deducted will be recaptured and taxed as ordinary income.

EXAMPLE: Using the amounts in the previous example, but now presuming the property is commercial (such as offices, stores, or warehouses), the entire $20,000 fifteen-year 175 percent accelerated depreciation deducted will be taxed as ordinary income at the time the property is sold.

Obviously, Congress wants to discourage commerical property owners from using the new 175 percent accelerated depreciation method since *all* such depreciation is recaptured and taxed as ordinary income. So unless the taxpayer saves a huge amount of income tax dollars by using 175 percent accelerated depreciation on his commercial property, in most cases it will pay to use straight-line fifteen-year depreciation on commercial buildings acquired in 1981 or later years.

Although it may seem disastrous to some property investors to have part of their resale profit recaptured and taxed as ordinary income tax rates, it should be remembered that the taxpayer has the tax-sheltered use of that profit money from depreciation (actually, the income tax dollars saved) until the property is sold.

For residential property owners electing the 175 percent accelerated depreciation method, it is also important to note that the longer the property is owned before sale, the less the recapture amount will be because the difference between accelerated and straight-line depreciation declines annually. By the fifteenth year, both methods fully depreciate the building.

HOW TO AVOID DEPRECIATION RECAPTURE

Smart taxpayers who own either residential or commercial property, however, can forget the recapture problem if they never sell. Another way to avoid recapture of depreciation deductions as ordinary income is to make a tax-deferred exchange.

Internal Revenue Code Section 1031 approves property trades as a continuous investment, rather than a sale and reinvestment in a second property. The happy result for traders is avoidance of accelerated depreciation recapture if the easy requirements of IRC 1031 are met.

As explained in Chapter 9, tax-deferred exchanges are virtually the only method of pyramiding your wealth without paying income taxes as you do so. Such exchanges allow a smart investor, for example, to start out with a small property (such as a two-family rental), build some equity in it, and later make a tax-deferred trade of that equity for a larger property to be held for investment or use in a trade or business.

BEWARE OF THE NEW ANTI-CHURNING RULES
FOR TAX-DEFERRED EXCHANGES

Although tax-deferred exchanges are a great way to avoid depreciation recapture and profit taxation when disposing of one property and acquiring another, the 1981 Tax Act has an exchange pitfall to avoid. It is called the "anti-churning rule."

If you own investment or business real property acquired before 1981, you probably would like to dispose of it and acquire other property so you can take advantage of the 1981 Tax Act's generous depreciation deductions. So you might think you can exchange your pre-1981 property (thus deferring the profit tax) for post-1981 property (to use the new depreciation rules).

But Congress anticipated this desire because it did not want taxpayers to both defer profit tax upon disposal of property and be able to take advantage of the new generous depreciation rules for the replacement property.

Greatly simplified, the 1981 Tax Act's anti-churning provisions say that if you make a tax-deferred exchange of business or investment real estate for another such property, your old basis and its old depreciation method carry over to the newly acquired property. The new fifteen-year, 175 percent accelerated depreciation methods can only be used on the increased depreciable basis of the property acquired in the exchange.

EXAMPLE: Suppose you own a $100,000 depreciable building which you have depreciated down to $20,000. If you sell it, you will owe long-term capital gains tax on your $80,000 profit. So you decide to trade for a $300,000 property. The anti-churning rule requires you to use your old depreciation method on the $20,000 basis carried over to the $300,000 property. But the new fifteen-year, 175 percent accelerated depreciation methods *can* be used on any increased depreciable basis in the acquired property.

However, if the owner of property acquired before 1981 has a depreciated book value adjusted cost basis only slightly less than the property's market value, he might be better off selling his old property, paying a small long-term capital gains tax on his small profit, and reinvesting in another property that can fully qualify for the new rapid depreciation.

EXAMPLE: Suppose you own a $100,000 depreciable building which you have depreciated down to $90,000 adjusted cost basis (book value). If you sell, you will have a $10,000 long-term capital gain with a maximum 20 percent tax of about $2,000. You can reinvest the $8,000 remaining into another depreciable property and use the new depreciation methods on the new acquisition's entire depreciable basis. But if you make a tax-deferred exchange instead, the 1981 Tax Act's anti-churning rule requires you to carry over your old $90,000 adjusted cost basis and its old depreciation method (perhaps a twenty-five- or thirty-year useful life) to the acquired property.

To maximize tax shelter from the new depreciation rules, and to avoid the adverse results of the anti-churning rule in the 1981 Tax Act:

1. If you own low basis pre-1981 property, use a IRC 1031 tax-deferred exchange to defer your large profit tax and carry over your old, low basis and old depreciation method (but just on the old basis amount) and use the new fifteen-year depreciation rules for the amount of the increased basis.
2. If you own a high basis pre-1981 property, consider selling it, paying the long-term capital gain tax on your profit, and acquiring another property which can be fully depreciated using the new fifteen-year depreciation rules (with no carry-over of your old basis and old depreciation method).

A SPECIAL TAX BONANZA—NEW PERSONAL PROPERTY DEPRECIATION RULES

In addition to the new fifteen-year depreciatin rules for depreciable buildings and other real property improvements, the 1981 Tax Act improved the rules for depreciating personal property used in a trade or business.

The tax law requires depreciation of business personal property such as equipment and furnishings. In real estate, examples include apartment house furniture and appliances used by the tenants of the apartment rentals.

EXAMPLE: Howard bought $10,000 of furniture and appliances for his apartment house. Using the new ACRS depreciation method, he can select a five-, twelve-, or twenty-five-year useful life for this personal property. Like most realty investors, Howard selects the five-year useful life because he then maximizes his depreciation tax deductions and this depreciation bookkeeping write-off will approximate the rate at which the furniture and appliances drop in actual market value as they wear out.

ACCELERATED DEPRECIATION ALLOWED FOR PERSONAL PROPERTY

The 1981 Tax Act allows taxpayers to select either straight-line or accelerated depreciation for personal property. The accelerated depreciation tables provided in the new tax law are equivalent of 150 percent declining balance accelerated depreciation. It does not matter if the personal property is new or used.

Further note should be made of the so-called "half-year convention." Regardless of whether you acquire depreciable personal property in January, July, or December, in the year of acquisition you get a prorated depreciation deduction as if you had bought the personal property on July 1. But this half-year convention applies only to personal property using accelerated depreciation. All real property and personal property depreciated on the straight-line basis does not use the new half-year convention provided for in the following ACRS depreciation chart.

150 PERCENT RAPID DEPRECIATION FOR PERSONAL PROPERTY

YEAR	3-YEAR VEHICLES	5-YEAR PERSONAL PROPERTY
1	25%	15%
2	38%	22%
3	37%	21%
4		21%
5		21%

Remember, this chart only applies to business personal property *after* the allowable write-off (up to $5,000, $7,500, or $10,000) has been first subtracted from the cost. So if you buy $3,500 of personal property in 1982 or later for your apartment house, it should be fully expensed in the year of purchase and you will not have any depreciation schedule for that acquisition. Also, please note that it is not necessary under the 1981 Tax Act to consider any salvage value for business personal property.

INVESTMENT TAX CREDIT

Although the investment tax credit will not apply to personal property acquired by most real estate investors for use in their properties, the investment tax credit does apply to vehicles (such as a car used in supervising your properties). This tax credit is a direct subtraction from your income tax liability as follows:

Vehicles	6% credit
Other personal property	10% credit

The reason the investment tax credit does not apply to most real estate investors is that the tax law specifically excludes from eligibility personal property used in connection with lodging facilities unless used by transients more than half the time (IRC 48(a)(3); Reg. 1.48-1(h)). However, nonlodging commercial facilities open to the public, such as coin-operated laundry machines or vending machines in an apartment house, qualify for the investment tax credit.

If the personal property, on which an investment tax credit was claimed, is sold before it is fully depreciated, the taxpayer can keep 2 percent for each year the property was owned.

EXAMPLE: Betty claimed a 6 percent investment tax credit on her new car acquired in 1982. She keeps it two years and disposes of it in 1984 before it is fully depreciated. Betty can keep 4 percent of her investment tax credit but the remaining 2 percent will be recaptured on her 1984 tax returns.

SUMMARY

The 1981 Tax Act is a tax bonanza for real estate investors who understand how to take advantage of its provisions. The rapid fifteen-year, 175 percent accelerated depreciation useful life methods will further enhance real estate's inherent advantages, which are unmatched by alternative low-risk investments. But what Congress giveth, Congress can take away. The sooner you acquire depreciable real estate, the sooner you can benefit from these tax benefits of owning depreciable property.

SUMMARY OF THE "TAX MAGIC" DEPRECIATION APPLICABLE TO INVESTMENT REALTY

The goal of tax-wise property investors should be to own total holdings which at least break even on a cash basis. After deducting the paper loss from depreciation, the properties should lose money to give the owner "tax shelter" for his other ordinary income, such as job salary. If your real estate produces an after-tax profit, rather than a paper loss, it is time to trade up to larger properties which will give higher depreciation deductions and, hence, tax shelter.

Depreciation tax magic occurs when the building's cash flow is exceeded by its depreciation deduction. The result is a tax loss. A tax loss should be every investor's goal!

But the best news is that while the building is depreciating in book value, in the real world it should be appreciating in market value. When the owner sells his building, the difference between his net sales price and depreciated book value is profit (taxable at the low, long-term capital gain tax rates ranging from 5.6 percent to 20 percent of the total profit, except for any recaptured depreciation taxed as ordinary income.).

A footnote should be added, however. Another advantage of owning depreciable real property is *it is just about the only investment that can be sold at a profit even if the price attained is the same as the investor paid for the property*. It is all due to the *tax magic of depreciation that converts ordinary income into long-term capital gains*.

For example, suppose your $100,000 building is depreciated down to $80,000 book value when you resell it for $100,000. That $20,000 difference between the adjusted sales price and the adjusted cost basis is profit. It is long-term capital gain if the property was owned over twelve months. During ownership, the $20,000 depreciation deduction sheltered $20,000 of ordinary income (such as rents or job salary) from income taxes. At resale time, that profit is taxed at the lowest possible rates for long-term capital gains.

The happy result is conversion of ordinary income (taxed at the highest income tax rates) to long-term capital gain (taxed at the lowest rates).

There is nothing wrong with paying income taxes. But smart investors pay those taxes at the low, long-term capital gains rates. This is made easy for investors who understand the tax benefits of owning depreciable real property.

QUESTIONS AND ANSWERS

UNLOCK HOME EQUITY TO BUY DEPRECIABLE INVESTMENT PROPERTY

Q. We sold our stocks at a substantial loss. After reading your newspaper articles about how it costs money to keep cash in a savings account, after considering inflation and income tax on the interest, we decided to buy an apartment house. The first agent showed us a ten-unit building we saw advertised in the newspaper. When we told him we had about $25,000 to invest, he asked if we would like to buy a twenty-seven-unit building instead. Of course, we told him we were interested (because we want to maximize our tax shelter from the depreciation) but that we have only $25,000 to invest. He suggested we "create" a second mortgage on our home equity for the rest of our down payment. This sounds like a good idea. Is it?—*Charles R.*

A. Yes. By giving the seller of the twenty-seven-unit building a second mortgage on your house for part of your down payment, in addition to your $25,000 cash investment, you are unlocking your idle home equity.

Most homeowners should unlock their home equities. The more property you control, the better protected you will be against inflation. If you buy that twenty-seven-unit building, you will own two properties (your home and the apartments) which are probably going up in value at least as fast as the inflation rate. In addition, that apartment house should give you a "tax loss" or "paper loss" to shelter the rents and some of your other ordinary taxable income from income taxation.

WHERE TO GET CASH TO BUY INVESTMENT PROPERTY

Q. I own my home, valued at $55,000. My mortgage at 7 percent interest rate is about $13,500. I have over $6,000 in my savings account. To buy income property, probably apartments, should I take the $6,000 for my down payment, or should I refinance my home mortgage to raise the cash for the down payment? I want to acquire as much income property as possible. I have heard that to get a mortgage on income property, you must live in the building. Is that true? Does FHA make apartment-house mortgages?—*Mr. D. K.*

A. To raise cash for your down payment, instead of refinancing that beautiful 7 percent mortgage, consider adding a second mortgage instead. Weigh both alternatives before deciding. Unless you have good borrowing power, keep adequate cash in savings for emergencies.

No, you do not have to live in the apartment house to get a mortgage on it. But FHA mortgages on one- to four-family buildings require owner occupancy of one apartment. FHA loans on over four units do not require you to live in the building.

However, your best finance source is the property's seller. In your first purchase offer, provide for the seller to carry a first or second mortgage to help finance your purchase. Many sellers will do so. Also, please remember to make as small a cash down payment as possible to maximize your leverage yield per dollar.

DO CONDOS MAKE GOOD HOMES AND INVESTMENTS?

Q. Last winter we visited Florida for a month. We are thinking of retiring there. While we were there, we looked at several new developments of retirement houses and condominiums. The condo idea appeals to us, as we can just lock the door and drive away without having to worry about maintaining the property while we're gone. But we are two years away from retirement. Would it be smart to buy a retirement condo now, rent it for two years, and then move into it as our retirement home? I guess what I really want to know is whether or not condos make good homes and investments?—*Marty R.*

A. Yes, condominiums can be excellent homes and investments. But they can also be lousy if you buy the wrong one.

Before you buy, talk to current residents of the development. Find out what they like most and least about it. Ask if they would buy there again.

Some condos are well built and extremely satisfactory. Others are cracker boxes. Personally, I have done well with condo investments. But I strongly suggest you double-check the soundproofing before you buy. Lack of adequate soundproofing is the number one complaint of condo owners.

As investment property, condos can be extremely profitable due to their high building-to-land ratio. Unless the condo development has lots of open space, you may be able to depreciate up to 90 or 95 percent of the purchase price for the cost of the condo unit (land value is nondepreciable). Your tax adviser can further explain the tax benefits of condo investing.

VACATION OR SECOND HOMES
ARE RARELY GOOD TAX SHELTER INVESTMENTS

Q. We bought a second home in a vacation area. The summer season lasts about sixteen weeks, and there is winter ice fishing and some skiing too. The realty agent will try to rent it to tenants as much as possible except when we use it for about three weeks each July. Will we be able to take depreciation on this property so we can get some tax shelter from it? —*Woody M.*

A. For income tax purposes, if your personal use of your second home exceeds fourteen days per year or 10 percent of its rental period, it cannot qualify as "investment property." That means no tax shelter benefits for you.

Your mortgage interest and property tax are always deductible on your income tax returns even if they exceed the second home's rental income. But if your personal use time exceeds the limits above, then your tax deductions for the second home cannot exceed the rent received.

Suppose your house earns $4,000 annual rent and $3,000 is the total of the annual mortgage interest and property taxes. If your personal use exceeds the time limits above, you can then only deduct up to $1,000 of other expenses, including any depreciation.

In other words, no "tax loss" is allowed on second homes if your personal use exceeds the fourteen-day or 10 percent limits. But you can get tax loss benefits for your vacation home if your personal use time is below these limits since the cabin then qualifies as investment property.

NO INFLATION PROTECTION IF YOU
DO NOT INVEST IN REAL ESTATE

Q. I am sixty-four, one year away from retirement, and have about $20,000 excess funds to invest. I own my home free and clear and am a widow. My son suggests I invest my $20,000 in several second mortgages. What do you think?—*Laura M.*

A. I think you should first decide what your investment goals are. Income? Inflation protection? Pride of ownership? Tax shelter?

All these goals can be accomplished with real estate. But usually not at the same time with just one investment. If you invest in second mortgages, for example, you will probably maximize your income. That is why so many retirees invest in second mortgages. But there is no inflation hedge protection and no tax shelter for the excellent interest earnings.

If you buy a small rental property, however, it may appreciate in market value at least as fast as the inflation rate. But such property will not give you immediate cash income equal to what you could have earned investing in second mortgages.

To help decide which form of real estate investment is best for you, consult a local real estate counselor. If you do not know such a person, you can find one through your local board of realtors. For a fee, you will be objectively counseled and guided to the best type of realty investment for you.

YOUR PROPERTY CAN PROVIDE
YOUR RETIREMENT INCOME

Q. In 1975, when you first started writing your newspaper articles in Washington, D.C., I said to myself "There's a guy who knows what he's talking about." This was long before real estate obviously became such a good inflation hedge. In 1976, my wife and I took $10,000 of savings and bought a run-down house which we fixed up. We bought it to live in. But a real estate agent dropped by while we were working on it and offered us such a fantastic price we couldn't refuse to accept. To make a long story short, we followed your ideas. Today we still live in our bargain-rent Washington apartment where we pay only $325 per month rent, but we have over $750,000 in equities in various properties. Keep up the good work telling people what a great investment real estate can be.—*Jess R.*

A. Thank you for sharing your success story. I believe that reader comments like yours do more to motivate people to invest in good property than I ever can. When you are ready to retire, you can gradually sell off your properties to provide your retirement income security.

To illustrate how vital it is to buy good property while you are young, let me tell a personal story. I recently bought a rental house being sold by an elderly lady who now lives with her children. I offered to buy it with $15,000 cash down payment and a mortgage for the balance payable at $1,030 per month. That house was the major asset the seller owned. Thanks to its sale, she will receive money to live comfortably for the rest of her life. Clearly, you are in a much better position for your retirement in a few years since you own several properties.

WOULD GOLD, SILVER, OR REAL ESTATE BE A BETTER INVESTMENT?

Q. We have saved about $6,000. My husband wants to invest it in gold or silver, but I think we should put it as down payment on a small rental house. Which investment do you think will offer the greatest long-run security?—*Frannie M.*

A. Gold and silver market values can fluctuate wildly, but home values are relatively stable. Homes are necessities; gold and silver are not.

Gold and silver prices are subject to market fluctuations beyond your control. On the other hand, people must have homes to live in. For this reason, only a tiny fraction of homes are sold in any one year so this stabilizes their value.

If you want long-run security, without worry, invest in rental houses whenever you get a little extra cash to invest. In addition to the joy of ownership, you will probably benefit from the house's market value appreciation which, in recent years, has averaged 10 to 15 percent per year on a nationwide average. Gold and silver investments are for speculators. True investors buy good real estate for long-term security.

INVEST, DO NOT SPECULATE, IN REAL ESTATE

Q. I would like to speculate in rental house investments. Being a salaried insurance company clerk, I can spare up to $200 per month to make up any negative cash flow for up to one year. Do you think I should speculate in rental houses even though they won't produce enough rent to cover the mortgage payments, property taxes, insurance, and maintenance?—*Joseph M.*

A. Don't speculate. Invest. Buyers who will have to sell in a year or so can get themselves in a jam if the local home sale market is slow when they have to sell.

A better approach is to buy property in need of upgrading. After you improve the property, thereby raising its market value, you can almost surely resell for more than you paid. The result is you have turned yourself from a speculator, depending upon inflation to give you a profit, into an improver who raises the property's value regardless of what happens to inflation.

LIFETIME PROPERTY PLAN PROVIDES FOR COLLEGE, RETIREMENT COSTS

Q. I sure wish our newspaper had been running your articles when we first started investing in real estate back in 1968. We could have used your advice, but somehow we got over the hurdles. As a result we now own twelve properties, all bought as a result of a $6,000 initial investment. Today, due to inflation, I think it would take about $10,000 to get started, however. Perhaps our experience can help others. Our goal was to buy one investment property each year. By refinancing our existing holdings, we've managed to do that. In 1978, we sold one small duplex apartment to give us cash for our son's college tuition. Next year we'll sell another building to pay for more tuition. In four years we'll sell another building on an installment sale to provide for our retirement income. Then we'll sell off buildings as we need the cash. That's not too bad for a taxi driver with a ninth-grade education is it?—*Claude R.*

A. Thank you for your marvelous letter. It shows how wise property investment can provide long-term security. Your example should be an inspiration to others to get busy in real estate investing.

DEPRECIATION RECAPTURE EXPLAINED

Q. What does "depreciation recapture" mean? When we did our last year's income tax returns, our accountant told us not to take accelerated depreciation on a fourplex we bought. He gave his reason as "depreciation recapture."—*Amos M.*

A. Depreciation recapture applies only when you sell your property held for investment or for use in a trade or business. Recapture means the difference between accelerated depreciation deducted and the lower amount you could have deducted using the straight-line depreciation method, and it is taxed as ordinary income at the time of sale.

To illustrate, suppose when you sell your fourplex you have deducted

$20,000 of accelerated depreciation, but you could have deducted only $15,000 using the straight line depreciation method. The $5,000 difference will be "recaptured" and taxed as ordinary income. This really is not such a "bad deal" since you had the use of the tax savings until the time of the resale.

IS IT BEST TO SELL OR RENT FORMER HOME?

Q. In November 1979, we bought a $50,800 house with an 11.5 percent interest rate mortgage. The Air Force has advised my husband he is to be transferred to Alaska for a minimum of three years. Would it be best for us to sell or rent our house? The monthly payment is $609. Realtors tell us it will rent for about $400 per month. We fear that if we sell we may not be able to afford to buy another house when we return to the continental U.S. What do you advise? Our realty agent says "sell," but I think he wants the sales commission?—*Barbara M.*

A. Your house can be an excellent investment if you do not sell. If you can afford the $209 monthly negative cash flow, after considering your income tax dollar savings from the deductions and depreciation, plus the home's probable future appreciation in market value over the next three years, it can be very profitable for you to keep that house. As rents go up in future years, your negative cash flow will probably decrease.

Your biggest problem will be management of the house. Do you have someone who can rent it when it becomes vacant? Is someone available locally to arrange repairs? Many realty agents are glad to do so for a nominal fee.

If you sell your house now, after ownership for such a short time, you may have little net profit after paying the sales expenses. A home sale within a year or two after purchase generally is not very profitable unless home values have risen rapidly in your neighborhood.

ARE VACATION HOMES GOOD INVESTMENTS?

Q. Do you think investment in a vacation home would be profitable? I am considering buying a cabin on a lake that is also near a winter sports area. I can buy it for just $23,000 down payment. The agent says he can rent it when I'm not using it.—*John N.*

A. Never, never, never buy recreational property with any hope of resale profit. Buy such property only for personal use. Your chances of keeping the cabin rented year around are very slim. The tax advantages are not good either if you make considerable personal use of the vacation home.

If you have $23,000 to invest, you will probably do much better investing in depreciable income property close to your home. Rental houses, commercial property, or rental condos usually make much better investments than risky vacation property.

IS DEPRECIATION ALLOWED ON AN APPRECIATING PROPERTY?

Q. I own a triplex three-family house. You told another reader he must depreciate the value of his apartments. Would this apply to me too even though my triplex is actually going up in market value?—*Jim D.*

A. Yes. Depreciation is a noncash bookkeeping expense deduction on your income tax returns for wear, tear, and obsolescence. Uncle Sam allows this deduction even if your property is actually going up in market value.

Depreciation is a primary motivation for investing in income real estate. It is required even if the property is appreciating in value or if the seller had fully depreciated the building before selling it to you.

MUST DEPRECIATION BE DEDUCTED?

Q. I am retired now with little taxable income. Last year I inherited two small apartment buildings from my late sister. My tax man says I must deduct depreciation on them even though that depreciation doesn't save me any income taxes. Is this correct?—*Mrs. L. L.*

A. Yes, your tax man is correct. Depreciation must be deducted on improved property held for investment or for use in a trade or business even if you receive no resulting income tax savings.

However, you may be eligible to use your net operating loss to get an income tax refund if you paid income taxes in any of the last three years. Ask your tax man if he considered this tax advantage of the depreciation deduction.

ARE PROPERTY INSPECTION TRIPS TAX DEDUCTIBLE?

Q. We own a farm in North Dakota which we lease to a farmer there. If we go to inspect this property next summer, can we take a tax deduction for our trip expenses?—*Sylvia D.*

A. Yes. Reasonable travel expenses to inspect investment property or real estate used in your trade or business are tax-deductible expenses.

But if your trip is part of a vacation, only the expenses directly related to the inspection are deductible. This is a "gray area" of tax law, so consult your tax adviser for exact details.

CAN INVESTOR DEPRECIATE HOME CONVERTED TO RENTAL?

Q. We bought a new house and are considering renting our old home for the tax benefits and value appreciation rather than selling it. The old house cost us about $60,000 and is worth at least $125,000 today. Can we depreciate the $60,000 or the $125,000?—*Joe M.*

A. Neither. You can depreciate the lower of your home's fair market value or your adjusted costs basis (usually purchase price plus capital improvements added during ownership) as of the date of conversion from personal use to rental status.

That means you start out with your $60,000 cost basis. Assuming you did not add any capital improvements, you must then allocate the $60,000 between nondepreciable land value and depreciable value of the structure. Only the value of the building qualifies for depreciation tax deductions when the house is rented to tenants.

IS VACANT LAND OR INCOME PROPERTY A BETTER INVESTMENT?

Q. We realize we should be investing in real estate. But my wife and I can't agree on whether to buy rural land, which needs no management, or city property, such as apartments or a commerical building. What do you advise?—*Charles F.*

A. First, decide your investment goals. Perhaps you want to invest for appreciation in market value, tax shelter, pride of ownership, leverage profits, or some other motive.

If you invest in land, it must appreciate in value at least 20 percent per year just to keep even with inflation and carrying costs. Land offers no tax shelter as there is nothing to depreciate (except maybe a fence).

But investing in depreciable buildings, such as apartments, offices, stores, or warehouses, offers potential for future value appreciation as well as immediate tax shelter. Another advantage is rental properties usually earn enough rental income to pay their carrying costs, so you do not have to meet payments out of your pocket as you usually would with vacant land. I vote for investing in depreciable buildings.

5.

How to Find
the Best Properties to Buy

Up to this point, we have looked at why real estate (including your home and income property) is your best investment opportunity, the tax benefits of home ownership, and reasons why income property is so profitable.

Now the focus changes. This important chapter gets down to the nitty gritty of how to find the best properties.

If this chapter had to be summarized in one word, it is "persistence." Do not give up. The right property for you will not have a flashing neon sign saying "This is it!" Instead, each successful property buyer has to work to locate and sometimes create the bargain properties. If it was easy to buy the best properties, everyone would be doing so. Since it is not always simple to locate good properties, this limits your competition. In fact, if you are competing with another buyer for the same property, it is usually smart to walk away because competition makes the purchase terms less desirable.

HOW TO START YOUR PROPERTY SEARCH

Before rushing off to look at homes for sale or income properties offered by local realty brokers, take at least one hour to analyze your personal financial situation. *Do this alone—be 100 percent honest with yourself.*

Do not let your spouse or friends see what you write down.

First, list all your financial assets and their true market value today if you had to sell them to raise cash. For example, your gas guzzler car which cost $8,000 last year may only be worth $4,000 as a used car today.

Next, list all the ways you can raise cash. Although not part of your financial statement, your cash-raising ability is an important asset. Include your credit card lines such as Visa and MasterCard, bank credit lines, and department store charge cards (which are handy for property improvements).

101

Lastly, list the liabilities you owe. Examples might include your auto loan, your charge account balances, and any college tuition debts.

The difference between the value of your assets and what you owe on your liabilities is your net worth. Add to your net worth the amount of cash you can raise within thirty days. This total is the maximum amount you can afford to invest (although you will probably invest something less than this sum).

Here is a quick summary of this procedure of financial self-analysis:

ASSETS	$___
Cash in checking and savings accounts	$___
Accounts receivable	$___
Mortgages owned	$___
Marketable securities owned	$___
Cash surrender value of life insurance policy	$___
Real estate owned (today's market value)	$___
Automobiles (today's market value)	$___
Personal property (today's market value)	$___
Other assets	$___
TOTAL ASSETS	$___
LIABILITIES	
Accounts payable within thirty days	$___
Notes payable beyond thirty days	$___
Income taxes payable	$___
Loans on life insurance policy	$___
Mortgages or liens on real estate	$___
Installment loan total balances	$___
Auto loan	$___
Other liabilities	$___
TOTAL LIABILITIES	$___

To arrive at your net worth, subtract your total liabilities from your total assets:

Total assets	$___
Minus: Total liabilities	$___
NET WORTH	$___

Add to this amount the amount of cash you can raise within thirty days by borrowing. This is the maximum amount you can invest, although you should probably invest less. As you acquire more properties, your net worth and borrowing power will increase, allowing you to acquire still more properties.

Next, check your income and expenses to see if you can afford to make the payments on your realty acquisitions.

ANNUAL INCOME $___
Job salary—gross income from employment $___
Interest income $___
Dividends $___
Rental income (net after expenses and mortgage payments) $___
Alimony, child support, separate maintenance $___
Other income $___
TOTAL ANNUAL INCOME $___

ANNUAL EXPENDITURES $___
Housing costs: mortgage payments or rent $___
Property taxes $___
Income and other taxes $___
Loan payments $___
Insurance payments $___
Living expenses $___
Alimony, child support, separate maintenance $___
Charity donations $___
Other expenses $___
TOTAL ANNUAL EXPENSES $___

The excess income over expense is the "savings" in your budget. This is the amount you can set aside for your real estate investments. Of course, keep a cash reserve or, better yet, an emergency borrowing credit line at the bank.

WHAT CAN YOU OFFER A PROPERTY SELLER?

Your financial analysis was probably very revealing. If you did not fully complete your self-survey, stop now and do it. It is always a surprise to find out how little or how much your net worth really is. But without this basic knowledge of your current financial position, you are not ready to start acquiring real estate.

Now consider what you can offer to a property seller besides your charm and good looks. Property sellers know they own something valuable. The reason they are selling is they think they will be better off after the sale than before. This may or may not be true.

But if you get nothing else from this book, remember:

SMART PROPERTY BUYERS OFFER THEIR SELLERS A WAY TO IMPROVE THEIR SITUATION WHILE, AT THE SAME TIME, IMPROVING THE BUYER'S POSITION TOO.

Normally, the way most buyers improve the situation of the seller is to offer a cash down payment. But this is not always what the seller wants. If you are a multimillionaire, for example, more cash is not always what you want.

In other words, smart property buyers offer sellers the benefit the seller is seeking from the property sale. Usually, this benefit is cash and the buyer makes a down payment to satisfy the seller's need. But smart buyers look beyond the seller's obvious or stated needs. Many sellers will not confide their true needs to the real estate agent who has the listing on the property offered for sale. Do not always believe the reason the agent gives as the seller's motivation. The agent may not know the full story.

Make a list of what you can offer a property seller in return for his selling to you. Your list might include:

Cash down payment

Personal property—auto, boat, RV (recreational vehicle), furniture, appliances

Personal services—carpentry, plumbing, wiring, legal services, dentistry, or whatever else you can do

Payment of seller's debts—this can often be done at a discount by contacting the seller's creditors (with his permission after you have a binding sales contract to buy the property)

Cash raised from borrowing on your present properties or on the property to be acquired

Offering the seller a mortgage secured by property you already own

Trading property you already own for the property you want to acquire

You can probably think of many other creative benefits to offer to a property seller for the down payment. For example, recently a professional property investor told me he bought an out-of-town property for nothing down from a seller who did not want to sell to local buyers. "Saving face" is another seller motivation, and it is often very easy for a creative buyer to satisfy this need.

When you spot a property you would like to own, try to find out what will motivate the seller to sell to you on your terms. Although many realty agents try to prevent it, often there is no other way to learn the seller's true motivation than to sit down, face to face, with him to get acquainted. While I prefer to let the listing agent do my negotiating, if this fails, I do not hesitate to suggest a meeting with the seller to learn if I can offer him something which will meet his needs. At this point, if the traditional method of keeping the buyer and seller apart does not work, *there is nothing to lose and everything to gain* by having the buyer and seller meet each other.

Often the seller's needs can be satisfied with something other than cash. For example, I have purchased several rental houses from elderly sellers who were selling so they could move closer to their children. These sellers, I learned, did not need large amounts of cash. What they wanted was security. By offering them a small cash down payment and a first or second mortgage on the property they were selling to me, I satisfied their security needs in the form of monthly income payments (paid by my tenant's rent).

One elderly seller told me the monthly payment I send her of over $1,000 per month is more money than she ever earned in her life. That payment will provide her with more than adequate retirement income, so she will not be dependent on her children for living expenses.

HOW TO LOCATE THE RIGHT PROPERTY FOR YOU

Now that you have (1) analyzed your financial position so you know how much you can afford to spend and maintain your property purchase and (2) decided what you can offer to induce property sellers to sell to you, you are ready to start the property selection process.

Hopefully, by now you have decided what kind of property you want to seek. If you are looking for condominiums, for example, do not waste time looking at single-family homes for sale. Similarly, if you want to invest in apartments, save time by not investigating office buildings, warehouses, or vacant land.

There are several property-locating techniques which work well for different buyers. Depending upon your personal inclinations and time available for the search, you may want to use one or all of these suggestions.

THE BEST PLACE TO START

Most property buyers start their searches in the newspaper classified want ads. This is a highly efficient marketplace for sellers and buyers to get together. If possible, check more than one newspaper in your area. The smaller papers, especially the weekly community papers, often have special bargain ads by do-it-yourself sellers who are too cheap to place a want ad in the more expensive city daily newspapers.

Each community usually has one leading newspaper which carries most of the real estate want ads. This is usually the best source, but do not overlook the smaller papers with cheaper ad rates that most other realty buyers may not be checking.

As you read the want ads, remember why those ads were placed there. If the advertiser is a realty agent, the purpose is twofold. One motive is to sell the advertised property. But the second motive, often more important, is to make the realty agent's phone ring.

Most realty agents have many listed properties that they are not advertising. The properties that get advertised often are the ones that are (a) overpriced, (b) seriously deficient in some respect, (c) listings about ready to expire, or (d) owned by sellers who pester the agent to advertise their property.

When phoning a realty agent on a want ad, if the advertised property turns out not to be what you want to buy, be sure to ask the agent if he has another listing which better meets your requirements. The best agents who have "floor duty" time answering "cold calls" will have prepared a "switch sheet." A switch sheet lists alternative listings similar to the advertised property, usually in the same price range. The properties on the agent's switch list are often better bargains than the advertised properties.

But if it turns out the agent you talk to does not have any alternative listings, be sure to leave your name and phone number. Some agents are so lazy you will have to force them to write down your name and phone number. If you are lucky, and if you tell enough agents what you want to buy, eventually an agent will phone you when he learns of a property meeting your requirements.

For example, today an agent I met four months ago at a Sunday open house phoned me about her new listing that she hopes I will buy. Unfortunately, this agent did not take good notes as to what financing I want, but at least she has not forgotten my buying interest. The more people you tell of your buying desire, the greater your chances of finding exactly the right property for you. Property buying is not easy, so widen your chances of success.

IS IT BEST TO DEAL WITH ONLY ONE REAL ESTATE AGENT?

While we are talking about real estate agents, the question often is asked whether it is best to deal with only one real estate agent. When looking for a personal residence, I find it is best to start out dealing with just one agent. Let that agent know you are relying on him (or her) to find you a perfect home to live in. Give the agent plenty of time to produce results. One to two months, however, should be adequate.

If the agent you select to deal with exclusively has not come up with suitable property within a month or two, however, do not hesitate to start dealing with other agents. The problem is if one agent knows you are dealing with that agent exclusively, the agent tends to become lazy. Competition does wonders to bring out the best in realty agents. But if your agent is doing a first class job, deal with that agent exclusively because many agents uncover "insider deals" that they present only to their best, exclusive clients.

ANOTHER WAY TO LOCATE GOOD REALTY AGENTS

In addition to the newspaper want ads, another good way to find realty agents with listings that meet your requirements is to write letters. I recall once writing to all the realty agents listed in San Francisco, describing the particular type of property I wanted to buy. Out of several hundred letters, less than a dozen agents bothered to contact me. However, one of those agents had a bargain property that I immediately bought. It had been listed over six months, but the agent was too cheap to advertise it.

OTHER METHODS OF FINDING BARGAIN PROPERTIES

In addition to using the want ads, and writing or phoning realty agents, another profitable technique is to "cruise." That means drive around neighborhoods where you would like to buy property. Jot down the addresses of any properties with "for sale" signs and phone the agent (or owner if it is a "for sale by owner" FSBO). Better yet, jot down addresses of properties that look like they might be for sale. Telltale signs include need for paint, vacant-looking windows with no shades or curtains, overgrown lawns, and other signs of absentee ownership. Then check the ownership at the court house or other local place where the owner's name can be easily obtained. In my county, I find the tax collector's office offers the easiest access to owner's names and addresses, but you may find a better place where you live.

One technique used by a friend of mine is he buys a master list of property owners in the area where he wants to buy properties. About four times a year he sends mass mailings to all owners of appropriate properties asking if they might like to sell "on flexible terms." He tells me each mailing usually produces lots of flakey phone calls but at least a dozen serious sellers who want to sell but have not yet listed their properties for sale with an agent. Although this technique takes time and organization, the results can be very profitable, especially since you have no competition. To locate a source for a master list of property owners in your area, check with local title insurance companies, realty agents, or real estate attorneys.

THE MULTIPLE LISTING TECHNIQUE

Still another technique for finding good properties for sale is to borrow a local realty agent's multiple listing book. Once you get to know an agent well, he or she will usually agree to loan you the current multiple listing book overnight. Better yet, ask the agent to give you last week's multiple listing book so you can study the listings. Although giving the multiple listing book to a nonmember technically violates the multiple listing service's monopolistic rules, it is done all the time. If your agent will not give you access to a current or recent multiple listing book, find an agent who will.

Once you have the current or recent multiple listing book, go through it carefully. Note the properties that interest you. Drive by them. Check recent sales prices for neighborhood homes (recent comparable sales prices are often in the back of the multiple listing book). Then make many offers (through the agent who gave you the multiple listing book, of course), contingent upon your inspecting the properties.

Many professional realty investors make purchase offers before they inspect the property. This saves many hours of inspection time. Of course, such purchase offers are contingent upon inspection and approval of the property. One investor I know bought a $2,000,000 industrial property this way, sight unseen. First he works out the purchase price and terms. Then he spends time inspecting the property to see if it as good as the listing agent says it is.

OTHER BARGAIN-FINDING TECHNIQUES

Ways of finding realty bargains are virtually unlimited. One friend of mine, a social climber who goes to lots of cocktail parties, is constantly asking people he meets "Have you got any property you want to sell?" He is a medical doctor, and he even asks his patients. Although he misses some great bargains advertised in the newspapers and available through realty agents, this doctor probably makes more money from his realty investments than from his medical practice, thanks to his technique of asking people what they own and want to sell.

Another technique for locating bargain properties is to run a newspaper want ad under "Real Estate Wanted" or similar title. I have tried this method and was bombarded with phone calls from flakey people. Only one serious seller surfaced in the month I ran my ad. But this method works if you run your ad long enough and can put up with all the unusual phone calls. Many real estate agents buy properties or get listings this way. One local realtor runs a productive ad reading "I'll buy your property, any condition, within 48 hours." He has been running this ad for years so it must pay off. Of course, the ad does not say that the realtor will buy the property at his price and on his terms.

Still another property-finding technique is to phone owners who have placed newspaper want ads under "for rent." To illustrate, if you want to buy a house, phone advertisers trying to rent houses. First, find out over the phone where the house is located and what the rent is. If you would like to live there, make an appointment to inspect it *with the owner*. Once you see the house, if you like it and would really like to own it, ask the owner if he would lease to you with an option to buy. If so, you have found yourself a bargain.

Why? Because today it is cheaper to rent a house than it is to buy it (unless you make a huge cash down payment to reduce the mortgage payments). But an owner can afford to lease to you, with an option to buy, because he probably bought the house years ago, and his mortgage payments are less than you would incur if you buy today.

Many owners of rental houses would like to sell. But when the house becomes vacant, instead of listing it for sale with all the inconveniences of selling, the owner decices to rent it because that is usually much easier. It is surprising how often an owner will sell when he receives an unsolicited purchase offer. Owners of empty rental houses are especially good candidates for this technique.

DISTRESS SALES

Another fruitful source of property bargains is distress sales. This category includes properties in what I call "special situations." Examples include probate or estate sales, foreclosures, property tax sales, divorces, deaths, bankruptcies, out of town owners, and sheriff's or marshall's sales. Checking these sales takes considerable time and large amounts of cash, but the competition from other buyers is practically nil. Cash talks. If you have lots of cash with which to buy properties, look into local procedures for distress property sales. Most of these sales will be advertised in legal notices published in local newspapers. Your county clerk or other local official can show you which newspapers carry these notices, and there is also usually a bulletin board at the courthouse where notices of such sales are posted. It takes considerable time and work to follow these distress property sales, but if you work faithfully at it, you will soon discover shortcuts. Frankly, I have not had good experience buying distress property, but some of my investor friends say it is the best way to find the bargain properties.

STILL MORE SOURCES OF BARGAINS

Wherever you go, if you want to buy good properties, talk about real estate. Do not be afraid to bring up the subject. You will be surprised to find it is one topic on which most people freely share their knowledge. People who especially like to talk about real estate include your attorney, banker, and barber or beautician. They often know who wants to sell or who has to sell. Let everyone you know understand that you are buying real estate. Within a few weeks or months, you will have so many properties offered to you that you cannot possibly buy them all.

But if you sit back and wait for the bargains to come to you, you will be waiting forever. Get busy. Make contacts, starting with the newspaper want ads. You will be surprised how much fun finding and buying property can be.

WHAT TO LOOK FOR IN A BARGAIN PROPERTY

Smart investors not only know the sources of bargain properties, but they know how to recognize one when they see it. A big problem with novice investors is they faithfully look for properties to buy, but they never actually buy. Novice buyers have a list of criteria, such as good location, good structural condition, and good financing. Rarely will all the requirements be met in one property. THERE IS NO SUCH THING AS A PERFECT PROPERTY. EVERY PROPERTY HAS SOMETHING WRONG WITH IT. The secret of buying the right property is to *avoid incurable defects.* An incurable defect is a drawback that is offensive to a majority of property buyers.

It is true there is a buyer for every property. But that buyer will buy at his price and on his terms. If the price and terms do not match those acceptable to the seller, no sale takes place.

Examples of incurable defects include (1) bad neighborhood (such as one with high crime rate, poorly maintained neighboring properties, or heavy street traffic), (2) poorly planned physical layout (such as a home with its bathroom located off the living room), (3) defective physical characteristics (such as a defective foundation or drainage toward the building rather than away from it), (4) economic or social obsolescence (factors outside the property that affect its usefulness, such as a home located downwind of a smelly sewerworks), and (5) high maintenance costs (such as an uninsulated building in North Dakota that can be insulated only at great cost).

Although defects such as these are called incurable defects, they really are curable. But the cost is so great that it is uneconomic. To illustrate, a beautiful home located adjacent to a noisy highway has an incurable defect. But if you had enough money, you could pay to relocate the highway or build sound barriers along the highway to cut down the noise. The cost of such corrective action, however, is beyond its worth to the homeowner.

In addition to avoiding incurable defect properties, smart investors buy only in good locations. Please notice I did not say "best locations." Usually the greatest real estate profits are made in locations other than the very best ones. For example, if your town has a (1) wealthy neighborhood, (2) a middle-class neighborhood, and (3) a lower-class slum neighborhood, the greatest realty profits can probably be earned by buying in the middle-class neighborhood. Money can be made in the wealthy neighborhood too, but it often takes more cash to invest there and the returns per dollar invested may not be as great as in the middle-class neighborhood. Of course, stay away from the lower-class slum neighborhood because it is considered a "poor location."

WHAT IS A GOOD LOCATION?

Every book on real estate investments says to buy only well-located property. That is true. But those books do not tell what a good location is. The truth is a good location depends on the people who use or can use the property. Good locations either already exist or can be created by the property owner. Bad locations usually already exist and are obvious, but they occasionally are created (such as when a new highway is built, thus chopping up adjoining land parcels and creating lower property values due to heavy noise or traffic congestion).

Is it wise to buy cheap, poorly located property for improvement so it can be profitably resold? NO! Unless you have a vast fortune and can buy up all the properties in a bad location and redevelop the neighborhood, stay away from bad locations. They are too costly to try to improve. Of course, if you see a well-established neighborhood trend developing, such as Chicago's famous Old Town area, buy in the bad location before everyone else realizes what is happening. Smart investors buy in such improving locations only (1) with high leverage (small cash down payments) and (2) if they can afford to lose their small investment if things do not turn out as expected.

Good locations are those that are highly useful or are considered desirable by the majority of people in the community. That does not mean those people live or work in those good locations. But they consider good locations to be where they want to live or work. Consider, for example, your town's busiest commercial intersection. It is called a "100 percent location" because it is the most desirable in town. The value of real estate at that intersection is probably also the most expensive in town too. Since most investors cannot afford to buy there, they buy in lesser locations which are still considered "good" by most people in the community.

In fact, the largest real estate profits are usually not made by purchasing property at a 100 percent location. The biggest realty profits are made buying in lesser locations and creating value by improving the property. This is called "forced inflation." An example would be buying a run-down house in a middle-class neighborhood, fixing it up, and reselling it at a profit. Doing the same thing in a bad location, such as a slum neighborhood, probably would not produce any profit because smart investors do not buy in bad locations no matter how attractive the property is made to appear.

SUMMARY

Summing up this chapter on how to locate good properties involves three key ingredients. (1) Use many sources to locate desirable properties. (2) Avoid buying properties with incurable defects. (3) Buy only in good locations; avoid neighborhoods which are not considered desirable by a majority of the people in the local community.

QUESTIONS AND ANSWERS

HOW TO FIND PROPERTY BARGAINS

Q. How do you find bargain properties? You make it sound so easy. —*Bill M*.

A. My major source of property bargains is knowing many top real estate agents who contact me when they find properties meeting my requirements. Although I am a real estate broker, I never split a sales commission with these agents. The commission is all theirs to keep. As a result, they bring me their best bargains.

But if my "bird dog agents" do not produce enough property bargains, and I am desperate to buy a property, I (1) check newspaper want ads daily in several local newspapers, (2) phone agents advertising property that sounds interesting (I always ask about their unadvertised listings which are often better bargains than those advertised), (3) get to know many realty agents and make sure they know my property desires and do not forget me, and (4) drive around neighborhoods where I would like to own property, noting addresses of neglected-looking property, and then contact the owners to see if they would like to sell. Lastly, when I see a property I like that meets my buying criteria, I make a purchase offer immediately before someone else beats me out of the bargain.

HOW ZONING CAN HELP OR HURT PROPERTY'S VALUE

Q. We own a vacant lot on a busy street. The city is proposing to rezone from commercial to residential apartment house district. Some of the neighbors oppose this change, others favor it. Will it hurt or help the value of my property?—*Susan A*.

A. Commercially zoned property is usually worth more than a similar residentially zoned parcel. In the residential zoning category, apartment zoning is generally more valuable than single-family zoning.

But these are general rules of thumb which may not apply to your situation. The fact that your lot is vacant might indicate there is not much demand for it as commercial property. Yet if the zoning is changed to apartment zoning, you might find your lot is in great demand for apartment or condominium construction.

Go to the public hearings on the proposed zoning change. Listen to the arguments on both sides. If you feel strongly one way or the other, voice your opinion at the hearing. Zoning changes are generally made by local zoning or planning boards only after careful consideration of all viewpoints.

REINSPECT PROPERTY PURCHASE
JUST BEFORE CLOSING SETTLEMENT

Q. My husband says we should insist in reinspecting our home purchase a day or two before the closing settlement. Is this necessary?
—*Mary Ann T.*

A. While reinspection is not necessary, it is a very smart idea. Let the seller know you plan to reinspect before the sale closing. You will be pleasantly surprised at how much cleaner the house will be, and the seller will not try to play games, such as switching light fixtures and substituting cheap items for those that were in the house when you first inspected it. You have maximum leverage over the seller before the sale closes. After closing, when the seller has received his money, he could care less.

AVOID INCURABLE PROPERTY DEFECTS

Q. My cousin has agreed to sell us his home for $79,000. We like the location, but the floor plan is bad. There are three bedrooms, but to get to one bedroom you have to walk through another bedroom. While this would be all right for our two children, when we want to sell I think this would be a drawback. If my cousin was selling to us at a bargain price, I would buy in a minute. But he's asking top dollar for our town. Do you think we should buy in spite of the bad floor plan?—*Roger D.*

A. I think you have already answered your question. Bad floor plans are known as incurable defects or incurable obsolescence. I suspect your cousin is having trouble selling his home, and that is why he is being so generous in offering it to you.

Of course, even though your cousin is not offering a bargain price, if he is offering special terms, such as a small down payment and seller financing, then you might wish to buy the home in spite of its defects. But if you can do just as well buying another house, buy the other house. Sometimes it does not pay to make business transactions a family affair.

BUY INADEQUATE, WELL-LOCATED HOME
RATHER THAN GOOD, POORLY LOCATED ONE

Q. The last four weekends we have been looking at homes for sale. After we got over the shock of today's prices, we realized we'll either have to buy a home we like in a "not so good" location or a less-than-adequate home in a better, close-in location. Which do you think is the better home to buy?—*Martin E.*

A. Always go for the well-located home. The reason is that when you want to resell your home in the future, location will be a big part of its value. A "perfect" home in a bad location will always suffer in value. It usually will not go up in value as fast as the well-located home. A more expensive home in a good location is almost always a better buy than one in a second-rate location.

Remember, most home buyers stay in the home an average of less than seven years before selling. Even if you buy that "less-than-adequate" home in a top, close-in location, you probably will not be living there the rest of your life. Chances are you will sell it in a few years and buy a home that more closely meets your needs.

That technique is called "home pyramiding." Young couples use it to buy a small cottage where they live a few years before moving up to a better home. Older people use it to buy a second or third home that is their "dream home." Elderly people use this method to buy their retirement home, often in a community offering special amenities such as golf courses, swimming pools, or other extras. But whatever home you buy, always choose one that is favorably located in a popular resale area.

HOW TO FIND PROPERTY FORECLOSURE BARGAINS IN YOUR MAILBOX

Q. On the ABC-TV program "20/20," they recently showed how some properties are being bought in Los Angeles just before they go into foreclosure. But the details weren't shown. While I don't want to operate the way the people were shown on that TV program, I would like to learn where to find out about foreclosure sales. It seems to me that bargains can be bought, and the owners can be paid a fair price for their properties before they lose them by foreclosure.—*Roy A.*

A. Most of the properties on which foreclosure notices are filed never go to foreclosure sale. The reason is smart buyers contact the defaulting owners and buy out their equity before the sale. This gives the financially troubled owner some cash with which to get started again, and it gives the buyer a bargain purchase.

I do not approve of the techniques shown on that "20/20" telecast. But investors who contact defaulting owners can often perform valuable services in buying their homes. These defaulting borrowers often have no other way to save their equity.

To learn about foreclosures in your area, contact the county clerk or other local official who records notices of mortgage default. You can check the records to find out which lenders have filed notices against which borrowers. In many urban areas you can have information on these defaults delivered to your mailbox by subscribing to a local public recording summary service. The county clerk or recorder, title insurance firm, or realty office can tell you if such a service exists in your area.

THE CHEAPEST WAY TO BUY YOUR NEXT HOME

Q. We don't have very much cash for a down payment on a home. Just about $4,500. We talked to an old-time real estate agent. She suggested we buy a home on a lease with option to purchase. It just happened she had a home available on a lease-option. The way the deal works, she says, is we put up $4,000 "consideration for the option." It is to be a three-year option at purchase price agreed upon today. We would pay $550 per month rent, half of which applies to the option purchase price. But we are to pay all maintenance and property taxes on the house. We're wondering if there is some "catch?"—*James M.*

A. Consider yourself fortunate to find a smart real estate agent who understands lease-options. Many do not, so they discourage potential buyers from even thinking about lease-options. Grab that "good deal" before someone else like me does.

For the buyer, lease-option advantages are (1) you lock up the home's purchase price today, (2) it is usually cheaper to pay rent than to make mortgage payments, (3) you will benefit from the appreciation in market value between now and the time of option exercise, (4) it takes little cash to get into a lease-option, and (5) if you decide not to buy, the option can be assigned (sold) unless prohibited by its terms.

For the seller, lease-option advantages are (1) tax-free use of the option consideration money until either the option is exercised or it expires unused, (2) monthly rent payments cover the payments on the existing mortgage, (3) tenant pays the maintenance and property taxes, thus reducing or eliminating the negative cash flow problem, (4) with a substantial option consideration payment, you can consider the house sold, and (5) tax advantages of a delayed sale and installment sale taxation of the profit.

I have used lease-options for many years. They work out very well. However, I have found realty agents resist them because they often have to wait for all or part of their sales commission until the option is exercised. But as you found out, smart agents suggest lease-options to increase their sales and to provide for future commission income.

MAKE AN OFFER, ANY OFFER, IN TODAY'S BUYER'S MARKET

Q. Recently you said we're in a "buyer's market" for home sales. Please explain further. Do you mean this is a good or bad time to buy a home? I ask because my wife and I are waiting to buy a home until mortgage interest rates come down.—*Conrad C.*

A. A "buyer's market" means there are more homes listed for sale than there are active buyers seeking a home to purchase. Although I do not have exact statistics, I estimate in most communities there are four or five homes listed for sale for each one which has sold in the last month.

This means it is a terrific time to buy a home. While you probably will not get much of a price reduction from the seller, you will find home sellers are now very flexible on terms they are offering. Low down payments, low interest rates, and low monthly payments are not uncommon today if the seller is motivated and will help finance the sale.

Start making offers. Do not get discouraged. Provide for seller financing in your offers. Forget about getting a new mortgage because they are too expensive. Buy only if the seller will finance your purchase.

There are so many ways to buy homes today on terrific seller-financed terms I cannot list them all. Work with a good realty agent who understands creative finance so the terms can be tailored to your circumstances.

Ideas to consider include lease with option to buy later, land contracts, wrap-around mortgages, deferred down payments, and trading unwanted cars, boats, RVs, or land as your down payment. The important things to remember when buying a home today are (1) think creatively and (2) make offers.

IS TODAY A BAD TIME TO BUY REAL ESTATE?

Q. My parents have what I call "depression mentality." They never take any chances, and they keep warning me not to take any either. But I don't want to wind up like them. They are retired, barely existing on social security and a tiny pension. Dad worked thirty-four years for the same company. All he got was a handshake and a gold watch when he retired. I am twenty-eight, a bachelor. It seems to me real estate is the safest and potentially most profitable investment. Do you think today is a bad time to buy real estate? I'm considering buying a condominium apartment. Is this wise today?—*Morrow T.*

A. Unless you want to wind up like your parents, barely one step away from welfare, plan ahead. Investing in good real estate can be your retirement security. When you are young, buy sound, well-located property. When you are old, sell it and take back mortgages for retirement income. Today is a great time to buy because fantastic seller financing terms are available.

Condominiums can be excellent first investments. But check the particular condo complex very closely. Ask current residents if they would buy there again.

Find out from the residents and your realty agent the recent annual percentage increase in market value of the condominiums. If this annual increase in value has been less than the inflation rate, maybe you should buy elsewhere. Also, ask current residents if there are any drawbacks, such as poor soundproofing or bad management.

After you buy your home, then start buying investment property. I like small residential income property such as rental houses and apartments.

Other investors favor commercial and industrial buildings. To learn more about investment property, take real estate courses at a nearby college. Also, read every real estate book you can so you will understand the tax, income, and other benefits of owning real estate.

TO MAXIMIZE PROPERTY PROFITS, AVOID "RED RIBBON DEALS"

Q. I inherited about $45,000 that I want to invest in real estate as I think it offers the best inflation hedge and income tax benefits. But I am undecided whether to buy income property that is in good shape or should I buy "fix up" buildings?—*Hilda P.*

A. If you buy buildings in perfect condition, called "red ribbon deals," your profits come only in the form of possible future market value appreciation. When you are selling, of course, offer a "red ribbon deal" because that is what most naïve buyers want to buy. They are willing to pay top dollar for "red ribbon" property in top condition.

But if you buy run-down property and fix it up, then your profit opportunities are much greater. The reason is you benefit from both increased value due to the improvements and increased value due to inflation. The property thereby acquires a double profit potential.

THE FOUR-WAY CHECKLIST FOR BUYING YOUR NEXT HOME

Q. Do you have a checklist of things to look for when buying a home? We are first-time home buyers who are worried we'll make a bad buy.—*Marlis A.*

A. Fortunately, real estate is a forgiving investment. If you should make a "bad buy," inflation will probably bail you out. But to prevent making a mistake, here are the most important home-buying considerations.

1. *Neighborhood.* Before buying any home, inspect at least ten houses in various locations throughout your community. Of course, do not waste your time looking at $200,000 homes when your budget can afford only a $75,000 home. Buy in a stable or improving neighborhood, never in a declining one. Also, be sure the particular house does not have incurable location defects such as adjacent railroad tracks, smells, or freeways.

2. *School quality.* Never buy in an area where the public schools are bad. If you buy in an area with poor public schools, good quality middle-class families will not buy a home there, thus limiting your resale market to singles and people without school-age children.

3. *Financing.* Before you inspect a house, ask the realty agent "What financing is available on this house?" In today's market, try to find

a home where the seller will carry all or most of the financing at a reasonable interest rate. This is far cheaper than getting a new mortgage at a bank or savings and loan association.

Many shrewd realty agents will not even show listings today where the seller wants an all-cash sale requiring a new mortgage because so few buyers can qualify for new mortgages at today's interest rates.

4. *Physical condition.* Unless you or your husband are construction experts, provide in your purchase offer for an inspection clause. In termite-infested areas, insist on a termite inspection report, with the seller to pay for any necessary repairs.

Better yet, include an offer contingency such as "This offer contingent upon buyer's inspection and approval of the property." Then hire a professional building inspector if you have doubts. Also, try to get the seller to pay for a one-year home warranty (available through most realty agents) for repairs to built-in appliances, plumbing, wiring, and furnace.

COMPETITIVE MARKET ANALYSIS AVOIDS OVERPAYING FOR PROPERTY

Q. How can I be sure I'm not paying too much when I buy a house or investment property?—*Julius M.*

A. Your first profit from a property is earned by buying it for the right price. To avoid overpaying for a property, before you make your purchase offer, ask your realty agent to prepare a "competitive market analysis" for you.

This is a written summary of (1) recent sales price of similar nearby properties, (2) other comparable properties now for sale that have not sold yet, and (3) properties that were recently listed for sale but which did not sell.

Your agent can easily prepare such a written analysis from records available at the local Board of Realtors, title insurance companies, or mortgage lenders. Only by analyzing such a comparison of similar properties can you be sure you are not offering too much for a property.

If you are buying investment property, such as apartments or commercial buildings, to avoid paying too much ask your agent to find the "capitalization rate" (that is net income divided by the sales price) for similar nearby properties which sold recently. Then apply that "cap rate" to the investment property you are considering buying. Make your purchase offer at that indicated market value.

DO REALTY AGENTS BUY UP ALL THE GOOD PROPERTIES?

Q. We've decided real estate is the best place to invest our money. But we're having trouble making our first income property purchase. It seems all the real estate brokers buy up the bargains. Do you think I should get my real estate sales license so I can learn of the best buys when they first come on the market for sale?—*Hugo L.*

A. It is true that real estate brokers and salespeople do invest in many of the best properties which come up for sale. But realty agents cannot possibly buy all the good properties.

If your only reason for getting a real estate sales license is to get first crack at good properties, I would not bother getting a realty sales license. A better approach is to get to know a dozen or more realty agents who specialize in the type of property you want to buy. Let them know you will act fast when they notify you of a "hot" new listing. You should not have to wait long before you will be buying your first investment property.

IS IT WISE TO BUY A LESS-THAN-IDEAL HOME?

Q. For some time we've read and enjoyed your articles on why it pays to buy a home. But my husband is still in college. So our only income is from my job as a bank loan officer. We both hate paying our $325 per month apartment rent as we know that money is wasted. So we've been trying to find a home we can afford to buy. The best we can find is a tiny three-room cottage which is in, shall we say, less than the best neighborhood. But the cottage is in perfect condition even though it was built in 1932. The original owner is the seller. He will let us buy for only a 10 percent down payment and he will carry the mortgage for ten years. Should we buy?—*Joanne G.*

A. Unless there is something very bad about the neighborhood, it usually pays to buy just about any home rather than continuing to waste money on apartment rent. Even if the cottage does not appreciate much in market value, you will have the income tax savings from mortgage interest and property taxes.

But ninety-nine out of a hundred homes go up in market value at least as fast as the inflation rate, currently about 12 percent per year.

You probably will not spend the rest of your lives in that three-room cottage. But it can be an excellent starter home until your husband graduates and starts earning an income. By then your cottage may have gone up in market value 10 or 20 percent, perhaps more. Buy now before prices go higher. The seller's attractive easy financing is another reason to buy that cottage.

HOW TO BEGIN BUYING PROPERTY

Q. We have about $2,000 for the down payment on a home. I earn about $24,000 per year. Can I afford to buy a home?—*Steve R.*

A. Yes. Start reading the newspaper want ads. Sooner or later you will find a home for sale advertising "low down payment" or "no down payment," or other attractive terms. Phone the agent on every ad that remotely interests you and tell him your situation.

Most realty agents know of at least one "starter home" that can be bought for little cash. The sooner you buy, the sooner you will start building equity so you can eventually sell and buy a better home. The important thing is to buy your first home now before prices go higher.

6.

Secrets
of Financing
Property Purchases

There is an old real estate maxim, never truer than today, that says "If you can't finance it, you can't sell it." Adapting that truism to today's real estate market changes it to "If you can't finance it creatively, you can't buy it."

Although it is important to understand the tax and leverage benefits of owning real estate, financing is the key to opening the real estate door. Without a firm understanding of financing opportunities, chances of successful real estate investing are nil.

Some real estate buyers, especially older people, think the best way to buy property is with all cash. This was correct when annual inflation was only 2 or 3 percent. But paying all cash is downright stupid in today's highly inflationary economy. Borrowing other people's money (OPM) is vital to profitable real estate purchases. If you cannot stand to borrow money, change your thinking, because borrowing money is the prime profit method in real estate.

At the other extreme from the 100 percent cash buyers (who are few and far between, by the way) are realty buyers who think the best way to buy is with 100 percent financing and little or no cash investment of their own money. While this goal is attainable and is being achieved every day, 100 percent financing is not desirable for every situation. If something goes wrong with a property in which the owner has little or no equity, he is too easily tempted to walk away and let the mortgage holder foreclose. Thousands of FHA and VA home loan foreclosures are testimony to the risks, for the lender, of financing with little or zero cash down payment.

THE TRUTH ABOUT
REAL ESTATE MONEY LENDERS

Most real estate lenders hate to foreclose. When they must, if the owner does not make his loan payments, the lender has failed in his primary job

121

of maximizing profits. Realty lenders are usually very good at making big profits by lending money. But, next to bank trust departments, lenders are usually the poorest property managers you can find. That is why they are so cautious making real estate loans. *Most realty lenders never, never, never want to end up owning the property, by foreclosure, on which they loan money.*

But lenders must make loans to earn profits. Never forget that. Although real estate lenders often lead loan applicants to believe otherwise, if lenders do not loan money, they soon have big trouble with declining profits. The recent huge losses of eastern savings banks and many savings and loan associations are due in large part to lack of new loan volume and mortgage loan fees charged to borrowers.

NEVER FORGET THAT LENDERS NEED BORROWERS, JUST AS BORROWERS NEED LENDERS

Persistence is the key to successful real estate financing. Arranging financing terms for any property, from a small cottage to a multimillion dollar high-rise building, is like shopping for groceries. To find the best terms and price (interest rate), *you have to shop around.* Call it "comparison shopping" or whatever you like, but realty lenders are not all the same.

Most lenders do not advertise their loans vigorously, so it is usually necessary to phone or visit realty lenders to find which one is offering the best terms at the moment if you need financing money.

For example, one bank or savings and loan association may offer terrific terms on improvement loans (which are extremely profitable for lenders, by the way) but high interest rates and short terms on first mortgage loans. It is obvious such a lender wants one type of loan business, but not the other. The only way to find out the facts of life in real estate financing is to shop around and make many contacts with loan officers at different loan sources.

DO NOT BE SURPRISED IF YOUR LOAN REQUEST IS REJECTED

The most successful real estate investors have had dozens of their loan applications rejected by lenders. It happens to the best people! They just do not happen to fit the lender's loan formula. Those formulas change constantly and will even vary between loan officers working for the same lender, depending upon the loan officer's authority and willingness to bend the rules. I recently heard of a successful realty developer in my area who was turned down by twenty-one banks, savings and loan associations, and insurance companies before the twenty-second lender agreed to finance his new office complex! Persistence pays.

THE FIRST STEP TO SUCCESSFUL REALTY FINANCING

All lenders ask, before they make a loan, (1) will it be profitable, (2) what will the money be used for, and (3) where will the funds come from to repay the loan. Once the lender is satisfied with the answers, the loan is approved.

But even if the answers to questions two and three are not satisfactory, many lenders will still approve the loan if there is sound security for its repayment. These "equity lenders" loan on the security of the real estate rather than the borrower's apparent financial ability to repay the loan. Most second mortgage lenders are "equity lenders," whereas banks and savings and loan associations are more conservative and look at both the equity and the borrower. These "credit lenders" loan primarily on the borrower's income.

So if your credit or income is not the greatest, borrow from an "equity lender." The cost will be higher, but the inquiry into your ability to make the payments will be less probing.

The security for a real estate loan, of course, is a mortgage, deed of trust, land contract, or other security device on the property. Unsecured loans can be made by banks, but other lenders insist on security of some type, most often the property itself.

As we have seen, *the first step to successful real estate financing is satisfying the lender.* One way or another, the lender gets his answers to his "big three" questions before a loan is approved. Even though the property is the security for real estate loans, lenders qualify borrowers for trouble-free repayment. Old-time lenders looked solely at the mortgaged property for repayment in the event of default. But they learned in the Great Depression of the 1930s that the borrower's financial status is often more important than the property securing the mortgage. That is why today most lenders look at both the property and the borrower closely.

WHERE DO YOU STAND TODAY FINANCIALLY?

In Chapter 5 you prepared your asset-liabilities and income-expense statements. If you have not completed those financial surveys, do it now.

Even if you are not planning to apply for any loans today, it is sound financial planning to prepare your financial balance sheet and earnings statement at least twice a year, preferably on January 1 and July 1. Comparisons can be made each six months to see how your financial position is improving. If it is not getting better, corrective action should be taken.

It is easy to prepare a financial statement. Use the format shown in

Chapter 5. A good place to keep your financial reports is in a notebook where you can compare your progress each six months. Some lenders will accept a neatly typed copy of your financial statement, but others insist it be transferred to their own loan application forms. Below each category on your personal balance sheet enter the details, such as name of the bank that has your savings account. You may think of assets you had long forgotten about.

Here is a sample of how a typical financial report might look. It is important to know how to prepare such a statement because most lenders require you to prepare one. The only exceptions are (1) some equity lenders who loan on just the security of the property and (2) some property sellers who finance the sale of the property without inquiring closely into the buyer's finances.

YOUR BALANCE SHEET

NAME   John and Mary Investor   DATE   January 1

Assets

Cash in checking and savings accounts	3,900
Accounts Receivable	1,150
Mortgages owned	14,000
Marketable securities owned	6,600
Cash surrender value of life insurance policy	400
Real estate owned (today's market value)	54,000
Automobiles owned (today's market value)	1,500
Personal property (today's market value)	2,000
Other assets	$1,150
TOTAL ASSETS	$84,700

Liabilities

Accounts payable within thirty days	800
Notes payable beyond thirty days (installment contracts total)	4,500
Income taxes payable (state and federal)	1,000
Loans on life insurance policy	0
Mortgages of liens on real estate	36,450
Other debts and liabilities	450
TOTAL LIABILITIES	43,200
NET WORTH*	$41,500
TOTAL (Must equal total assets)	$84,700

*Net worth equals Assets minus Liabilities

The totals at the bottom of the asset and liabilities columns must agree.

If they do not, any lender sees a red flag that he is dealing with a novice borrower.

No matter how good your personal balance sheet looks to a lender, he also wants to see an equally important financial report—your income statement. Be sure to show current income information. Last year's earnings might be substantially different from this year's. If both husband and wife are employed steadily, show the earnings of each separately. Lenders must accept total annual earnings of both spouses, even if the wife is pregnant and expects a baby next week. Include income from all sources in your family total.

YOUR INCOME STATEMENT

ANNUAL EARNINGS

Job salary (husband's and wife's) gross employment income	$16,000
Interest income and dividends	450
Rental income (net after expenses and mortgage payments)	1,425
Fees or commissions	0
Alimony, child support, separate maintenance	0
Other income	0
TOTAL ANNUAL INCOME	$17,875

If a significant part of your income comes from self-employment, most lenders want to see a copy of your income tax returns for the latest one or two years. Although such information may be irrelevant to your current year's income, lenders use this method to verify self-employment income. Often just the front and back pages of IRS Form 1040 will satisfy most lenders. But some nasty ones insist on seeing all the supporting schedules too. Frankly, much of the information on your tax returns is not the lender's business, but if you want the loan, you have got to play by their rules.

Wage earners on a salary should bring a copy of their W-2 form when applying for a loan. This verification will speed the loan approval since many employers will no longer give employment earnings verifications to lenders. Some employers will not even verify employment status unless the employee makes a written request. Smaller employers are usually more cooperative with lenders who seek to verify employment and earnings status.

In addition to providing a potential lender with your balance sheet and income statement, many lenders will ask four key questions you should be prepared to answer:

1. Do you have any contingent liabilities as endorser or guarantor, any taxes past due, any damage claims against you not covered by insurance, or any other lawsuits against you?

2. Have you ever filed bankruptcy or compromised a debt?
3. Are any assets shown on your financial statement the separate property of one spouse?
4. What assets are pledged other than those shown on your statement?

TYPES OF REAL ESTATE FINANCING

Now that you have a good picture of your financial status and ability to repay loans, it is time to look at the different types of real estate financing available.

Traditionally, the mortgage (or deed of trust in some states) is the most frequently used real estate finance device. Most property buyers use some type of realty financing that is secured by a mortgage or trust deed. Very few pay 100 percent cash for real estate because of the tax and leverage drawbacks of doing so. Even if you can afford to pay all cash for a property, don't (unless you get a huge price discount for your cash payment).

The most common formula for buying real estate is to make a cash down payment of 5, 10, 15, or 20 percent of the sales price, plus a first mortgage for the balance of the purchase price. A second mortgage may be used to fill any finance gap between the amount of the down payment and the first mortgage amount.

But there are many alternatives to this traditional finance formula. However, before discussing these alternatives, let us take a quick look at the three basic types of mortgage financing used today.

INTERIM OR CONSTRUCTION FINANCING

Construction financing is usually a temporary loan to finance costs of erecting a building. It may or may not include the cost of buying the land. Payments are made periodically by the lender, often a bank, to the contractor, or the materialmen may be paid directly by the construction lender. The security for the construction loan is the value of the underlying land plus the increasing value of the building under construction. Today most construction loans have a floating interest rate, such as the prime rate (the bank's best interest rate for unsecured loans to its best customers) plus two or three points (each point equals one percent of the amount borrowed).

Sometimes a riskier type of loan is used where the construction loan is converted by the lender, after construction completion, into a long-term permanent mortgage. Costs of a construction loan, due to the high interest rate, are usually much greater than for the permanent mortgage, which involves no lender problems with mechanic's liens, cost overruns, or uncompleted work.

Because of the risky nature of construction loans, many Real Estate Investment Trusts (REITs) specializing in this high-risk, high-earnings type of loan are today either bankrupt or far from healthy. The importance of having a permanent mortgage loan commitment to take out (pay off) the construction lender cannot be overemphasized for the safety of the lender.

DEVELOPMENT FINANCING

This really is a variation of the construction loan. Here a mortgage is used to finance purchase of a tract of land where a builder plans to construct homes or, perhaps, a commercial development. A lender takes a mortgage on the entire project and then releases individual parcels from the loan as they are sold to buyers.

For example, upon payment of an agreed sum to the lender (the money comes from the parcel buyers), the development lender releases his mortgage on that parcel sold. A major disadvantage of this type of financing is the developer has his profits tied up in the project until the last parcels are sold. The profits are not fully realized until these last, sometimes difficult-to-sell parcels are finally sold (which may take years). Needless to say, development loans are expensive, due to the high risk for the lender.

PERMANENT FINANCING

The first mortgage or deed of trust is the most common form of real estate financing. This loan is secured by a particular property. It is often used to finance the buyer's purchase of that property. Or it may be used to refinance an existing loan or loans already against the property.

Due to increasing property values, many property owners refinance their mortgage loans every four or five years to take tax-free money out of their property for other uses.

Second mortgages are another form of permanent mortgage financing. Because they have secondary claim against the property in the event of default by the borrower, they are riskier than first mortgages. Upon foreclosure, the first mortgage is paid off; any remaining money realized at the foreclosure sale is paid toward the second mortgage.

To compensate for this greater risk, the interest rate on second mortgages is usually 1, 2, or 3 percent (sometimes more) higher than that of the first mortgage, depending upon state usury laws.

Second mortgages are often carried back by the seller of the property. Such a loan is called a "purchase money mortgage." Many individual investors and finance companies make "hard money" second mortgage loans because of the high interest rate they usually yield. To further maximize their return, second mortgage investors often buy existing second mortgages at substantial discounts off the balance due from individuals who wish to sell their second mortgages to raise cash. Returns on invested dollars of 15 percent to 20 percent or more are not unusual when buying discounted second mortgages.

THE HIGHER THE INTEREST RATE, THE HIGHER THE RISK

In real estate lending, the maxim "The higher the interest rate, the higher the risk" applies. Since second mortgages are usually riskier than first mortgages, they usually carry a higher interest rate to compensate the lender for his risk.

LENDING STANDARDS

All mortgage lenders (called mortgagees) have lending standards. Some are more conservative than others. The interest rate charged varies with the lender's risk, the borrower demand for loan funds, and the lender's loan standards.

Lenders usually charge the lowest interest rate on single-family home loans. Higher rates are usually charged on income property loans, such as apartments and stores. Construction loans have the highest interest rates because of the high lender risks during construction.

The lender's appraisal of a property's fair market value is the key to the decision to make or reject a loan application. Without the underlying value of the property to secure the mortgage loan, a lender will not risk his funds. Most lenders also consider the borrower's ability to repay the loan, as discussed earlier, but there are some "equity lenders" who do not even run a credit report on the borrower. They look strictly to the property for their loan security.

SECURITY—THE ABSENCE OF RISK

Security is defined as the absence of risk. If a loan is 100 percent secure, it is riskless. An example would be a loan secured by the cash in your bank savings account. But if you think carefully about it, even a loan secured 100 percent by cash is a risky loan for a lender today. The reason is inflation.

Today it is impossible to have a 100 percent riskless loan because of the loss of purchasing power caused by inflation. The major cause of our high inflation rate, of course, is government deficit spending. Nobody knows how high the inflation rate will go. As a result, long-term lenders demand high interest rates to compensate for their risk of high future inflation rates.

Mortgages are regarded as relatively safe investments if the appraised value of the property security does not decline (as it rarely does). The major factors considered by all mortgage lenders in evaluating their risks are:

1. Location of the property—the community and the specific neighborhood.
2. Building activity, stability, or expected growth in the area, or lack of growth.
3. The subject property—its condition of repair, its cost of reproduction, and the suitability of the improvement for the neighborhood.
4. Loan to value ratio (percentage of the loan balance to the property's market value).
5. Borrower's credit history and his financial ability to repay the loan.
6. Income property: stability of its income and ability of the property to repay the loan from income rentals.
7. Operating expenses of the subject property and if increases can be passed along to tenants.
8. Term of the loan in years, its amortization schedule, and ability of the lender to compensate for inflation (variable rate loans).

Various lenders apply their own lending standards to each loan request. Even though a lender may have written guidelines for its loan officers, these guidelines are often violated, especially for good customers. Exceptions are also made if the property security is outstanding.

For example, a real estate broker friend of mine contacted seventeen banks, mortgage brokers, and savings and loan associations for financing the sale of a well-located downtown office building. All turned him down because the building was about forty years old. But when his buyer opened a large savings account with one of the S&L lenders that had previously said no, the answer suddenly changed to yes.

KNOW YOUR MAJOR SOURCES OF REAL ESTATE LOANS

Today there are more sources of real estate loans than ever before. But much of this money is ultraexpensive. It pays to shop carefully for the best financing source. Saving just one percentage point on a long-term mortgage can save thousands of dollars.

THE BEST MORTGAGE SOURCE OF ALL

Usually the reason a mortgage is being sought is to finance the purchase of a property. Too often the buyer and real estate agent overlook the best and most obvious finance source of all—the seller. Especially in the home sale market, the individual seller is the cheapest and best source of a mortgage loan. Especially good sources are "motivated sellers" who are anxious to sell and will do anything reasonable to get the property sold.

To tap this financing source, a few guidelines will help. (1) If the realty agent says something like "The seller won't carry a first or second mortgage," do not believe it until you have made a written purchase offer which the seller has rejected. (2) Before making a purchase offer, find out the seller's true motivation for selling (this will help you tailor your purchase offer to meet the seller's needs). (3) Make your purchase offer on terms you can live with, such as a low interest rate, deferred payments, and long term. Beware of "short fuse" mortgages, such as a one- or two-year mortgage carried by the seller, that just postpone your finance problem. (4) Do not get discouraged if your first seller finance offer is rejected; there are thousands of other properties for sale, and many of them can be bought with seller financing.

More about the important area of seller-finance techniques will be explained later. For now, it should be regarded as the most important and best finance source of all.

SAVINGS AND LOAN ASSOCIATIONS

Until recently savings banks and savings and loan associations made about 60 percent of all conventional home mortgage loans in the United States. But due to their financial problems brought on by high interest rates, which most mortgage borrowers cannot afford, S&Ls have cut their loan volume substantially. But they will continue to be an important finance source, especially for home loans. They can make a limited number of commercial property mortgage loans too, but most of their loans are secured by single-family houses.

Nationwide, there are over 6,000 S&L offices and they invest about 85 percent of their assets in mortgages. Maximum loan-to-value ratios go up to 95 percent of the appraised value of single-family homes. However, on amounts over 80 percent of the property's market value, most S&Ls insist on "private mortgage insurance" (PMI). These high-ratio home loans are often called "magic loans" because of the initials of the largest private mortgage insurer, Mortgage Guaranty Insurance Corporation of Milwaukee.

Most home loans are made for 75 percent to 80 percent of the house's appraised value at the time of a sale. For refinancing of existing mortgages, S&Ls tend to be more conservative, often making loans up to 75 percent of their appraised value.

MUTUAL SAVINGS BANKS

There are about 500 mutual savings banks which function like savings and loan associations. Only eighteen states allow mutual savings banks. Both mutual savings banks and S&Ls, as well as banks and mortgage brokers, make FHA and VA insured home loans, although they jump in and out of the FHA-VA market depending upon yields available.

COMMERCIAL BANKS

Banks in some communities are a major factor in real estate finance, especially for commercial and construction mortgage lending. But their role in home mortgage financing fluctuates wildly, depending upon yields available and if the loans can be sold. Banks like to originate home loans and then sell them to other lenders, but they retain the servicing for which they earn a fee of about ¼ percent.

Many banks make home mortgage loans only to their customers who have established accounts. Surprisingly, the nation's largest home mortgage lender is a bank, Bank of America. But as a general rule, banks tend to be very conservative on home loans, and they are usually not an outstanding home loan source.

INSURANCE COMPANIES

Insurance companies used to be major lenders on home mortgages. Today, because other investments offer higher yields, few insurance companies make direct home loans. Some, however, will buy packages of home loans originated and serviced by other lenders, such as banks and savings and loan associations.

Since insurance companies are less regulated than banks and S&Ls, they can be more flexible in financing special or unusual real estate properties. But their interest rates are usually higher than mortgages from banks or S&Ls. That is because the risk is usually higher, and the insurance company may be the only available financing source, so they charge what the traffic will bear.

Many insurance companies want a share of the project's gross or net income (called a "kicker"). Insurance companies usually make their loans through mortgage brokers, known as "correspondents." Their loan processing time is often long, as compared to banks and S&Ls which make loan decisions in a few days. Some correspondents demand the loan fee be paid at the time the insurance company loan is requested. If the mortgage broker requests the advance fee, the borrower should obtain written evidence the fee is fully refundable if the mortgage loan is not approved as requested. Be especially aware of crooked mortgage brokers who request advance loan fees for "shopping the loan application" because it is these brokers who often are unable to refund the loan fee if their loan source search is unsuccessful. Any mortgage broker who demands a nonrefundable loan fee should be avoided.

PENSION AND TRUST FUNDS

Although they control billions of dollars of long-term money, the pension and trust funds have been slow to invest in real estate mortgages. These lenders operate much like insurance companies in mortgage lending. They usually arrange their loans through mortgage brokers, or they buy existing mortgages originated by mortgage bankers. As these huge pension and trust funds diversify their investments for safety, and as they realize the high and safe yields available in first and second mortgages, more pension and trust fund money is becoming available for mortgages.

But these lenders have high-minimum loans, usually at least $1,000,000. They are not interested in home mortgages, except to occasionally buy packages of home loans originated and serviced by the original lender such as a bank, mortgage broker, or savings and loan association.

MORTGAGE LOAN BROKERS AND BANKERS

Mortgage loan brokers are often the local correspondents for insurance companies and pension or trust funds. Mortgage bankers, however, use their own funds (often borrowed from a bank) to originate mortgage loans which are then sold to institutional mortgage investors such as insurance companies.

Loan fees of mortgage bankers and brokers tend to be the highest of all the lending sources listed. But these people are often the only source of mortgage money for difficult-to-finance projects. Many will not look at a loan under $500,000 or $1,000,000 because it is not worth their time.

INDIVIDUAL LENDERS

Every town and city has individuals who will make mortgage loans. They make such loans for a variety of reasons such as (1) high return on invested dollars, (2) opportunity to participate in project profits, and/or (3) profits from occasional foreclosures. These individuals often buy first or second mortgages at large discounts to further enhance their return on investment. Some seek security of investment with a low loan-to-value ratio. Others want a higher interest rate in return for a higher loan-to-value ratio.

Many individual lenders become involved in mortgage financing by carrying back the first or second mortgage when they sell their property to a new owner. Some individual lenders make direct loans to borrowers. But most work through a mortgage loan broker who collects a loan fee from the borrower for arranging the loan. Such mortgage brokers often service the loan, usually a second mortgage, without charge and handle any delinquent loan collection problems or foreclosures.

Newspaper want ads frequently carry notices of individual lenders who have funds to loan. Loans for sale are also often advertised in the want ad pages of newspapers, especially in larger cities.

OTHER MORTGAGE SOURCES

There are many other sources of mortgage money. They vary in each community. Some include finance companies (a big factor now in the second mortgage market), credit unions, and cash-by-mail personal property brokers. State usury laws that regulate maximum interest rates often determine whether or not these secondary real estate loan sources do business in a particular state.

THIRTY WAYS TO FINANCE VIRTUALLY ANY PROPERTY

There is no limit to the creative methods which can be used to finance the acquisition and operation of real estate. The major methods are often combined and adjusted to meet the requirements of the parties to the transaction. When using these methods, *think creatively.* There is no such thing as an impossible realty financing situation. Keep an open mind. Seek help from real estate finance specialists in your community. Listen, learn, and prosper by understanding the basic and advanced methods of financing real estate.

1. The Traditional First Mortgage

All of the loan sources listed above will make first mortgage or deed of trust loans. By being well prepared when approaching your most logical lender for the type of property you want to finance, you will save lots of time and work. Even though it pays to search several sources for the best loan terms and interest rates, do not become known among mortgage lenders as a "shopper."

A "shopper" is a borrower who plays one lender off against another lender. Lenders do not like this. Even though it pays to shop and compare for the best mortgage finance terms, do not tell the lenders you are doing this.

When you find reasonable terms on a firm mortgage commitment, *take it!* Don't fool around and run the risk of losing a choice loan commitment. Real estate brokers and agents, working to finance their sales, often know the best local mortgage sources so encourage them to assist you as part of their service when purchasing a property. But double-check with other lenders to be sure you are actually getting the best terms, not just the easiest loan.

Of course, when purchasing a property, always provide in your initial purchase offer bid for the seller to finance your purchase. Even if the agent says this is impossible, insist the agent write up your offer providing for seller financing. In the last four years, with only one exception, all my property purchases have been seller-financed. On most of them, the agent was as surprised as I was when the seller accepted my offer. Never hesitate to make a purchase offer that provides for seller financing. The worst that can happen is the seller will make a counteroffer that requires outside financing.

2. Second, Third, Fourth, etc., Mortgages

The same rules apply here as when seeking a new first mortgage. If you cannot arrange a large enough first mortgage, or if you are buying "subject to" or "assuming" an existing first mortgage, a second mortgage can fill the finance gap between your down payment and the first mortgage.

In some situations, the second mortgage can take up *all* the slack and make 100 percent financing (no down payment) possible. Of course, the further down a mortgage is on the chain of priority, the higher the risk for the lender. Naturally, the interest rate on a second or third mortgage will be higher than on a first mortgage. The seller is usually the best source for second, third, or fourth mortgages (because he does not actually have to advance any cold, hard cash) although outside individuals and mortgage brokers often make or arrange these secondary mortgages too. Again, shop carefully among local hard money lenders because interest rates and terms vary widely. Depending upon local loan conditions, sources of secondary "hard money" mortgages include banks, S&Ls, finance companies, credit unions, and mortgage brokers.

A WORD ABOUT A COMMON MISUNDERSTANDING

It is important, while considering second mortgages, to explain a common misunderstanding regarding the safety of such loans. In the Great Depression of the 1930s, many second mortgage holders were wiped out when a first mortgage lender had to foreclose because the borrower did not make his loan payments. In those days a second mortgage lender had to pay off the entire first mortgage balance to protect his second mortgage from being wiped out when the first mortgage lender foreclosed.

These laws have been changed. Today if a borrower defaults on *either or both* a first and/or second (or third, fourth, etc.) mortgage, *only the missed payments* need be paid up by the secondary lender to protect his mortgage. No longer are large amounts of money needed to protect a secondary mortgage in the event of foreclosure by a prior mortgage lender in the chain of priority. Even today many potential secondary mortgage lenders do not understand this important fact of mortgage life. Many homesellers refuse to carry back a second mortgage due to misunderstanding this mortgage concept.

To summarize, if you hold a second mortgage and the borrower defaults on either your mortgage or the first mortgage, or both, to protect your loan from being wiped out at a foreclosure sale by the first mortgage lender, you must make up any missed payments on the first loan. Then you can declare a default and begin foreclosure on your second mortgage. But do not wait to do so. If a borrower falls behind on his loan payments, begin foreclosure immediately, otherwise keeping up the payments on the prior mortgages may become a financial burden.

Of course, any amounts advanced by a second mortgage lender on behalf of the borrower to make up missed payments on a prior mortgage are added to the balance owed on the second mortgage.

3. Purchase-Money Mortgages

Although we have just discussed first, second, third, etc., mortgages, special attention must be directed toward such a mortgage that is financed by the property seller at the time of sale. These are called "purchase-money mortgages," whether they are a first, second, third, etc.

In some states, such as California, purchase-money lenders cannot collect any deficiency loss from the borrower if, after foreclosure, the property does not bring enough foreclosure sales proceeds to pay off the debt owed to the lender. Anti-deficiency laws vary from state to state, so secondary mortgage lenders should check with their attorneys as to local law.

But foreclosure deficiencies are rarely important unless property values drop below the amount owed on the mortgage at the time of foreclosure. Sellers who carry back purchase-money mortgages usually get higher sales prices for their property than if they demand 100 percent cash from the buyer.

Although the seller does not get all-cash if he helps finance the sale, he can earn excellent return on his loan to the buyer. In most states, except where barred by usury laws, yields of at least 10 percent to 15 percent are possible on purchase-money mortgages. Some state laws, such as California, have no interest rate usury limit on purchase-money mortgages from the property seller. Purchase-money mortgages not only give the seller excellent interest income, but they also qualify the sale for deferred-payment installment-sale tax savings.

But a word of caution is in order. If the seller does not want the property back in the event of the borrower's default and foreclosure, he should insist on a substantial cash down payment. This is called "protective equity." But if the seller would not mind receiving the property back someday, so he can sell it for another profit, a low or no down payment sale could be advantageous. Of course, the lower the down payment, the greater the amount of loan money at risk for the seller and the greater the interest income he will receive.

4. Special FHA and VA Home Mortgage Programs

The Federal Housing Administration (FHA) and the Veteran's Administration (VA) have many special home loan programs that require no or a minimum cash down payment. While these insured or guaranteed mortgage programs involve lots of government red tape delays, the low investment rules can make the frustrations worthwhile. Loan processing has been greatly improved in recent years so the drawbacks aren't as severe as formerly.

For the latest information on FHA and VA home loans, check with your local approved FHA-VA lender such as a bank, S&L, or mortgage broker. As of this writing, VA no-down-payment loans are generally available up to $110,000. VA mortgages above this amount usually require a 25 percent down payment, but the lender has considerable flexibility on VA loan terms.

As of this writing, FHA home loans are available up to $67,500, but there are higher loan amounts available in high-cost communities. The cash down payment required is 3 percent of the first $25,000 plus 4 percent of the balance.

With both FHA and VA mortgages, the home buyer can pay more than the loan amount in cash as second mortgages are not allowed at the time of FHA or VA mortgage origination (except VA sometimes allows a fully amortized second mortgage).

The big drawback of FHA and VA home loans is the government sets the maximum interest rate. Usually this interest rate is below the prevailing open market interest rate that lenders can obtain on conventional home loans. Since lenders are not fools, they charge "loan fees" or "discount points" to raise their yield on FHA and VA mortgages. A one-point loan fee equals 1 percent of the amount borrowed. For each one-point loan fee charged, the lender raises its true yield about ⅛ percent. To illustrate, if the government-set FHA-VA interest rate is 13 percent and a lender charges a three-point loan fee, the lender really earns 13⅜ percent yield.

Unfortunately, by law the FHA or VA borrower cannot pay his own loan fee (as do borrowers obtaining conventional home mortgages from lenders such as banks and S&Ls). Since the buyer cannot pay the loan fee, that leaves the seller the "opportunity" to pay the loan fee. Many home sellers refuse to pay their buyer's loan fee. Some will pay only if they can raise their sales price by a corresponding amount. When this is done, however, the home may not appraise at a market value including the inflated loan fee added on.

Many realty agents have had unfortunate incidents with FHA and VA home loan appraisers who tend to be very conservative in their appraisals. If you do offer to buy a home contingent upon obtaining a VA or FHA home loan, be sure your realty agent accompanies the VA or FHA fee appraiser and points out to him recent comparable sales prices of similar neighborhood homes that reflect true market value.

5. Trade-ins and Exchanges

There is no law saying the down payment to purchase real estate must be in cash. It can be just about anything the seller is willing to accept.

Typical real estate trade-ins and exchanges involve autos, boats, motor homes, other real estate such as lots, cabins, and houses, corporate stocks or bonds, and just about anything of value the owner wants to get rid of. Many realtors offer guaranteed trade-in plans or guaranteed sales programs so a potential home buyer can be sure of the minimum price he will receive for his old home.

Exchanges involving investment property, such as a trade of a vacant lot for an apartment house, are frequently arranged to avoid paying income tax on the profitable disposal of the smaller property. A direct trade is necessary to defer the tax on the trade up (with the exception of Starker and Biggs "indirect exchanges" which are discussed in Chapter 10). But after the swap is completed, the owner of the larger property who accepts the smaller property as a down payment often sells the smaller property for cash. Such a trade is then called a three-way exchange because there are three parties, the up trader, the down trader, and the cash-out buyer.

When disposing of one personal residence to buy another, however, it is not necessary to go through the "exchange game." As discussed in Chapters 2 and 3, an owner must defer paying his profit tax when selling his principal residence and buying a more expensive one within eighteen months before or after the sale.

6. Assigned, Transferred, and Assumed Mortgages

Another method of paying for property to be acquired is to assign, transfer, or assume a mortgage. There are important differences in the meaning of these terms.

An assigned mortgage is one that you already own. In other words, someone owes you money, and your security is a mortgage on a property which can be foreclosed if the debt is not paid to you as agreed. You could assign this mortgage, as your down payment, to the seller of the realty you want to acquire. Another example of a mortgage assignment occurs when a construction lender, after the building is completed, assigns the construction loan to a permanent lender thereby converting the mortgage into long-term financing. This saves considerable escrow and recording fees. However, there may be tax aspects to consider on a mortgage assignment, so check with your tax adviser.

A transferred mortgage changes the borrower but keeps the original lender. This is frequently called a mortgage assumption if the new borrower assumes the legal obligation to make the loan payments and the lender releases the previous borrower from further liability. If the buyer merely takes over the loan payments, without any formal arrangement with the lender, this is called buying the property "subject to" the mortgage. Problems can develop with "subject to" mortgages if the loan contains a legally enforceable "due on sale clause." This is a hot real estate topic now as the legal enforceability of due on sale clauses differs in each state.

7. Hypothecated Mortgages

If you hold a mortgage on a property now and want to acquire a property, but the seller will not accept a mortgage assignment, hypothecate instead.

Hypothecate means to pledge as security or borrow against. For example, I held a seven-year second mortgage at 7 percent interest on an apartment house I sold. As there has not been much of a demand from investors to buy 7 percent mortgages, and I did not want to sell the mortgage because the discount would be at least 50 percent, I borrowed on it instead. The $15,000 mortgage was collateral for a loan of $7,500 at 10 percent interest. Sure, I took a 3 percent interest rate loss on the $7,500, but when the $15,000 loan paid off in seven years, I then used $7,500 to pay off my hypothecated loan. Hypothecation is a great way to obtain tax-free money secured by a mortgage you will not want to sell at a big discount.

8. Blanket Mortgages

There are many ways to use blanket mortgages, including buying property with little or no cash down payment. However, to use this finance technique, you must already own one or more properties.

Lenders love to get the maximum security for their mortgage loans. Often a bank or S&L will suggest you give a blanket mortgage on two or more properties you own as security for their mortgage loan. If the properties are in poor repair or in undesirable locations, the lender wants to spread the risk over as many properties as possible.

To illustrate, a friend of mine owns several duplexes in a not-so-hot neighborhood, a run-down hotel, and a small office building. He wanted to raise cash by refinancing his mortgages on these properties. But no lender desired to loan on these marginal properties. However, a lender would make a blanket mortgage on all of them. If my friend does not make the payments, the lender can then foreclose on all the properties. Without a blanket mortgage it would be next to impossible to borrow on these properties.

Another use for blanket mortgages is for buying property. Suppose you find a house for sale where the elderly seller does not need a cash down payment, but he or she wants secure monthly income. So you offer to buy the house, take over its existing first mortgage, and give the seller a blanket mortgage for the balance of the purchase price (no cash down payment). The blanket mortgage would be secured by the property you are buying as well as another property you already own. The blanket mortgage lets you acquire another property for no cash and gives its seller the security he or she seeks.

9. Lease With Option to Buy

This is such a powerful finance method for buyers and sellers, it is a special topic in the next chapter about short- and long-term lease-options. In the last year there has been considerable interest from my newspaper readers in this creative finance technique. The next chapter includes explanations and sample forms for this special finance method that can accomplish many real estate goals.

10. Ground Leases

Some of the sharpest, shrewdest real estate investors never buy or sell land. They lease it. The ground lease is a finance method that gives the landowner safe, secure income. The lessee (tenant) does not tie up cash in a nondepreciable asset but rather turns it into a tax advantage. If the land-leased property is other than the lessee's personal residence, land rent payments are tax deductible.

Special mention should be made of redeemable ground leases. If a land lease is for at least fifteen years and the lessee has an option to buy the land, then Internal Revenue Code Section 1055 allows the lessee to deduct his ground rent payments on his tax returns as interest. That may sound crazy, but even the IRS recognizes a redeemable ground lease as a finance device, similar to a mortgage.

11. Sale-Leasebacks

This finance method often produces 100 percent financing for the buyer. The property seller sells the property, usually business property, to an investor, such as a pension trust fund or an insurance company, at the fair market value. Often there is an option to repurchase the property when the lease expires, sometimes before.

By using the sale-leaseback method, the lessee-seller obtains cash and can now deduct his rent payments for a building he may have owned many years and fully depreciated before the sale. Stores, banks, factories, apartments and many other types of commercial properties are suitable for sale-leasebacks. But a tax adviser should be consulted because the tax require proper structuring of the sale-leaseback transaction.

12. Land Contract, Contract of Sale, Contract for Deed, and Agreement of Sale

All these names refer to the same type of transaction. Using this finance method, the property's seller retains legal title to the property until all or an agreed part of the sale price is paid by the buyer to the seller. This method is often used where the buyer makes no or a very small cash down payment. The seller feels more secure in such a transaction if he still holds the deed to the property.

But in the event of the buyer's default on the payments, the seller may have problems getting back possession of the property or clearing up the title. The status of land contract sales varies in each state, and an attorney should be consulted before using this technique. Although land contracts are used to finance otherwise "impossible transactions," they can be risky if not properly structured to protect both buyer and seller.

Another land contract sale problem can occur after the buyer has made all his payments and is entitled to receive the deed from the seller. Legally the seller is required to convey marketable title to the buyer at this time. But what if he cannot? Of course, the buyer can sue the seller for damages, but this can be costly and nonproductive. Many attorneys suggest, to avoid title problems, that the seller's deed should be held in escrow or a trust until the buyer completes his payments.

13. Commercial Loans
14. Chattel Loans
15. Personal Loans

Any one or a combination of these loan types can be used to finance the cash portion required for a down payment to buy a property. If the realty to be acquired needs immediate improvements, part of the money can be used to make those improvements. If you have built up a good credit history, you can probably borrow $5,000 to $20,000 from a bank or finance company on your signature alone. Sometimes the lender will record a lien on your household goods as security, but this is just to meet lending requirements and you can be 99 percent sure the lender never wants to foreclose on your furniture if you default on the loan.

16. Improvement Loans

An often overlooked finance source is the improvement loan. It can be either on property you already own or on the property you want to acquire. One of the first loans I ever obtained was a home improvement loan. The friendly old-time banker was extremely successful making these loans. He knew the money was not going to improve the property, and he did not care. All he wanted was good security for his loan in case of default.

Today, some lenders are sticky about improvement loans and want to see how the money will be spent to improve the property. Others do not care as long as there is sufficient equity in the property which secures the loan.

Since banks and S&Ls no longer play games and now make second mortgage loans readily, there really is not much need to call such loans improvement loans anymore. Improvement loans are really second mortgages. As bankers change their thinking and loan on the security of the property rather than on the borrower's credit, expect to see more second mortgages from banks and S&Ls and fewer improvement loans. Of course, if the owner lacks sufficient property equity to justify a second mortgage, and if the money really is going to finance improvements that will increase the property's value, then an improvement loan solves the problem. In such a situation, the lender will make sure the money really is spent on improvements which will increase the market value of the property.

17. Wrap-around mortgages

Another way to finance property acquisition is by use of a wrap-around mortgage. Such a loan is really a second mortgage. It can be either "hard money" (actual cash obtained from a mortgage lender) or "soft money" (loaned by the property seller to the buyer without cash actually changing hands). This finance technique can be good for buyers and sellers. But it is badly misunderstood and is often used in the wrong circumstances. Along with lease-options, wrap-around mortgages are fully discussed in the next chapter.

18. Syndication of Limited Partnerships

Often you will locate excellent investment property that is beyond your financial ability to buy and maintain. This is the time to consider forming a partnership with other investors. There are thousands of investors who want to invest in real estate but who lack the time and ability to find and buy properties. Examples include wealthy doctors, dentists, and lawyers who can better use their time making money than renting to tenants.

Many successful realty investors started out, as I did, investing with partners. This combination can work out very successfully if it is clearly understood, in a written partnership agreement, that the general partner will manage the property and will consult the investors (limited partners) only on major decisions such as selling or refinancing the property.

My first partnership ended by my buying out my partner. When we got our first vacancy, I wanted to fix up the unit so it could command higher rent. But my partner wanted to milk the property and take out as much cash as possible by putting in minimal maintenance. This fundamental clash of management philosophy should have been ironed out before buying the property. Thankfully, my partner was willing to sell out to me without any hassle, but it could have been a sticky problem if he had resisted.

A limited-partnership syndication should be entered into only after consultation with an attorney who should draw up the documentation. Investors should invest in such partnerships only if they will not need their investment money for the agreed number of years of the partnership's life. Some major stockbrokers offer huge limited-partnership offerings, based mostly on tax shelter benefits, but the "front end" load fees of such offerings diminish the limited-partner profit potential. Before investing in any limited partnership, check the general partner's experience and track record as that is some indication of probable future results too.

Frankly, I would never invest in the large, nationwide, partnership offerings. The tax shelter and investment returns are better, I find, on local properties that I can see, touch, and smell.

19. The Equity Release Technique

There are thousands of homeowners and other property owners who have idle equity in their properties. For example, if your home is worth $100,000 and you have a $60,000 mortgage on it, you have $40,000 of idle equity that is doing you absolutely no good just sitting there. It produces no income, no tax shelter, and no other benefits.

Equity is the difference between a property's fair market value and the amount owed on that property. To illustrate, suppose your home is worth $75,000 and it has a $25,000 first mortgage and a $10,000 second mortgage. The difference between the $75,000 value and the $35,000 total loans is the $40,000 idle equity that can be fully or partially used to buy more realty.

To release this idle equity, the property owner simply creates a promissory note, secured by a mortgage or trust deed on the property owned.

EXAMPLE:

Home's Current Market Value	$95,000
Old First Mortgage Balance	$40,000
New Second Mortgage Created	$40,000
Owner's New Equity in Home	$15,000

This homeowner can now go shopping for another property to buy, knowing he can use his $40,000 created second mortgage for his down payment. If he adds a little cash to "sweeten" the transaction for the seller of the property the homeowner wants to buy, his chances of getting a "good deal" are appreciably enhanced. To illustrate, suppose this homeowner finds a $200,000 apartment house he wants to buy. The financing might look like this:

Purchase Price	$200,000
Existing First Mortgage	$100,000
Buyer's Down Payment Created Second Mortgage	$40,000
New Second Mortgage Taken Back by Seller	$60,000

However, this buyer should be careful to structure the payments on the second mortgage created on his home and the second mortgage to the seller secured by the apartments. If the payments exceed the rents minus operating expenses, a negative cash flow results. To avoid this problem, perhaps one of the second mortgages can be structured to allow interest to accumulate, with no monthly payments and a balloon payment due in five or ten years.

20. The Life Estate Finance Method

Many older homeowners would like to (1) sell their homes to produce cash or monthly payments and (2) remain in their homes until they die or are physically unable to care for themselves. Although these desires are conflicting, they occur very frequently among elderly homeowners. The solution can be the life estate finance method.

A life estate allows a property user to retain use of a property as long as he or she is alive. For example, it is common for a husband in his will to provide a life estate for his surviving widow in the family home, but at her death the home is to go to the children.

When an investor buys a home subject to a life estate for the seller, it means the seller is guaranteed the privilege of living there for the rest of his or her life. If the property is being sold by husband and wife, the life estate can be for their joint lives.

The buyer-investor in such a house, which is subject to a life estate in the seller, would agree to pay the life tenant an agreed monthly payment based on that person's life expectancy at the time of the sale to the buyer-investor. This buyer will, of course, need an outside source of funds for these payments, such as purchasing an annuity based on the seller's life expectancy.

Advantages for the seller: Small cash down payment plus monthly income for living costs so occupancy of the home can be retained for life.

Advantages for the buyer: Little cash required. The property is bought at today's market value which will surely increase with inflation.

Disadvantages for the seller: Cannot will the property and may die before receiving the property's full value in payments from the investor-buyer.

Disadvantages for the buyer: Seller may outlive the life expectancy tables; resale or refinance of property subject to a life estate is very difficult so such property should not be bought with the thought of quick resale.

EXAMPLE: Investor wants to buy a $50,000 house owned by an elderly lady. He offers her $1,000 down payment and agrees to pay her $300 per month for life. To finance his purchase, the investor could get an open-end mortgage, adding to the mortgage balance periodically as need for funds arise. Or the buyer could purchase an annuity that would pay $300 per month for the seller's life, but this could be very expensive.

21. Foreclosures Purchased From the Lender

Although this is not a finance device, because of the seller's unique position, REO (real estate owned) foreclosures bought from lenders such as banks and savings and loan associations offer special financing terms.

Mortgage lenders do not like to admit it, but they make mistakes occasionally. These mistakes are called foreclosures. After the lender becomes the owner of a foreclosed property (if there are no cash bidders at the foreclosure sale), it is called REO property. Most banks, real estate investment trusts, savings and loan associations, and insurance companies own REO property which they would love to sell.

To get rid of these REOs (never call them foreclosures when talking to the lender because they do not like it known they make mistakes), 90 percent, 95 percent, and even 100 percent mortgage loans are made by the lender "to facilitate the sale." It is called "basket money." Such REO properties can be located in two ways. One is to phone all the S&Ls and banks in your area and ask to speak to the lender's officer in charge of real estate owned. If that person says the lender does not have any REOs at the present time, that may be the truth. Leave your name, address, and phone number. Better yet, follow up your phone conversation with a short typewritten letter on your letterhead reinforcing your buying interest. If you are lucky, when an REO comes available, the lender's REO officer may phone you.

The second method is to get a copy of the lender's latest quarterly financial statement. On that report you will see an item headed "real estate bought in settlement of loans" or some similar, misleading asset title. That is REO property. Regulated lenders want to get rid of this property because they have to set aside special reserves for such property. If you see that item on a lender's financial statement, you will know they have REO property to sell. Then contact the lender to find out what the property is, and then decide if you are interested in it.

But do not be misled! If the item on the lender's financial report statement says something like "Real estate held for investment," that is not REO property, and the lender may not want to sell it.

Lastly, keep checking back with lenders monthly to see if they have any new REO property. The best bargain property I ever bought was an REO sold by a large S&L that was so desperate to sell it they had even listed it with a real estate broker. Most lenders will not list REOs with realty agents because they do not want to play favorites, and they do not want to pay a sales commission. I found out about the REO from the realty broker, but I probably could have bought it cheaper before he got the listing if I had bought direct from the lender and if I had regularly phoned the lender for new REO offerings.

22. The Sandwich Lease

This finance technique is much like the lease-option method to be discussed in the next chapter. But it is even better. Its application is usually limited to commercial properties, but it could also be used on apartment houses.

An example will illustrate how a sandwich lease works. Suppose there is a vacant supermarket building in your town. Due to competition from newer stores, it is no longer suitable for a supermarket. But the building is basically sound. It is most likely being leased by a major supermarket chain that has several years remaining on its lease, plus an option to renew.

This abandoned supermarket might be a terrific location for several small shops—perhaps a "Farmer's Market" of restaurants, such as Chinese, Italian, German, Mexican, fast-food, and pizza, for example. So you go to the supermarket chain's real estate manager and obtain (1) a master lease on the store and (2) maybe, an option to purchase the property if the supermarket's lease contains such a purchase option. Frankly, the option is not important.

Suppose you master lease the store for $10,000 per month. You then divide it into perhaps ten smaller stores renting for $1,500 per month each ($15,000 total monthly rent). You will then have a $5,000 per month profit for being "sandwiched" between the owner and the shopkeepers. Your investment is minimal, unless you agree to make the improvements (for which higher rent can be charged, of course). Ideally, when you negotiate your master lease with the supermarket chain, you will have an option to purchase the building, so if the project is very successful, the property's value will appreciate. If it does not, you don't have to exercise the purchase option.

23. The Option

The cheapest yet potentially most profitable finance technique is the bare, naked option. Six- to twelve-month options often can be bought for 1 to 5 percent of the market value of a property. If the option expires but you have not exercised your purchase option, you lose your option money. But hopefully by the time the option is ready to expire, you have found a buyer who will purchase the property from you for a substantial profit. Or you may decide to buy the property to hold it as an investment.

To convince a property owner to sell you an option to buy his property, be sure to point out the tax advantages to the owner. Your option payment, perhaps $10,000, is nontaxable to the property owner until either (1) you exercise the purchase option or (2) the option expires unexercised. Either way, the property owner has the tax-free use of the option money. If the option is exercised and the option money is applied toward the purchase price, that option money becomes long-term capital gain to the seller. If the option expires unexercised, the option money is ordinary income to the seller. But until one of those events happens, the seller can use the option money as he pleases without any tax consequences.

24. Tax-deferred Exchanges

If you already own property held for investment or for use in your trade or business, your equity in that property can be used to trade toward a larger such property. In such an exchange, the tax on your profit is deferred if you meet the simple conditions of Internal Revenue Code Section 1031. The details on tax-deferred exchanges are explained in Chapter 10.

25. The Deferred Down Payment Method

When you are ready to buy a property, with lots of cash in your bank account, may not be the time when a property meeting your requirements is for sale. What often happens is you will hear of a property you would like to own, but at the time you do not have available cash for a down payment. Unless the seller is willing to sell for no down payment (such a seller is highly motivated and not easy to find), you may have difficulty buying that property.

But here is an idea which may convince the seller to sell to you now with little or no cash down payment. It is called the deferred down payment. The method of deferral can take several forms.

If you can afford high monthly payments to the seller, provide in your purchase offer for such high payments on the second mortgage the seller takes back to finance your purchase. In other words, your monthly payments will consist of interest on the unpaid principal plus abnormally high principal payments (your deferred down payment).

Another approach, if you are expecting to receive a large amount of cash in a few months, is to use a "short fuse mortgage" which has its balloon payment due in six or twelve months. But this can be dangerous if your expected source of the balloon payment does not materialize as expected. So be very careful before committing yourself to a short fuse mortgage for the deferred down payment.

Still another variation of the deferred down payment is to provide in your purchase offer for 100 percent financing to the seller but with prepayment of the first six monthly payments at the time of the closing.

To illustrate, suppose you find a $100,000 investment property that has a $60,000 existing assumable mortgage. You might offer the seller his full $100,000 asking price if he will finance your purchase with a $40,000 second mortgage. Most sellers will not accept such an offer. But if you pay the first six month's payments on that $40,000 second mortgage at the time of closing (which would be a $2,400 payment if it was a 12 percent interest-only second mortgage), that might sweeten the deal for the seller. Better yet, offer to prepay the entire year's monthly payments at the close of escrow.

The happy result for the buyer of this variation of the deferred down payment is the entire "down payment" becomes tax deductible interest.

26. Borrow the Realtor's Commission

Sometimes the buyer does not have enough cash for the down payment and he has no readily available source for borrowing that money such as a bank, S&L, cash-by-mail company, or "plastic money" from credit cards.

The last hope for the buyer may be the realty agent. Although they like to be paid their sales commission in cash, many real estate agents will loan their buyers all or part of their commission to finance the purchase.

To protect the agent, the promissory note should be secured by a mortgage or deed of trust either on the property being purchased or on other property owned by the buyer. Smart agents realize it is wise to take sales commission notes because this evens out the peaks and valleys of cyclical real estate sales commission income. If an agent builds up a portfolio of secured commission notes, he does not have to worry where his next dollar is coming from.

But a word to realty agents is in order. Never, never, never loan your sales commission to a buyer without getting adequate security. I recall selling a large apartment house where the seller did not have enough cash out of the sale to pay all the debts he owed on the building. He asked the two agents involved to loan him $7,000 so the sale could close. Although we were glad to make the loan (we got the rest of our commission in cash), we did not have time before the closing to check the seller's title on the property he offered as security. Unfortunately, he did not have clear title to it, so we wound up with an unsecured $7,000 commission note. When it came due in six months, the seller was now broke and either could not or would not pay us. We had to sue on the unsecured promissory note, get a court judgment, and then try to collect. We are still looking for assets to attach. Does anybody want to buy an unsecured $7,000 promissory note?

27. Refinance Before or During the Sale

If you find a property you want to buy, and the seller absolutely must have more cash from the sale than you have available, provide in your purchase offer for either (1) seller to refinance the mortgage before the sale or at the time of sale, or (2) at the time of sale you will take over payments on the existing first mortgage, obtain a new "hard money" second mortgage to give the seller the cash he needs, and seller will take back a third mortgage for the balance of the purchase price (thus giving you a no down payment purchase).

Last year I used this technique to acquire a rental house for practically no down payment. The seller said he needed $30,000 down payment. That was more than I wanted to invest in the house, which was worth about $115,000. So my purchase offer provided the following: (1) seller to refinance his $45,000 existing first mortgage for $80,000 and (2) seller to take back a second mortgage for the balance of the purchase price. The seller counteroffered that I was to make a $5,000 cash down payment, and I accepted. The happy result was a highly leveraged purchase, maximum tax shelter for me, and the seller got the cash he needed (to buy another house).

The same result could have been obtained by leaving the old first mortgage intact, adding a new "hard money" second mortgage, and the seller could have carried back a third mortgage for the balance of the sales price.

28. Borrow on Something You Already Own

In many property purchases there is often no adequate substitute for cash from the buyer to the seller. To raise this cash, consider what you already own (but do not want to sell) and can raise cash from. Examples probably include your auto, summer home, boat, common stocks, bonds, house, condominium, or furniture. By borrowing on the security of these items from your bank or finance company, you can acquire the necessary cash for the down payment on the real estate you want to acquire. Of course, be sure you can make the total payments on all your loans, otherwise this could be foolish borrowing.

29. The Right Day of the Month to Buy Income Property

Smart buyers of income property cut down the cash needed to finance their purchases by closing their purchase on the right day of the month.

What is that day? It is the day after the rents are due. For example, if you are buying a ten-unit apartment house where each tenant pays $250 per month rent on the first of the month, if you close the sale on the second of the month, you will receive a prorated rent credit for $^{29}/_{30}$ (assuming it is a thirty-day month) of $2,500 which is $2,416.66. In addition, you will be credited at the closing settlement with the amount of the tenant's security deposits. Depending upon state law, you may or may not be able to use the security deposits to reduce your cash needed to close the purchase. In most states, you can use the security deposits, and they do not have to be held in separate trust accounts for the tenants.

Of course, as the new owner you must be prepared to refund tenant security deposits when the tenant moves out. But since you will soon be renting to a new tenant who will pay a new security deposit, the money to return the old tenant's security deposit, in essence, comes from the new tenant.

30. Other Creative Ways to Finance Your Purchase

There are dozens of other creative, innovative methods of financing your property purchase. Examples include using the cash value of your life insurance policy (the cost is usually only 5 percent or 6 percent); giving the seller prepaid rent so he can remain in the property, free, for an agreed period in return for a no or low down payment purchase; selling part of the property acquired to raise cash for the down payment (works very well if the property can be split into two or more lots); or taking in a rich partner who puts up the down payment cash in return for a 50 percent or 75 percent of the property you found and will manage.

The key to financing real estate today is to think positively and do not be afraid to innovate. Of course, do not take unnecessary or unreasonable risks. Your reputation is extremely important. Do not do anything to tarnish it. Be sure you can meet your payments on time because if you once default, it harms your credit and your future ability to finance property acquisitions creatively.

Listen to other real estate investors. Attend meetings of your local property owner's association, which is usually very inexpensive to join. Spend money attending real estate seminars. Buy books on real estate investments. An excellent one on creative finance is Robert G. Allen's *Nothing Down,* published by Simon and Schuster.

There is no real estate finance technique that will work in every situation on every property. Although the traditional buying formula of a 20 percent cash down payment and an 80 percent new mortgage is not gone, it is dying fast. Those buyers who understand innovative finance will be the ones who prosper in real estate. But buyers and their realty agents who do not understand the new finance methods will miss profit opportunities. You will be a winner if you keep up with the changes in real estate finance and adapt to changing conditions.

QUESTIONS AND ANSWERS

SELLER CAN NAME OWN PRICE
IF HE WILL CARRY THE MORTGAGE

Q. We are selling our home so we can move to a condominium we have already purchased in south Florida. As we are retiring, income will be very important to us. I want to maximize my retirement income. Does this idea make sense? Our home should sell for about $125,000. It presently has a $24,000 FHA mortgage at 8 percent interest. I would like to sell for $20,000 cash down payment and take back a $105,000 "wrap-around mortgage" at 10 percent interest only (no principal payments). This would give me $875 monthly income without touching the principal. What do you think?—*Joseph M.*

A. I think you have got an outstanding idea. More sellers should follow your suggestion. Sellers who are willing to carry the purchase-money mortgage for their buyers can practically name their own price in today's market. By offering easy financing, you should be able to get a sales price higher than for similar recent home sales in your neighborhood.

Be sure to have your attorney draw up that wrap-around mortgage to be sure it does not violate any usury law in your state, however.

WHY FHA AND VA MORTGAGES
DO NOT APPEAL TO MANY SELLERS

Q. We own a rental house in a low income part of town. It is listed for sale with a nearby real estate agent. He brought us a purchase offer from a GI buyer who wants to get a 100 percent VA home loan. That's fine with us, but the agent says if we accept the purchase offer we must pay the buyer's loan fee. This sounds stupid to me. Why should I, the seller, pay the buyer's loan costs? The agent says the law prohibits the buyer from paying such loan fees. Is this true or is the agent lying?—*Ed R.*

A. The agent is telling the truth. I agree with you that it is a stupid law which prohibits VA and FHA mortgage borrowers from paying the loan fee on their own home loan. Borrowers using conventional mortgages pay their own costs, why cannot FHA and VA borrowers do so too?

Lenders are charging extra-high loan fees on FHA and VA mortgages now because the government-set interest rate on these loans is below that lenders can get on conventional home mortgages. For this reason, few FHA and VA home loans are being made now. You are not alone in refusing to pay those outrageous loan fees for the buyer.

IS BUYING "SUBJECT TO"
OR "ASSUMING" OLD EXISTING MORTGAGE BETTER?

Q. Our real estate agent has shown us several homes that have large existing mortgages. She said we can either take title "subject to" these mortgages or "assume" them. I'm not clear on the difference. Which is better for us?—*Bruce R.*

A. Buying "subject to" an existing mortgage means the buyer takes title to the property and takes over the payments on the old mortgage. But he does not legally assume any liability on that mortgage. Of course, if he does not keep up the payments, he loses the property by foreclosure.

Assuming an existing mortgage means the buyer takes title to the property and legally assumes the responsibility for paying the mortgage. The lender will then usually release the original borrower from further liability on that mortgage. However, some lenders blackmail buyers into paying an increased interest rate when they assume the old mortgage. But FHA and VA loans can be assumed without change of interest rate or terms.

IS VARIABLE INTEREST RATE MORTGAGE
GOOD FOR BORROWER?

Q. I know you dislike variable interest rate mortgages. But with mortgage interest rates so high today, don't you think they will come down in six months or so? We have just been transferred here and must buy a home quickly. Should we request a variable interest rate mortgage? —*Moses S.*

A. That is a difficult question. Please understand that interest rates on variable rate mortages (VRMs) will drop only if the lender's cost of funds drops. While that cost is near all-time peaks today, there is no guarantee it will drop. It could go up further if inflation is not brought under control.

Canada, for example, has had high interest rates for many years. Maybe we are due for a similar period of long-term high interest rates.

Even if interest rates drop on mortgages, that does not mean the lender's cost of funds will drop, thereby reducing the interest rate on VRMs already existing. With lenders under extreme pressure to raise interest rates paid to savers, I see little hope of lender fund costs dropping much if any within the next twelve months.

In spite of what you read in the newspapers, fixed interest rate mortgages are still available if you shop hard enough. For example, as of this writing FHA and VA fixed rate thirty-year mortgages are readily available. Considering their advantages, and their assumability by a subsequent buyer, that fixed-rate mortgage is far more attractive than a VRM.

HOW SOME MORTGAGE LENDERS USE
PREPAYMENT PENALTY RIP-OFFS

Q. We are trying to sell our home. Our mortgage, from a savings and loan association, has a prepayment penalty which is 4 percent of our $74,000 balance. That's $2,960. In our area, most lenders waive the prepayment penalty if the new buyer gets his mortgage from the same lender. Our house sold for $136,000, subject to the buyer's getting a new mortgage for $100,000. But our present lender refuses to make the loan to the new buyer, even though it only means a $26,000 increase and a raise in the interest rate. I'm told this lender has a policy of wanting to collect the prepayment penalty, and it rarely makes new loans for buyers of properties on which it has existing loans. What can we do to save the $2,960 prepayment penalty?—*George P.*

A. You have encountered a classic mortgage lender rip-off practiced by many savings and loan associations. I have been a victim of it twice from lenders in my area. Of course, I will not do business with those lenders again, but there was nothing I could do, other than not sell.

It is highly unethical for a lender to refuse to make a new loan to your buyer, but there is no law violation unless the lender is illegally redlining or discriminating. Many unscrupulous lenders refuse to make loans to property buyers where that lender already has the loan because the lender knows the prepayment penalty must be paid if the loan is obtained elsewhere.

Prepayment penalties add millions of dollars to lender earnings. In addition, prepayments wipe out old, low interest rate mortgages so that money can be reloaned to another borrower at today's higher interest rates. Unfortunately, it is all prefectly legal.

WATCH FOR MORTGAGE GIMMICKS ON NEW HOMES

Q. My wife and I are trying to find a home to buy. We've looked at several brand new home projects where the mortgage interest rates are about 10 percent. But realtors tell us mortgage money to buy an older house costs at least 14 percent in our area now. Why the big difference? Do the builders have some secret source of cheap money we can tap? —*Simon U.*

A. Those below-market interest rates on new homes are gimmicks. The builders, months ago, bought mortgage commitments from lenders for their entire project. The cost may have been one to five points (each loan point equals 1 percent of the amount borrowed), which, you can be sure, is passed along to buyers in the form of inflated home costs.

Although you will only pay the advertised interest rate on the new homes, lenders make their profit on such loans up from when the builder pays the loan commitment fee. Many lenders wish they had not made such mortgage commitments a few months ago. But now they are stuck with the low interest rates they agreed to charge the borrowers.

P.S. Watch out for below-market interest rates which only prevail for the first year or two, with the interest rate then reverting to market levels.

HOW TO TAKE THE SHOCK OUT OF
HIGH MORTGAGE INTEREST RATES

Q. I am a worried real estate agent. My fear is the high mortgage interest rates will dry up the market for home sales, and I won't make any commissions. So far I've managed to keep up my sales volume using "creative finance" ideas such as wrap-around mortgages, land contracts of sale, and lease-options. How long do you think these high interest rates will last or should I look for another job?—*Lottie M.*

A. I share your concern. In some communities, home mortgage money is not available at any price. In most others, it is available but very expensive.

When mortgage interest rates eventually decline, be ready for buyer demand to soar. So will home prices because there will only be a limited supply of homes for sale then.

To take the shock out of high mortgage interest rates, point out to your buyers their true after-tax mortgage cost. To illustrate, suppose a home buyer gets a new mortgage at 14 percent interest. If he is in a 30 percent income tax bracket (combined state and federal taxes), his tax dollar savings for the interest deduction are about 30 percent of 14 percent which is 4.2 percent. Fourteen percent minus 4.2 percent is 9.8 percent. Considering that the home is probably appreciating in value at least 10 percent per year, that mortgage is virtually cost-free for the buyer. If more buyers understood this, they would not wait to buy, even if interest rates drop a little in the next few months.

TIME AND INFLATION RULE OUT
BIG HOME CASH DOWN PAYMENT

Q. Like many apartment dwellers, we are saving for the down payment on a home of our own, probably a condominium. So far we've saved about $6,000. But it seems at our rate of saving, prices of houses and condos are going up faster than we can save. We were hoping to make a 25 percent cash down payment to hold down the monthly mortgage payments. Do you think we're doing the right thing?—*Elizabeth D.*

A. No. It is smart to save up for your down payment, but time and inflation are against you. Buy as soon as you can, so you will benefit from inflation instead of being its victim.

You probably realize your $6,000 sitting in a savings account or money market fund is costing you lost purchasing power due to inflation (about

12 percent per year at current inflation rates). Since prices of houses and condos usually go up at or faster than the inflation rate, the sooner you buy a home the sooner you will participate in the appreciation in market value of your home.

A $6,000 down payment will not buy a very fancy home or condo, but it is enough to buy a "starter home." By use of creative finance ideas, you can buy a home now. Your benefits will include income tax savings for mortgage interest and property tax deductions, protection from rising rents, and the joy of building equity in your own home instead of helping your landlord buy his building. Work with a good realty agent to find and finance the right home for you.

ARE MORTGAGE PRINCIPAL PAYMENTS TAX DEDUCTIBLE?

Q. Is it true that mortgage interest, but not principal, payments are tax deductible?—*Fred D.*

A. Yes, it is true. Mortgage principal payments are never itemized income tax deductions for home owners or property investors.

HOW TO BUY A HOME IF YOU HAVE GOT BAD CREDIT

Q. Two years ago we went through bankruptcy. Since then, we have paid our bills and obligations on time. We talked to a loan officer at the bank where we have our savings account. She said we would have a hard time getting a home mortgage, even though we now have up to $9,000 for the down payment. Is there any way we can buy a house with our poor credit?—*Pat E.*

A. Yes. Your credit history should be no problem if you buy a home that the seller will finance. Many home sellers, especially retirees, want to carry back a first or second mortgage since this will give them safe, profitable interest income. Work with a good real estate agent. Explain your problem so the agent can concentrate on finding a seller-financed home for you.

FINANCING IS THE KEY TO REAL ESTATE SUCCESS

Q. I am a new real estate salesman and am mystified by all the property finance methods you discuss. Wrap-around mortgages, land contracts, and purchase money mortgages are some of the terms I don't understand. Is there any way to simplify home financing?—*Nathan E.*

A. Basically there are only five ways to finance property sales. (1) All cash (highly undesirable for buyers, due to inflation), (2) buyer "assumes" or takes title "subject to" an existing mortgage already on the property, (3) seller takes back a first or second mortgage or trust deed, or sells on a land contract, wrap-around mortgage, lease-option, or other innovative finance method, (4) buyer borrows on a new conventional, FHA, or VA mortgage from a bank, S&L, or mortgage broker, and (5) any combination of the above methods.

Financing is the key to real estate success. Learn all you can about real estate finance so you will prosper in real estate sales good times and bad. One good way to learn quickly is to take evening classes in real estate finance at a nearby college. Another good way is to read books on real estate finance, available at your local bookstore or library.

HOW TO PAY OFF HOME MORTGAGE BALLOON PAYMENT

Q. The seller of the house we are considering buying will help finance our purchase with a second mortgage. But he wants the payments to be "interest only" for six years at which time the entire balance of $24,000 will be due. Is this safe for us?—*Evan G.*

A. Yes. When that balloon payment comes due in six years, the balance on the first mortgage will probably be much lower than it is today. That first mortgage can probably then be refinanced to give you the cash to pay off the second mortgage's balloon payment. You may even have leftover tax-free cash from the refinancing.

Another alternative, in six years, would be to leave the old first mortgage alone and get a new second mortgage from an outside lender to pay the second mortgage balloon payment.

But a word of caution is in order. A six-year mortgage is safe, but large short-term second mortgages with balloon payments can be dangerous. For example, if your $24,000 second mortgage has its balloon payment due in only two years, then you might not be able to refinance the first mortgage or get a new second mortgage to produce the necessary $24,000 cash. If you cannot pay the balloon payment, of course, you lose the property by foreclosure.

As for the "interest-only" feature of the proposed second mortgage, that is good for you because all your payments will be tax-deductible interest. Although the interest only mortgage keeps your loan at a constant balance, you will be building equity due to the probable market value appreciation of the home.

TAKING OVER OLD HOME MORTGAGE
CAN HOLD DOWN COSTS

Q. We're in the process of buying a home, but we think the seller is taking advantage of us. When we made our purchase offer, it said we are to take title "subject to" the existing mortgage, and the seller was to give us a second mortgage to help finance the sale. The seller accepted in writing. Then about two weeks ago, the realty agent told us we'll have to "assume" the old mortgage as the seller wants to be released from liability on it. This will involve extra fees and the lender wants to increase the mortgage's interest rate. What do you advise?—*John G.*

A. See your attorney. Find out if the old mortgage has a legally enforceable "due on sale clause." If it does, when title to the property is transferred, the lender can demand full payment and foreclosure if you do not pay off the loan. When you assume such a mortgage, the lender can charge an assumption fee and raise the interest rate. Frankly, it is a lender's rip-off—also known as "legalized blackmail." After you assume the mortgage, the lender will probably agree to release the seller from further liability on the mortgage.

But if the old mortgage does not have an enforceable "due on sale clause" (FHA and VA mortgages do not), then you can take title "subject to" the old mortgage at its old interest rate and without a big assumption fee.

When a property buyer takes title "subject to" an old, existing mortgage, the seller remains liable on that loan if the buyer defaults. If you did not agree to assume the old mortgage in the sales agreement, however, it would appear the seller cannot require you to do so now. Be sure your attorney is up to date on the latest court decisions in this area as "due on sale clauses" are a hot real estate topic throughout the nation today.

FIFTEEN WAYS TO FINANCE HOME PURCHASE WITH LITTLE OR NO CASH

Q. My husband and I earn about $20,000 total per year. But we only have around $450 in our savings account. Any ideas how we can buy a home without waiting to save up a down payment?—*Tammie R.*

A. Yes. To build up your down payment savings account, always deposit your paychecks in your savings account, never in your checking account. Withdraw only for necessary living costs. Cut the frills. Then start looking for a home to buy. Keep making purchase offers until a motivated seller accepts one. Here are fifteen ways to buy a home with little or no cash. Your realty agent can probably suggest more.

(1) Lease a home with an option to buy it in twelve months, (2) VA no down payment mortgage, (3) FHA low down payment mortgage, (4) 90 percent or 95 percent PMI (private mortgage insurance) mortgage from over 22,000 banks and S&Ls, (5) buy a foreclosed FHA or VA home from HUD, (6) borrow the down payment from relatives, (7) borrow the down payment on your car or other personal property from a bank or finance company, (8) get seller to finance the sale on a first or second mortgage with minimal cash down payment, (9) buy an REO (real estate owned) foreclosed home from a bank or S&L, (10) "equity squeeze" by creating a down payment second mortgage on property you already own, (11) get a

group of friends to form a limited partnership syndicate to buy your home and give you an option to buy it for a higher price from them in a few years, (12) buy an option on a home, (13) buy out the owners' equity in a home that he is about to lose through foreclosure, (14) borrow the down payment on an unsecured loan at your bank (if your credit is good), and (15) buy on a land contract with little or no cash down payment.

7.

Wrap-Around Mortgage and Lease-Option Opportunities

Two of the most widely used and misunderstood real estate innovative finance techniques being used today are the wrap-around mortgage and lease-options. While these methods will not solve every realty finance problem, in the right circumstances they can be used profitably and creatively. This chapter will explain both methods in great detail. The section on lease-options, both the short-term and long-term types, contains actual forms which have been successfully used in lease-option transactions.

HOW WRAP-AROUND MORTGAGES BENEFIT PROPERTY BUYERS AND SELLERS

The wrap-around or all-inclusive mortgage is one of today's most popular real estate finance devices. Much has been written about the advantages of this technique but, unfortunately, much of that information is incorrect.

Some of the things being said about wrap-around mortgages include (1) they can overcome the "due on sale clause" problems with existing mortgages, (2) no prepayment penalty can be charged if there is a wrap-around mortgage, (3) they solve the "excess mortgage" problem in an installment sale, (4) they increase profits for the seller-lender, (5) they reduce costs for the buyer-borrower, and (6) they provide financing for otherwise impossible situations.

Only the last three are correct; the first three are not true. As we look at the pros and cons of wrap-around mortgages, think of situations where use of a wrap-around mortgage would be profitable. Unfortunately, wrap-around mortgages are still a mystery to most realty buyers, sellers, real estate agents, real estate attorneys, title insurance and escrow officers, and mortgage loan officers. As a result, wrap-arounds are not used as often as they should be.

WHAT IS A WRAP-AROUND MORTGAGE?

Wrap-around mortgages (WAM) have been used in Canada for over thirty years where they are called "blanket mortgages." (Do not confuse this with the U.S. useage of blanket mortgages which refer to a mortgage secured by two or more parcels of real property.) Wrap-around mortgages have been used in the U.S. since the 1930s, but they have achieved most of their popularity since 1960. They periodically become very popular as a method of overcoming our cyclical "credit crunches" when mortgage money becomes very expensive and hard to find.

It is impossible to use a WAM if the property involved does not already have an existing first mortgage on it. Of course, there can be an existing second and/or third mortgages too, in which case the WAM wraps around those old mortgage too. Any existing mortgage(s) on the property remain undisturbed.

The WAM, also called an all-inclusive mortgage, a hold-harmless mortgage, or an overriding mortgage, is really a second mortgage. It is the security device for a promissory note that states the debt owed by the borrowers to the lender. In many states, trust deeds are used instead of mortgages to secure the debt which is evidenced by the promissory note. Whether a trust deed or mortgage is used, the result is the same, although the details of mortgages and trust deeds differ slightly from a legal viewpoint.

The face amount of the WAM's promissory note is the *total* of the existing first (and second, and third, and fourth, etc.) mortgage *plus* the cash or equity loaned by the lender to the borrower. The interest rate of the WAM must equal or surpass the interest rate on the underlying old mortgage which remains undisturbed when the WAM is placed on the property. In other words, the WAM wraps around the old mortgage(s) already secured by the property.

A WAM borrower makes one mortgage payment monthly, quarterly, or annually to the WAM lender. That WAM lender then uses part of the borrower's payment to keep up payments on the old underlying mortgage(s). The leftover cash is the WAM lender's net payment.

EXAMPLE: Sam wants to retire in Arizona and sell his home in Illinois for $60,000. It now has a 7 percent FHA mortgage with a $25,000 balance. Sam wants to finance the sale for his buyer to (1) make an easy quick sale for top dollar and (2) provide extra interest income with excellent safety for his retirement years. Of course, Sam could take back a traditional second mortgage, but he wants the higher yield and simplicity offered by a WAM.

Sam sells his home for $60,000, taking a $9,000 cash down payment from his buyer. He also receives a $51,000 WAM at 10 percent interest. He decides on a twenty-five-year amortization payback schedule to keep the buyer's payments competitive with conventional mortgages, but he insists on a balloon payment of the unpaid balance due in ten years.

Because Sam takes back a WAM instead of a second mortgage, he earns 10 percent interest on his $26,000 loan ($51,000 minus the $25,000 existing FHA mortgage) to the buyer, plus the 3 percent interest differential on the underlying old $25,000 FHA 7 percent loan, which remains undisturbed.

This WAM is good for both the buyer (where else can he borrow so cheaply?) and for seller Sam (who earns a 12.8 percent total yield on his $26,000 net loan—$2,600 annual interest at 10 percent plus the 3 percent interest differential of $750 on $25,000 is $3,350 total yield which is 12.8 percent return on the $26,000 "at risk"). The buyer can pay the balloon payment in ten years by refinancing with a new conventional first mortgage if Sam will not extend the loan then.

This is a classic example of when a WAM should be used. It is much easier for a buyer to understand a $60,000 sale with $9,000 down payment and a $51,000 mortgage at 10 percent interest than it is to understand a $9,000 down payment, assumption of a $25,000 first mortgage, and the seller will carry back a $26,000 second mortgage at 12.8 percent. The result is exactly the same for the buyer and seller, but a WAM's simplicity makes the sale easy to understand.

Sam's sale was an example of a "soft money" WAM. It is called soft money because Sam did not physically loan the buyer any cold, hard cash. The entire transaction took place on paper. But WAMs can also be used for hard money loans too. In fact, many smart lenders are making hard money WAM loans instead of loaning on new conventional first mortgages.

EXAMPLE: Aaron owns a small shopping center worth $300,000. It has a $150,000 first mortgage at 7 percent from Friendly Insurance Company. This mortgage has a big prepayment penalty if Aaron pays it off early to refinance with a bigger new mortgage from another lender.

Aaron can secure a new AAA-rated tenant for his shopping center, but he must make $50,000 of improvements to obtain this new tenant. So Aaron goes to the local First National Bank to get a new hard money WAM for $225,000 at 12 percent (slightly below the "going rate" on such loans). The bank will earn their 12 percent interest on the $75,000 actual cash loan ($225,000 minus $150,000) plus a 5 percent interest differential on the underlying old $150,000 insurance company mortgage, which remains untouched.

The bank's total yield will be about 22 percent. Twelve percent is earned on the $75,000 cash loan ($9,000 per year) plus 5 percent on the $150,000 (about $7,500 per year) for which the bank advanced zero cash, a total interest income to the bank of $16,500 per year. This is a 22 percent annual return on the $75,000 "at risk" loan. This WAM is a "good deal" for both Aaron and the First National Bank.

WHEN SHOULD A WRAP-AROUND MORTGAGE BE USED?

The WAM can be used in many mortgage situations, but not in every case. The major circumstances when it can and should be used include (1) a purchase-money mortgage where the seller carries or takes back a WAM on the property being sold (as Sam did in the example above), (2) refinancing of the mortgage on a property with a commercial hard money lender (such as the First National Bank in the example above), and (3) purchase-money supplied by a third-party hard money lender, such as a bank or individual, to aid a buyer in purchasing property.

WRAP-AROUND MORTGAGE FEATURES AND PITFALLS

Although there are many WAM advantages for lenders and borrowers, there are pitfalls to watch for. In situations where these drawbacks are present, a WAM should not be used.

THE "DUE ON SALE CLAUSE" TRAP

Always be certain the existing first or other mortgage around which the WAM is wrapping does not contain a legally enforceable "due on sale clause." Such a clause means the existing first or other mortgage's balance is due in full if the property title is transferred without the lender's approval (such approval is usually granted if the buyer assumes the old mortgage's legal obligation and agrees to pay a higher interest rate than was originally written on the old mortgage).

The enforceability of these due on sale clauses is currently being litigated in almost every state. In the states still allowing enforcement, it is called "legalized blackmail" if the lender can demand a higher interest rate just because the fortuitous property transfer occurred. Many state courts have ruled these due on sale clauses are illegal restraints on the free transferability of title to real property.

This argument has been successful in some states, but not in others. The law is still developing on this topic, and consultation with an experienced real estate attorney is advised if the mortgage to be wrapped contains a due on sale clause that may be enforceable. If the existing first mortgage is from a federal savings and loan association (a S&L with the word "federal" in its name), watch out. These lenders are especially militant in trying to enforce due on sale clauses. They base their alleged ability to enforce due on sale clauses on a Federal Home Loan Bank Board rule allowing such clauses.

If the old existing mortgage contains a legally enforceable due on sale clause, do not risk using a WAM. The reason is if that lender decides to enforce the due on sale clause and "call" the loan because property title was transferred without the lender's approval, the WAM lender is then in a bad position. He then must pay off the underlying first or other mortgage to protect his WAM. But he cannot go out and get a replacement underlying first or other mortgage because he is not the title owner of the property.

Special Note: FHA and VA home mortgages do not contain due on sale clauses. They are freely assumable by the new owner upon payment of a modest assumption fee. FHA and VA mortgages therefore are excellent candidates for WAMs.

THE BALLOON PAYMENT TRAP

If the existing first or other existing mortgage on the property contains a balloon payment due in a few years, the WAM should provide for payoff of that balloon payment. The WAM should specify the borrower is to either pay off the WAM or come up with the cash to make the balloon payment on the old underlying mortgage. If this is not done, and the lender on the underlying mortgage forecloses, the WAM could be wiped out, since it was recorded after the underlying mortgage.

THE PREPAYMENT PENALTY TRAP

If the WAM is obtained from a commercial lender, such as a bank or insurance company, its terms often bar prepayment for ten or fifteen years. A penalty is often imposed for early repayment thereafter. The reason is a WAM lender wants to discourage early repayment. The WAM lender earns the maximum yield on its invested dollars after the underlying existing lower interest rate mortgage is paid down (if it is an amortizing loan). The longer the WAM exists, the higher the lender's yield rises.

Although the exact terms of WAMs are open to negotiation between the lender and the borrower, there are now preprinted standard forms for WAMs in most states. However, those forms should be carefully read to be sure they do not conflict with the terms of the transaction as the lender and borrower understand those conditions. On the next pages are examples of a typical WAM promissory note and a deed of trust, as used in California.

THE PURCHASE-MONEY TRAP

When a mortgage lender makes a mortgage loan to enable a buyer to purchase a property, it is called a "purchase-money mortgage." It can be a first, second, third, or a WAM. Some states, such as California, have laws barring a purchase-money mortgage lender from collecting any foreclosure loss deficiency from the borrower after default. In other words, the property is the sole security for a purchase-money mortgage in some states.

A seller who finances a purchase-money mortgage for the buyer, especially if the buyer makes a very low down payment, should be aware of this limitation in some states. In the low down payment situation, a land contract or a lease-option (where the seller retains legal title) might be a better alternative to a sale using a WAM.

THE TITLE INSURANCE TRAP

A few ultraconservative title insurance companies will not insure WAMs. But most title insurance firms insure WAMs like second mortgages. A WAM lender should check to be sure title insurance will be available and to see if any special WAM drafting requirements must be met to obtain title insurance for the lender.

THE USURY TRAP

The interest rate on the face of the WAM promissory note cannot exceed the applicable state usury interest rate. The usury problem arises with WAMs because, although the interest rate on the face of the WAM note must be below the legal usury limit, the lender's effective or actual total yield often exceeds the state's usury maximum allowable interest rate. This is due to the differential earned on the underlying old mortgage.

A second problem with usury is a WAM may run afoul of state laws prohibiting collection of interest on interest.

Almost every state has usury law affecting mortgage loans. Many exclude certain lenders, such as banks, S&Ls, corporations, and mortgage brokers. Others have differing tests for usury. Some calculate interest on the basis of actual dollars received by the borrower. For example, see *Mindlin* vs. *Davis,* a 1954 Florida case (74 So.2d 789) that held interest received by a lender is to be measured against the lender's net dollar investment in the loan, rather than on the face amount of the WAM note.

The unhappy result was the lender's total yield exceeded the state's usury limit at the time.

But there is considerable doubt if this reasoning would apply to a purchase-money WAM financed by a property seller if no cash funds are actually advanced to the buyer (a soft money loan). Since many states are now changing their usury laws to meet the realities of today's high

DO NOT DESTROY THIS ORIGINAL NOTE: When paid, said original note, together with the Deed of Trust securing same, must be surrendered to Trustee for cancellation and retention before reconveyance will be made.

ALL INCLUSIVE PURCHASE MONEY PROMISSORY NOTE SECURED BY LONG FORM ALL-INCLUSIVE PURCHASE MONEY DEED OF TRUST
(INSTALLMENT NOTE, INTEREST INCLUDED)

$ _____ _____ , California, _____ _____ , 19___

In installments as herein stated, for value received, I/We ("Maker") promise to pay to _____

_____

_____

_____

("Payee") or order, at _____

the principal sum of _____ DOLLARS,

with interest from _____ on unpaid principal at the rate of

_____ per cent per annum; principal and interest payable in installments of _____

_____

or more on the _____ _____ day of each _____ month, beginning

on the _____ day of _____ 19_____ , and continuing until said principal and interest have been paid.

Each installment shall be applied first on the interest then due and the remainder on principal; and interest shall thereupon cease upon the principal so credited.

The total principal amount of this Note includes the unpaid principal balance of the promissory note(s) ("Underlying Note(s)") secured by Deed(s) of Trust, more particularly described as follows:

1. (A) PROMISSORY NOTE:

Maker: _____

Payee: _____

Original Amount: _____

Date: _____

(B) DEED OF TRUST:

Beneficiary: _____

Original Amount: _____

Recordation Date: _____

Document No. _____ Book _____ Page _____

Place of Recordation: _____ , County, California

2. (A) PROMISSORY NOTE:

Maker: _____

Payee: _____

Original Amount: _____

Date: _____

(B) DEED OF TRUST:

Beneficiary: _____

Original Amount: _____

Recordation Date: _____

Document No. _____ Book _____ Page _____

Place of Recordation: _____ , County, California

By Payee's acceptance of this Note, Payee covenants and agrees that, provided Maker is not delinquent or in default under the terms of this Note, Payee shall pay all installments of principal and interest which shall hereafter become due pursuant to the provisions of the Underlying Note(s) as and when the same become due and payable. In the event Maker shall be delinquent or in default under the terms of this Note, Payee shall not be obligated to make any payments required by the terms of the Underlying Note(s) until such delinquency or default is cured. In the event Payee fails to timely pay any installment of principal or interest on the Underlying Note(s) at the time when Maker is not delinquent or in default hereunder, Maker may, at Maker's option, make such payments directly to the holder of such Underlying Note(s), in which event Maker shall be entitled to a credit against the next installment(s) of principal and interest due under the terms of this Note equal to the amount so paid and including, without limitation, any penalty, charges and expenses paid by Maker to the holder of the Underlying Note(s) on account of Payee failing to make such payment. The obligations of Payee hereunder shall terminate upon the earliest of (i) foreclosure of the lien of the All-Inclusive Purchase Money Deed of Trust securing this Note, or (ii) cancellation of this Note and reconveyance of the All-Inclusive Purchase Money Deed of Trust securing same.

Should Maker be delinquent or in default under the terms of this Note, and Payee consequently incurs any penalties, charges or other expenses on account of the Underlying Note(s) during the period of such delinquency or default, the amount of such penalties, charges and expenses shall be immediately added to the principal amount of this Note and shall be immediately payable by Maker to Payee.

Notwithstanding anything to the contrary herein contained, the right of Maker to prepay all or any portion of the principal of this Note is limited to the same extent as any limitation exists in the right to prepay the principal of the Underlying Note(s). If any prepayments of principal of this Note shall, by reason of the application of any portion thereof by Payee to the prepayment of principal of the Underlying Note(s), constitute such prepayment for which the holders of the Underlying Note(s) are entitled to receive a prepayment penalty or consideration, the amount of such prepayment penalty or consideration shall be paid by Maker to Payee upon demand, and any such amount shall not reduce the unpaid balance of principal or interest hereunder.

At any time when the total of the unpaid principal balance of this Note, accrued interest thereon, all other sums due pursuant to the terms hereof, and all sums advanced by Payee pursuant to the terms of the All-Inclusive Purchase Money Deed of Trust securing this Note, is equal to or less than the unpaid balance of principal and interest then due under the terms of the Underlying Note(s), Payee, at his option, shall cancel this Note and deliver same to Maker and execute a request for full reconveyance of the Deed of Trust securing this Note.

Should default be made by Maker in payment of any installments of principal, interest, or any other sums due hereunder, the whole sum of principal, interest and all other sums due from Maker hereunder, after first deducting therefrom all sums then due under the terms of the Underlying Note(s), shall become immediately due at the option of the holder of this Note. Principal, interest and all other sums due hereunder payable in lawful money of the United States. If action be instituted of this Note, I/we promise to pay such sums as the Court may fix as attorney's fees. This Note is secured by a LONG FORM ALL-INCLUSIVE PURCHASE MONEY DEED OF TRUST to FOUNDERS TITLE COMPANY, a California corporation, as Tustee.

_____   _____

_____   _____

_____   _____

_____   _____

(Maker)   (Maker)

The undersigned hereby accept(s) the foregoing All-Inclusive Purchase Money Promissory Note and agree(s) to perform each and all of the terms thereof on the part of Payee to be performed.

Executed as of the date and place first above written.

_____   _____

_____   _____

_____   _____

(Payee)   (Payee)

(THIS NOTE IS FOR USE ONLY IN PURCHASE MONEY TRANSACTIONS. IT IS RECOMMENDED THAT, PRIOR TO THE EXECUTION OF THIS NOTE, THE PARTIES CONSULT WITH THEIR ATTORNEYS WITH RESPECT THERETO.)

LONG FORM ALL-INCLUSIVE PURCHASE MONEY DEED OF TRUST AND ASSIGNMENT OF RENTS

This All-Inclusive Purchase Money Deed of Trust, made this _____ day of, _____
between _____,

herein called TRUSTOR, whose address is _____,
                                    (number and street)   (city)   (state)   (zip)
FOUNDERS TITLE COMPANY, A California corporation, herein called TRUSTEE, and

_____, herein called BENEFICIARY,

Witnesseth: That Trustor IRREVOCABLY GRANTS, TRANSFERS AND ASSIGNS TO TRUSTEE IN TRUST, WITH POWER OF SALE,
that property in _____ County, California described as:

TOGETHER WITH the rents, issues and profits thereof, SUBJECT, HOWEVER, to the right, power and authority hereinafter given to and conferred upon Beneficiary to collect and apply such rents, issues and profits.

For the Purpose of Securing:

1. Performance of each agreement of Trustor herein contained. 2. Payment of the indebtedness evidenced by one all-inclusive purchase money promissory note of even date herewith, and any extension or renewal thereof, in the principal sum of $_____ executed by Trustor in favor of Beneficiary or order.

Underlying Obligations:

This is an all-inclusive purchase money deed of trust, securing an all-inclusive purchase money promissory note in the original principal amount of

_____ Dollars ($ _____)

(the "Note") which includes within such amount the unpaid balance of the following:

(a) A promissory note in the original principal sum of _____ Dollars ($ _____)
in favor of _____
as Payee, secured by a deed of trust recorded _____, 19 ____ , as Document No. _____ , in Book _____ ,
Page _____ , Official Records of _____ County, California, and

(b) A promissory note in the original principal sum of _____ Dollars ($ _____)
in favor of _____
as Payee, secured by a deed of trust recorded _____, 19 ____ , as Document No. _____ , in Book _____ ,
Page _____ , Official Records of _____ County, California.

(The Promissory Notes secured by such deeds of trust are hereinafter called the "Underlying Notes").

To Protect the Security of This Deed of Trust, Trustor Agrees:

(1) To keep said property in good condition and repair; not to remove or demolish any building thereon; to complete or restore promptly and in good and workmanlike manner any building which may be constructed, damaged or destroyed thereon and to pay when due all claims for labor performed and materials furnished therefor; to comply with all laws affecting said property or requiring any alterations or improvements to be made thereon; not to commit or permit waste thereof; not to commit, suffer or permit any act upon said property in violation of law; to cultivate, irrigate, fertilize, fumigate, prune and do all other acts which from the character or use of said property may be reasonably necessary, the specific enumerations herein not excluding the general.

(2) To provide, maintain and deliver to Beneficiary fire, vandalism and malicious mischief insurance satisfactory to and with loss payable to Beneficiary. The amount collected under any fire or other insurance policy may be applied by Beneficiary upon any indebtedness secured hereby and in such order as Beneficiary may determine, or at option of Beneficiary the entire amount so collected or any part thereof may be released to Trustor.

Such application or release shall not cure or waive any default or notice of default hereunder or invalidate any act done pursuant to such notice. The provisions hereof are subject to the mutual agreements of the parties as below set forth.

(3) To appear in and defend any action or proceeding purporting to affect the security hereof or the rights or powers of Beneficiary or Trustee; and to pay all costs and expenses, including cost of evidence of title and attorney's fees in a reasonable sum, in any such action or proceeding in which Beneficiary or Trustee may appear, and in any suit brought by Beneficiary to foreclose this Deed.

(4) To pay: at least ten days before delinquency all taxes and assessments affecting said property, including assessments on appurtenant water stock; subject to the mutual agreements of the parties as below set forth, to pay when due, all incumbrances, charges and liens, with interest, on said property or any part thereof, which appear to be prior or superior hereto; all costs, fees and expenses of this Trust.

Should Trustor fail to make any payment or to do any act as herein provided, then Beneficiary or Trustee, but without obligation so to do and without notice to or demand upon Trustor and without releasing Trustor from any obligation hereof, may make or do the same in such manner and to such extent as either may deem necessary to protect the security hereof, Beneficiary or Trustee being authorized to enter upon said property for such purposes; appear in and defend any action or proceeding purporting to affect the security hereof or the rights or powers of Beneficiary or Trustee; pay, purchase, contest or compromise any incumbrance, charge or lien which in the judgment of either appears to be prior or superior hereto; and, in exercising any such powers, pay necessary expenses, employ counsel and pay his reasonable fees.

(5) To pay immediately and without demand all sums so expended by Beneficiary or Trustee, with interest from date of expenditure at the amount allowed by law in effect at the date hereof, and to pay for any statement provided for by law in effect at the date hereof regarding the obligation secured hereby any amount demanded by the Beneficiary not to exceed the maximum allowed by law at the time when said statement is demanded.

(6) That any award of damages in connection with any condemnation for public use of or injury to said property or any part thereof is hereby assigned and shall be paid to Beneficiary who may apply or release such moneys received by him in the same manner and with the same effect as above provided for disposition of proceeds of fire or other insurance. The provisions hereof are subject to the mutual agreements of the parties as below set forth.

(7) That by accepting payment of any sum secured hereby after its due date, Beneficiary does not waive his right either to require prompt payment when due of all other sums so secured or to declare default for failure so to pay.

(8) That at any time or from time to time, without liability therefor and without notice, upon written request of Beneficiary and presentation of this Deed and said note for endorsement, and without affecting the personal liability of any person for payment of the indebtedness secured hereby, Trustee may: reconvey any part of said property; consent to the making of any map or plat thereof; join in granting any easement thereon; or join in any extension agreement or any agreement subordinating the lien or charge hereof.

(9) That upon written request of Beneficiary stating that all sums secured hereby have been paid, and upon surrender of this Deed and said note to Trustee for cancellation and retention and upon payment of its fees, Trustee shall reconvey, without warranty, the property then held hereunder. The recitals in such reconveyance of any matters or facts shall be conclusive proof of the truthfulness thereof. The grantee in such reconveyance may be described as "the person or persons legally entitled thereto." Five years after issuance of such full reconveyance, Trustee may destroy said note and this Deed (unless directed in such request to retain them).

(10) That as additional security, Trustor hereby gives to and confers upon Beneficiary the right, power and authority, during the continuance of these Trusts, to collect the rents, issues and profits of said property, reserving unto Trustor the right, prior to any default by Trustor in payment of any indebtedness secured hereby or in performance of any agreement hereunder, to collect and retain such rents, issues and profits as they become due and payable. Upon any such default, Beneficiary may at any time without notice, either in person, by agent, or by a receiver to be appointed by a court, and without regard to the adequacy of any security for the indebtedness hereby secured, enter upon and take possession of said property or any part thereof, in his own name sue for or otherwise collect such rents, issues and profits, including those past due and unpaid, and apply the same, less costs and expenses of operation and collection, including reasonable attorney's fees, upon any indebtedness secured hereby, and in such order as Beneficiary may determine. The entering upon and taking possession of said property, the collection of such rents, issues and profits and the application thereof as aforesaid, shall not cure or waive any default or notice of default hereunder or invalidate any act done pursuant to such notice.

(11) That upon default by Trustor in payment of any indebtedness secured hereby or in performance of any agreement hereunder, Beneficiary may declare all sums secured hereby immediately due and payable by delivery to Trustee of written declaration of default and demand for sale and of written notice of default and of election to cause to be sold said property, which notice Trustee shall cause to be filed for record. Beneficiary also shall deposit with Trustee this Deed, said note and all documents evidencing expenditures secured hereby.

After the lapse of such time as may then be required by law following the recordation of said notice of default, and notice of sale having been given as then required by law, Trustee, without demand on Trustor, shall sell said property at the time and place fixed by it in said notice of sale, either as a whole or in separate parcels, and in such order as it may be determine, at public auction to the highest bidder for cash in lawful money of the United States, payable at time of sale. Trustee may postpone sale of all or any portion of said property by public announcement at such time and place of sale, and from time to time thereafter may postpone such sale by public announcement at the time fixed by the preceding postponement. Trustee shall deliver to such purchaser its deed conveying the property so sold, but without any covenant or warranty, express or implied. The recitals in such deed of any matters or facts shall be conclusive proof of the truthfulness thereof. Any person, including Trustor, Trustee, or Beneficiary as hereinafter defined, may purchase at such sale.

After deducting all costs, fees and expenses of Trustee and of this Trust, including cost of evidence of title in connection with sale, Trustee shall apply the proceeds of sale to payment of: all sums expended under the terms hereof, not then repaid, with accrued interest at the amount allowed by law in effect at the date hereof; all other sums then secured hereby; and the remainder, if any, to the person or persons legally entitled thereto.

(12) Beneficiary, or any successor in ownership of any indebtedness secured hereby, may from time to time, by instrument in writing, substitute a successor or successors to any Trustee named herein or acting hereunder, which instrument, executed by the Beneficiary and duly acknowledged and recorded in the office of the recorder of the county or counties where said property is situated, shall be conclusive proof of proper substitution of such successor Trustee or Trustees, who shall, without conveyance from the Trustee predecessor, succeed to all its title, estate, rights, powers and duties. Said instrument must contain the name of the original Trustor, Trustee and Beneficiary hereunder, the book and page where this Deed is recorded and the name and address of the new Trustee.

(13) That this Deed applies to, inures to the benefit of, and binds all parties hereto, their heirs, legatees, devisees, administrators, executors, successors and assigns. The term Beneficiary shall mean the owner and holder, including pledgees, of the note secured hereby, whether or not named as Beneficiary herein. In this Deed, whenever the context so requires, the masculine gender includes the feminine and/or neuter, and the singular number includes the plural.

(14) That Trustee accepts this Trust when this Deed, duly executed and acknowledged, is made a public record as provided by law. Trustee is not obligated to notify any party hereto of pending sale under any other Deed of Trust or of any action or proceeding in which Trustor, Beneficiary or Trustee shall be a party unless brought by Trustee.

The Undersigned Trustor requests that a copy of any Notice of Default and of any Notice of Sale hereunder be mailed to him at his address hereinbefore set forth.

Trustor and Beneficiary Mutually Agree:

(A) By Trustor's acceptance of this All-Inclusive Purchase Money Deed of Trust, Beneficiary covenants and agrees that provided Trustor is not delinquent or in default under the terms of the Note secured hereby, Beneficiary shall pay all installments of principal and interest which shall hereafter become due pursuant to the provisions of the Underlying Note(s) as and when the same become due and payable. In the event Trustor shall be delinquent or in default under the terms of the Note secured hereby, Beneficiary shall not be obligated to make any payments required by the terms of the Underlying Note(s) until such delinquency or default is cured. In the event Beneficiary fails to timely pay any installment of principal or interest on the Underlying Note(s) at the time when Trustor is not delinquent or in default under the terms of the Note secured hereby, Trustor may, at Trustor's option make such payments directly to the holder of such Underlying Note(s), in which event Trustor shall be entitled to a credit against the next installment(s) of principal and interest due under the terms of the Note secured hereby equal to the amount so paid and including, without limitation, any penalty, charges and expenses paid by Trustor to the holder of the Underlying Note(s) on account of Beneficiary's failing to make such payment. The obligations of Beneficiary hereunder shall terminate upon the earliest of (i) foreclosure of the lien of this All-Inclusive Purchase Money Deed of Trust, or (ii) cancellation of the Note secured hereby and reconveyance of this All-Inclusive Purchase Money Deed of Trust.

Should Trustor be delinquent or in default under the terms of the Note secured hereby, Beneficiary consequently incurs any penalties, charges, or other expenses on account of the Underlying Note(s) during the period of such delinquency or default, the amount of such penalties, charges and expenses shall be immediately added to the principal amount of the Note secured hereby and shall be immediately payable by Trustor to Beneficiary.

If at any time the unpaid balance of the Note secured hereby, accrued interest thereon, and all other sums due pursuant to the terms thereof and all sums advanced by beneficiary pursuant to the terms of this Deed of Trust, is equal to or less than the unpaid principal balance of the Underlying Note(s) and accrued interest thereon, the Note secured hereby, at the option of Beneficiary, shall be cancelled and said property shall be reconveyed from the lien of this Deed of Trust.

(B) Trustor and Beneficiary agree that in the event the proceeds of any condemnation award or settlement in lieu thereof, or the proceeds of any casualty insurance covering destructible improvements located upon said property, are applied by the holder of the Underlying Note(s) in reduction of the unpaid principal amount thereof, the unpaid principal balance of the Note secured hereby shall be reduced by an equivalent amount and be deemed applied to the last sums due under the Note.

(C) At such times as the Note secured hereby becomes all due and payable, the amount of principal and interest then payable to Beneficiary thereunder shall be reduced by the then unpaid balance of principal and interest due on the Underlying Note(s).

(D) Any demand hereunder delivered by Beneficiary to Trustee for the foreclosure of the lien of this Deed of Trust may be not more than the sum of the following amounts:

(i) The difference between the then unpaid balance of principal and interest on the Note secured hereby and the then unpaid balance of principal and interest on the Underlying Note(s); plus

(ii) The aggregate of all amounts theretofore paid by Beneficiary pursuant to the terms of this Deed of Trust prior to the date of such foreclosure sale, for taxes and assessments, insurance premiums, delinquency charges, foreclosure costs, and any other sums advanced by Beneficiary pursuant to the terms of this Deed of Trust, to the extent the same were not previously repaid by Trustor to Beneficiary; plus

(iii) The costs of foreclosure hereunder; plus attorneys fees and costs incurred by Beneficiary in enforcing this Deed of Trust or the Note secured hereby as permitted by law.

(E) Notwithstanding any provision to the contrary herein contained, in the event of a Trustee's sale in furtherance of the foreclosure of this Deed of Trust, the balance then due on the Note secured hereby, for the purpose of Beneficiary's demand, shall be reduced, as aforesaid, by the unpaid balance, if any, of principal and interest then due on the Underlying Note(s), satisfactory evidence of which unpaid balances must be submitted to Trustee prior to such sale. The Trustee may rely on any statements received from Beneficiary in this regard and such statements shall be deemed binding and conclusive as between Beneficiary and Trustor, on the one hand, and the Trustee, on the other hand, to the extent of such reliance.

Signature of Trustor

_____   _____

_____   _____

Signature of Beneficiary

_____   _____

_____   _____

STAPLE APPROPRIATE ACKNOWLEDGMENTS HERE

(THIS DEED OF TRUST FOR USE ONLY IN PURCHASE MONEY TRANSACTIONS. IT IS RECOMMENDED THAT, PRIOR TO THE EXECUTION OF THIS DEED OF TRUST, THE PARTIES CONSULT WITH THEIR ATTORNEYS WITH RESPECT TO SAME).

Title Order No._____ _____   Escrow or Loan No._____

——— **DO NOT RECORD** ———

REQUEST FOR FULL RECONVEYANCE
To be used only when note has been paid.

To FOUNDERS TITLE COMPANY, Trustee: Dated _____

The undersigned is the legal owner and holder of all indebtedness secured by the within Deed of Trust. All sums secured by said Deed of Trust have been fully paid and satisfied; and you are hereby requested and directed, on payment to you of any sums owing to you under the terms of said Deed of Trust, to cancel all evidences of indebtedness, secured by said Deed of Trust, delivered to you herewith together with said Deed of Trust, and to reconvey, without warranty, to the parties designated by the terms of said Deed of Trust, the estate now held by you under the same.

MAIL RECONVEYANCE TO:

_____   _____

_____   _____

_____   By_____

_____   By_____

Do not lose or destroy this Deed of Trust OR THE NOTE which it secures. Both must be delivered to the Trustee for cancellation before reconveyance will be made.

inflation rate, consultation with a real estate attorney is advised to avoid usury problems when using a WAM.

Many commentators feel usury laws do not apply to purchase-money WAMs because most usury laws apply to "loans or forebearances" and not to sales of real property. For example, this is the California view. In court decisions dating back to at least 1927, the California Supreme Court repeatedly has held that since a buyer and seller are free to adjust their sales price and terms to give the seller his desired return, the usury laws do not apply to purchase-money mortgages or credit sales of real property.

The theory is a sale or loan of credit in the form of a purchase-money "soft" mortgage is outside the usury laws because no cash is actually loaned. It seems the usury laws are to protect the penniless, desperate borrower, not an affluent property buyer. But this purchase-money mortgage exception from usury laws does not apply to third-party hard money cash lenders who make loans in excess of the applicable state usury limit.

By the way, this usury problem does not occur with Canadian WAM loans because Canada's usury law only prohibits "unconscionable interest."

THE INSTALLMENT SALE "EXCESS MORTGAGE" TRAP

A primary motivation for some sellers to take back a purchase-money mortgage to finance their buyer's purchase is they want to minimize their profit tax by use of an installment sale. An installment sale spreads out the profit tax over the years of the buyer's payments to the seller, thus avoiding a boost of the seller into a high income tax bracket in the year of the property sale.

The Installment Sale Revision Act of 1980, most provisions of which are retroactive to property sales made after January 1, 1980, eliminates the old 30 percent maximum installment sale limit for payments that the seller could receive in the year of property sale. Now deferred payments are taxed as they are received by the seller, regardless of the amount received each tax year.

In addition to eliminating the 30 percent year of sale payment limit, the new installment sale law (a) makes election of installment payment benefits automatic (but the taxpayer can pay all his profit tax in the year of the sale if he so desires) and (b) eliminates the requirement of installment payments in two or more tax years (thus making no down payment sales eligible for installment sale profit taxation even if no payment is received in the year of the sale).

But the new law did not solve the seller's potential problem with an "excess mortgage." If the seller's old mortgage(s) balance exceeds his adjusted cost basis and the buyer assumes or takes title "subject to" that financing, the "excess mortgage" amount is taxable to the seller in the sale year.

Unfortunately, use of a WAM will not overcome this bad result for the seller. Although a WAM can be used in an installment sale, just as a second mortgage can be used, the seller still owes tax on the profit portion of any excess mortgage. New IRS installment sale regulations issued in early 1981 indicate that use of a land contract or lease-option (where the seller retains legal title) will not avoid this excess mortgage problem either.

> EXAMPLE: Mary decides to sell her home for $80,000. The buyer makes a $16,000 cash down payment and gives Mary a $64,000 WAM for the balance at 10 percent interest for 25 years. Since there is currently a $20,000 FHA first mortgage at 6 percent interest on her house, Mary will earn 10 percent on her $44,000 loan ($64,000 minus $20,000) plus a 4 percent differential on the underlying old $20,000 FHA mortgage which will remain undisturbed. Mary's yield will be the $800 interest earned on the 4 percent differential on the $20,000 mortgage plus about $4,400 interest on the top $44,000, a $5,200 total annual return. This is an 11.8 percent yield on the $44,000 "at risk."
>
> If Mary's adjusted cost basis for her home is $16,000 (the FHA mortgage was a refinanced mortgage after Mary bought her house), this $4,000 "excess mortgage" ($20,000 minus $16,000) over Mary's $16,000 basis counts as an installment sale payment received in the year of sale. That $4,000 counts just as if the buyer had paid it as part of his down payment. In other words, Mary pays tax on the profit portion of the $4,000 in the year of selling the home.

THE PREPAID INTEREST TRAP

Until 1976, IRS Revenue Ruling 68–643 limited a taxpayer's deductions for prepaid interest to one year in advance of the current tax year if there was "no material distortion of the taxpayer's income." Using a WAM, however, permitted a greater opportunity to prepay interest because the face amount of the WAM is larger than would be a traditional second mortgage.

Taxpayers who abused this privilege, however, were not kindly treated by the tax court. See *James A. Collins* (54 T.C. 1656, 1970). In the 1974 tax court decision in *Kenneth D. LaCroix* (61 T.C. 471) prepaid interest on a WAM was disallowed because practically no principal payment was made toward the purchase price.

But the 1976 Tax Reform Act makes this history of prepaid interest tax deductions moot. No longer can interest be deducted on a taxpayer's income tax return beyond the amount of interest earned in the tax year. Of course, the interest can be prepaid for future years, but since it is not tax deductible for the taxpayer until the year it is earned by the lender, there is no longer any advantage in prepaying interest. (By the way, real estate property taxes can be prepaid for future years—if the tax collector is willing to accept prepayment—and deducted on the property owner's income tax return for the year the prepayment of property taxes is made.)

This 1976 tax law affects the deductibility of mortgage loan fees, often called "points," paid to obtain a mortgage. These fees are no longer automatically deductible in full as interest in the tax year of payment.

The 1976 Tax Reform Act now requires loan fees (advance prepaid interest) to be deducted over the life of the mortgage. *The one exception is for owner-occupied residences.* Loan fees (points) paid to a lender to obtain a home mortgage for purchase or improvement of one's primary residence are still fully tax deductible as interest in the year paid.

But loan fees paid to obtain a loan secured by any other type of property must now be amortized (deducted) over the life of the mortgage. To illustrate, suppose you pay a $1,000 loan fee to Greedy Savings and Loan Association to obtain a new thirty-year mortgage on your apartment house. For the next thirty years you will have a $33.33 annual interest deduction for this loan fee ($1,000 divided by thirty years).

Loan fees paid to obtain a hard money WAM follow the same deductibility rules as stated above. If the WAM lender customarily charges a loan fee, the taxpayer-borrower can deduct it fully in the year of payment only if the security for the WAM is his personal residence and if the purpose is purchase or improvement of that dwelling.

WHERE TO OBTAIN WAM MORTGAGES

WAM loans used to be difficult to obtain. But in the last few years they have become more readily available as more borrowers and lenders come to understand their advantages. Today WAMs are being made by many lenders. However, S&Ls have been slow to enter this field because of special reserve requirements placed upon WAM loans made by S&Ls.

THE BEST WRAP-AROUND MORTGAGE SOURCE

As with any property purchase, the property seller is the best and usually the cheapest source of mortgage financing. If a WAM is properly explained to the seller, so he understands why a WAM is better than a second mortgage, most sellers who do not need large amounts of cash from the sale will consider taking back a WAM. Not only does the WAM give a better yield than a second mortgage, but it can qualify the property seller for installment sale benefits too.

HARD MONEY WRAP-AROUND LENDERS

Depending upon state laws, commercial banks, insurance companies, real estate investment trusts, mortgage bankers and brokers, savings banks, and S&L associations can make WAM loans. These lenders often make WAM loans at interest rates ¼ percent to ½ percent below the "going rate" on conventional first mortgages. The reason the lender can afford to do this is the WAM will have a very high yield if it wraps around an old, low interest rate mortgage.

Until recently the problem has been that state laws required these lenders to hold a "first lien" on a property. But many lenders, especially state and national banks, have convinced their regulating agencies that a WAM *is* a first lien since the WAM lender undertakes to pay the existing, underlying first mortgage(s). In spite of the fact national banks can now make WAM loans, many such banks refuse to do so. So the borrower must shop for WAM financing, often with the aid of a mortgage broker.

SUMMARY OF WRAP-AROUND MORTGAGES

Wrap-around mortgages benefit all parties and harm none. They are the ideal lending device if there is an old, low interest rate mortgage on the property that does not contain a legally enforceable "due on sale clause."

WAMs are simple to use because the borrower makes just one payment to the WAM lender who, in turn, uses part of that money to keep up payments on the old underlying loan. Failure to make those payments, by the way, is "conversion," a crime which can subject the party letting the old loan go into default to criminal penalties. As with all real estate transactions, however, consultation with a real estate attorney is suggested for questions on the legal ramifications of WAMs. Tax attorneys and advisers can answer questions on the tax aspects of WAMs.

THE MOST OVERLOOKED
REALTY FINANCE TECHNIQUE

Today's buyers and sellers, and their real estate agents, are innovating as never before to create finance techniques for the sale of real estate. The shortage and high cost of traditional first mortgage financing has necessitated this result.

Probably the cheapest and most overlooked real estate finance technique, which is now coming out of the closet to meet a financing need, is the lease-option. There are two primary types of lease-options, the long-term lease-option of thirty years or more, and the short-term lease-option.

RESIDENTIAL LEASE WITH OPTION TO PURCHASE

RECEIVED FROM...

the sum of $ ....(....hereinafter referred to as Tenant,

evidenced by ....DOLLARS),

of the premises, hereinafter referred to as Owner, shall apply said deposit as follows: ...., as a deposit which, upon acceptance of this Lease, the Owner

	RECEIVED	PAYABLE PRIOR TO OCCUPANCY
Rent for the period from................................to....................................	$........................	$........................
Last ....month's rent	$........................	$........................
Security Deposit..	$........................	$........................
Key Deposit..	$........................	$........................
Cleaning charge...	$........................	$........................
Other	$........................	$........................
TOTAL	$........................	$........................

   In the event that this agreement is not accepted by the Owner or his authorized agent, within.............................days, the total deposit received shall be refunded.

   Tenant hereby offers to lease from the Owner the premises situated in the City of ...., County of ...., State of..................,

described as ....

and consisting of...

upon the following TERMS and CONDITIONS:

TERM: The term hereof shall commence on.., 19......, and continue for a period of................months thereafter.

RENT: Rent shall be $...per month, payable in advance, upon the.....................................day of each calendar month to Owner or

his authorized agent, at the following address: ....

or at such other places as may be designated by Owner from time to time. In the event rent is not paid within five (5) days after due date, Tenant agrees to pay a late charge of $10.00 plus interest at 10% per annum on the delinquent amount. Tenant agrees further to pay $5.00 for each dishonored bank check.

UTILITIES: Tenant shall be responsible for the payment of all utilities and services, except:..,

which shall be paid by Owner.

USE: The premises shall be used as a residence with no more than...adults and.....................................children, and for no other

purpose, without the prior written consent of the Owner.

PETS: No pets shall be brought on the premises without the prior consent of the Owner.

ORDINANCES AND STATUTES: Tenant shall comply with all statutes, ordinances and requirements of all municipal, state and federal authorities now in force, or which may hereafter be in force, pertaining to the use of the premises.

ASSIGNMENT AND SUBLETTING: Tenant shall not assign this agreement or sublet any portion of the premises without prior written consent of the Owner which may not be unreasonably withheld.

MAINTENANCE, REPAIRS OR ALTERATIONS: Tenant acknowledges that the premises are in good order and repair, unless otherwise indicated herein. Owner may at any time give Tenant a written inventory of furniture and furnishings on the premises and Tenant shall be deemed to have possession of all said furniture and furnishings in good condition and repair, unless he objects thereto in writing within five days after receipt of such inventory. Tenant shall, at his own expense, and at all times, maintain the premises in a clean and sanitary manner including all equipment, appliances, furniture and furnishings therein and shall surrender the same, at termination hereof, in as good condition as received, normal wear and tear excepted. Tenant shall be responsible for damages caused by his negligence and that of his family or invitees and guests. Tenant shall not paint, paper or otherwise redecorate or make alterations to the premises without the prior written consent of the Owner. Tenant shall irrigate and maintain any surrounding grounds, including lawns and shrubbery, and keep the same clear of rubbish or weeds, if such grounds are a part of the premises and are exclusively for the use of the Tenant.

ENTRY AND INSPECTION: Tenant shall permit Owner or Owner's agents to enter the premises at reasonable times and upon reasonable notice for the purpose of making necessary or convenient repairs, or to show the premises to prospective tenants, purchasers, or mortgagees.

INDEMNIFICATION: Owner shall not be liable for any damage or injury to Tenant, or any other person, or to any property, occurring on the premises, or any part thereof, or in common areas thereof, unless such damage is the proximate result of the negligence or unlawful act of Owner, his agents, or his employees. Tenant agrees to hold Owner harmless from any claims for damages no matter how caused, except for injury or damages for which Owner is legally responsible.

POSSESSION: If Owner is unable to deliver possession of the premises at the commencement hereof, Owner shall not be liable for any damage caused thereby, nor shall this agreement be void or voidable, but Tenant shall not be liable for any rent until possession is delivered. Tenant may terminate this agreement if possession is not delivered within ....days of the commencement of the term hereof.

DEFAULT: If Tenant shall fail to pay rent when due, or perform any term hereof, after not less than three (3) days written notice of such default given in the manner required by law, the Owner, at his option, may terminate all rights of Tenant hereunder, unless Tenant, within said time, shall cure such default. If Tenant abandons or vacates the property, while in default of the payment of rent, Owner may consider any property left on the premises to be abandoned and may dispose of the same in any manner allowed by law. In the event the Owner reasonably believes that such abandoned property has no value, it may be discarded. All property on the premises is hereby subject to a lien in favor of Owner for the payment of all sums due hereunder, to the maximum extent allowed by law.

   In the event of a default by Tenant, Owner may elect to (a) continue the lease in effect and enforce all his rights and remedies hereunder, including the right to recover the rent as it becomes due, or (b) at any time, terminate all of Tenant's rights hereunder and recover from Tenant all damages he may incur by reason of the breach of the lease, including the cost of recovering the premises, and including the worth at the time of such termination, or at the time of an award if suit be instituted to enforce this provision, of the amount by which the unpaid rent for the balance of the term exceeds the amount of such rental loss which the tenant proves could be reasonably avoided.

SECURITY: The security deposit set forth above, if any, shall secure the performance of Tenant's obligations hereunder. Owner may, but shall not be obligated to, apply all or portions of said deposit on account of Tenant's obligations hereunder. Any balance remaining upon termination shall be returned to Tenant.

DEPOSIT REFUNDS: The balance of all deposits shall be refunded within two weeks from date possession is delivered to Owner or his Authorized Agent, together with a statement showing any charges made against such deposits by Owner.

ATTORNEYS FEES: In any legal action brought by either party to enforce the terms hereof or relating to the demised premises, the prevailing party shall be entitled to all costs incurred in connection with such action, including a reasonable attorney's fee.

WAIVER: No failure of Owner to enforce any term hereof shall be deemed a waiver, nor shall any acceptance of a partial payment of rent be deemed a waiver of Owner's right to the full amount thereof.

NOTICES: Any notice which either party may or is required to give, may be given by mailing the same, postage prepaid, to Tenant at the premises or to Owner at the address shown below or at such other places as may be designated by the parties from time to time.

HEIRS, ASSIGNS, SUCCESSORS: This lease is binding upon and inures to the benefit of the heirs, assigns and successors in interest to the parties.

TIME: Time is of the essence of this agreement.

HOLDING OVER: Any holding over after expiration hereof, with the consent of Owner, shall be construed as a month-to-month tenancy in accordance with the terms hereof, as applicable. No such holding over or extension of this lease shall extend the time for the exercise of the option unless agreed upon in writing by Owner.

OPTION: So long as tenant is not in substantial default in the performance of any term of this lease. Tenant shall have the option to purchase the real property described herein for a PURCHASE PRICE OF $.......................... (.. DOLLARS), upon the following TERMS and CONDITIONS:

ENCUMBRANCES: In addition to any encumbrances referred to above, Tenant shall take title to the property subject to: 1) Real Estate Taxes not yet due and 2) Covenants, conditions, restrictions, reservations, rights, rights of way and easements of record, if any, which do not materially affect the value or intended use of the property.

The amount of any bond or assessment which is a lien shall be ☐ paid, ☐ assumed by ....

EXAMINATION OF TITLE: Fifteen (15) days from date of exercise of this option are allowed the Tenant to examine the title to the property and to report in writing any valid objections thereto. Any exceptions to the title which would be disclosed by examination of the records shall be deemed to have been accepted unless reported in writing within said 15 days. If Tenant objects to any exceptions to the title, Owner shall use all due diligence to remove such exceptions at his own expense within 60 days thereafter. But if such exceptions cannot be removed within the 60 days allowed, all rights and obligations hereunder may, at the election of the Tenant, terminate and end, unless he elects to purchase the property subject to such exceptions.

EVIDENCE OF TITLE: Evidence of Title shall be in the form of ☐ a policy of title insurance, ☐ other: .... to be paid for by ....

CLOSE OF ESCROW: Within .... days from exercise of the option, or upon removal of any exceptions to the title by the Owner, as provided above. whichever is later, both parties shall deposit with an authorized escrow holder, to be selected by the Tenant, all funds and instruments necessary to complete the sale in accordance with the terms and conditions hereof.

PRORATIONS: Rents, taxes, premiums on insurance acceptable to Tenant, interest and other expenses of the property to be prorated as of recordation of deed. Security deposits, advance rentals or considerations involving future lease credits shall be credited to Tenant.

EXPIRATION OF OPTION: This option may be exercised at any time after......................., 19...., and shall expire at midnight .... , 19.... unless exercised prior thereto. Upon expiration Owner shall be released from all obligations hereunder and all of Tenants rights hereunder, legal or equitable, shall cease.

EXERCISE OF OPTION: The option shall be exercised by mailing or delivering written notice to the Owner prior to the expiration of this option and by an additional payment, on account of the purchase price, in the amount of

$..(.. DOLLARS) for account of Owner to the authorized escrow holder referred to above, prior to the expiration of this option.

Notice, if mailed, shall be by certified mail, postage prepaid, to the Owner at the address set forth below, and shall be deemed to have been given upon the day following the day shown on the postmark of the envelope in which such notice is mailed.

In the event the option is exercised, ... percent from the rent paid hereunder prior to the exercise of the option shall be credited upon the purchase price.

The undersigned Tenant hereby acknowledges receipt of a copy hereof.

....Agent   DATED:...

By:...   ....Tenant

Broker:..   ....Tenant

....Address   ....Address

....Phone   ....Phone

ACCEPTANCE

The undersigned Owner accepts the foregoing offer.

NOTICE: The amount or rate of real estate commissions is not fixed by law. They are set by each Broker individually and may be negotiable between the Seller and Broker.

BROKERAGE FEE: Upon execution hereof the Owner agrees to pay to .... the Agent in this transaction, the sum of $..(... DOLLARS) for leasing services rendered and authorizes Agent to deduct said sum from the deposit received from Tenant. In the event the option is exercised, the Owner agrees to pay Agent the additional sum of $......................................(.. DOLLARS). This agreement shall not limit the rights of Agent provided for in any listing or other agreement which may be in effect between Owner and Agent. In the event legal action is instituted to collect this fee, or any portion thereof, the Owner agrees to pay the Agent a reasonable attorney's fee and all costs in connection with such action.

The undersigned Owner hereby acknowledges receipt of a copy hereof.

Dated...

....Address   ....Owner

....Phone   ....Owner

THE SHORT-TERM LEASE-OPTION

My favorite method of buying and selling single-family rental houses is the short-term lease-option. The reason it is the most underused home finance technique is real estate agents hate lease-options and discourage their use. There are two reasons for this: (1) most agents do not fully understand the short-term lease-option and (2) the agent does not receive his full sales commission until the purchase option is exercised in the future.

Lease-options are a great way to control property when buying. But they are also advantageous during ownership by (1) cutting or eliminating negative cash flow, (2) renting houses quickly in two hours or less, (3) assuring top quality tenants who treat the house as their own, and (4) giving the owner tax-free option money.

HOW THE SHORT-TERM LEASE-OPTION WORKS

A lease-option is simply a combination of a lease (usually for one to three years) and an option for the tenant to buy the property during the lease term. Although the lease conditions are the same as for a regular lease, the option terms can be as creative as the owner and tenant desire.

An outstanding lease-option form is available from Professional Publishing Corporation, 122 Paul Drive, San Rafael, California 94903. A copy of that form is on the preceding two pages. Please note that the first page is basically a lease. The reverse side contains the purchase option, with plenty of blank space to type in the conditions of the option.

The exact purchase terms of the option must be spelled out in the lease-option. Leave nothing to future doubt or negotiation. This is a key point to remember when creating a lease-option.

WHY USE A SHORT-TERM LEASE-OPTION?

There are many reasons for using a short-term lease-option. Usually the buyer wants to buy the property, but he is not yet in a position to do so. By use of the short-term lease-option, he "ties up" the property while he gets his finances in order so the purchase can be completed before the purchase option expires.

The circumstances of my purchase of my current home on a lease-option are probably typical. Before I sold my old residence I wanted to be sure I would be able to purchase a larger home. Yet, like many prospective sellers, I did not want to put my old home up for sale until I had the new one tied up.

The lease-option was the answer. With the aid of an outstanding realtor who never quit negotiating with the seller, Mrs. Betsy White of J. M. Tayler Company in Burlingame, California, a lease-option was negotiated that met my needs as a buyer, and it met the needs of the seller too.

Most sellers, and their realty agents, never think of a lease-option. But it can create those extra sales and purchase which otherwise would not occur. By giving the buyer time to arrange his financing, the lease-option practically assures the seller that the option will be exercised. More important, the short-term lease-option enables a buyer to buy a property he probably could not finance by any other method.

Another reason for using a short-term lease-option is for a property owner to collect immediate rental income, often at an above-market rate, while waiting for the tenant-buyer to purchase. Many rental house investors use lease-options to obtain high rentals while giving the tenant maximum incentive to properly maintain the property because he eventually plans to purchase it.

Still another reason for use of a short-term lease-option is to "sell" property which has been on the market a long time without any buyer materializing. As will be explained later, the lease-option makes property purchase easy. Once the potential buyer sees, feels, and smells the property (usually by living in it), he wants to own it. The lease-option gives him this opportunity.

THE HARDEST PART OF USING A SHORT-TERM LEASE-OPTION

The most difficult part of creating a lease-option is setting the purchase price of the property. When I purchased my home on a lease-option, it was not too difficult because the lease term was only six months. But we agreed on the home's purchase price at the time of the lease-option signing. While there is not much danger of a seller selling too cheaply on a six-month lease-option, a one-, two-, or three-year lease-option is another matter.

From experience, I have learned to set the purchase price on one-year lease-options at least 15 percent to 20 percent above today's fair market value of the property. Of course, this estimate would depend on the owner's expectations of future property price increases in the local market, usually based on price trends over the last few years in the neighborhood.

I once tried marketing a home on a lease-option that said "Purchase price to be determined by appraisal at the time of option exercise." While dozens of prospective buyers were interested in the house, they definitely wanted to pin down the future purchase price at the time of signing the lease-option.

Unfortunately, I have usually been too conservative when setting the purchase price. But a built-in sale profit, even though it turns out to be slightly less than the property's actual value in the future, is better than no sale.

In addition to setting the purchase price, a lease-option should also spell out the purchase terms. If the seller will carry back a first, second, third, or wrap-around mortgage, put those terms in the lease-option so nothing is left to doubt at the time of option exercise. However, I will not permit my lease-options to be recorded (only one tenant-buyer ever asked) because such recording clouds the title if the tenant does not exercise the purchase option.

LEASE-OPTION ADVANTAGES TO RENTAL HOUSE OWNERS

If you invest in rental houses, as I do, the short-term lease-option is ideal for both "buying" such property and for renting it to tenants.

To illustrate how the short-term lease-option advantages work for the owner (as well as for the tenant-buyer), let me use as an example a house I purchased in August of 1980 for investment. It cost me $135,000 with $13,500 down payment. The seller financed the $121,500 balance at 11 percent interest only for five years, payable at $1,113.75 "or more" per month. By the way, when buying property with seller financing, be sure those magic words "or more" are used on the promissory note as this gives the borrower the automatic right to prepay the note at any time.

This house rented within a week for $750 per month. The tenant is a sharp real estate broker who recognized a bargain when he saw it. Normal rent for this house would be about $650 or $675, but lease-option tenants are willing to pay a high rent in return for the lease-option. This house was advertised in the newspaper "$1,650 MOVES YOU IN—OPEN SUN-DAY 1–3 PM." In less than two hours, it was rented on a lease-option with two back-up applications.

Although my primary purpose for renting houses on lease-options is to get above-market rent from good quality tenants, some tenants will exercise their purchase options, others will sell them, some will ask for extensions (at a higher rent and purchase price, of course), and some just walk away at the end of their lease term without exercising their purchase option. If I wanted to assure a sale, I would require a large up-front "consideration for the option" such as $5,000 or $10,000.

I have found the one-year lease-option works best. But on this particular house in this example, I wrote a three-year lease-option with an escalating purchase price.

It is important to give lease-option prospects an information sheet spelling out the details. They usually will not understand your explanation, so it is important for them to have something in writing. The next illustration shows the information sheet I used on this house in the example.

This particular house can be bought in the twelfth month of the lease for the option purchase price of $158,500 with a rent credit of $4,500 for one-

<u>AVAILABLE FOR RENT or LEASE WITH AN OPTION TO PURCHASE</u>

Well-maintained two-bedroom home with living room, dining area, bathroom, two-car garage, kitchen with gas stove and refrigerator, kitchen breakfast area, fenced backyard with fruit trees and beautiful flowers. Forced air heat. Fresh paint in living room, bedrooms, and hallway. Hardwood floors in bedrooms. Drapes and curtains included. Rear view toward open space scenic hills. Underground sprinklers.

<u>RENT</u>: $650 per month, plus $1,000 refundable security deposit ($1,650 total)   <u>OR</u>

<u>LEASE WITH OPTION TO PURCHASE</u>: $750 per month rent on a 36-month lease, plus $900 refundable security deposit ($1,650 total to move in). One-half rent paid is applicable toward the purchase price if you wish to buy this home. The option purchase price is $158,500 if bought between the 12th thru 18th month of the lease, $173,500 if bought between the 19th thru 30th month, and $190,500 if bought between the 31st and 36th months of the lease.

<u>EXAMPLE #1</u>: $158,500 -- Option purchase price if bought in 12th month
            -4,500 -- ½ credit for rent paid for 12 months
          $154,000 -- Net Purchase Price
   <u>TERMS</u>:   If desired by tenant-buyer, with a $20,000 cash down payment, the seller will finance the $134,000 balance at 11% annual interest, payable $1,228.33 per month (interest only) or more, mortgage loan balance due June 1, 1985 (at which time the buyer must refinance to pay off the $134,000 balance).

<u>EXAMPLE #2</u>: $173,500 -- Option purchase price if bought in 24th month
            -9,000 -- ½ credit for rent paid for 24 months
          $164,500 -- Net Purchase Price
   <u>TERMS</u>:   If desired by tenant-buyer, with a $20,000 cash down payment, the seller will finance the $144,500 balance at 11% annual interest, payable $1,324.58 per month (interest only) or more, mortgage loan balance due June 1, 1985 (at which time the buyer must refinance to pay off the $144,500 balance).

<u>EXAMPLE #3</u>: $190,500 -- Option purchase price if bought in 36th month
           -13,500 -- ½ credit for rent paid for 36 months
          $177,000 -- Net Purchase Price
   <u>TERMS</u>:   If desired by tenant-buyer, with a $20,000 cash down payment, the seller will finance the $157,000 balance at 11% annual interest, payable $1,439.17 per month (interest only) or more, mortgage loan balance due June 1, 1985 (at which time the buyer must refinance to pay off the $157,000 balance).

<u>CONDITIONS OF THE LEASE WITH OPTION TO BUY</u>

1--Rent must be paid each month no later than 3 days after the due date or the purchase option becomes void and the ½ rent credit toward the purchase price is forfeited.
2--The purchase option is assignable and can be sold without the landlord's permission.
3--The lease cannot be assigned or sublet without the owner's permission (which will not be unreasonably withheld).
4--The tenant may cancel the lease (thereby cancelling the option) at any time.
5--Owner extends the special financing terms above only to the original tenant and he reserves the right not to extend these terms to any sublessee or assignee.
6--When the purchase option is exercised, the property is to be sold in its then "as is" condition, with no warranties or representations by the seller. Owner shall pay for routine maintenance until the time of option exercise.
7--Tenant shall receive a copy of the August, 1980 termite pest control clearance report.

For further information, please call Bob Bruss

half of the year's rent paid. Thus, $154,000 becomes the net purchase price. This is approximately 15 percent more than my purchase price paid for the house one year earlier. The option price goes up approximately 15 percent per year for the next two years (although I found the three-year lease-option is too complicated and I would not use it again, I am using it here for illustration).

To exercise the purchase option, the buyer can either obtain his own financing, or I will finance the purchase if the buyer makes a $20,000 cash down payment. Although I only invested $13,500 in this house, the extra $6,500 more than covers the negative cash flow. It is vital to spell out the purchase terms exactly in the lease-option because these terms are a major consideration for the tenant-buyer. Of course, he can obtain his own financing if he can do better elsewhere.

It is also important to spell out some lease-option conditions for the protection of the landlord. These are detailed on the information sheet as well as on the lease-option signed by the tenant and the owner.

While there are many variations of the short-term lease-option, it is an effective technique for (1) minimizing negative cash flow from a rental property and (2) selling a property that is otherwise hard to sell. If the owner's purpose for using a short-term lease-option is to get the property sold, he should require a reasonable "consideration for the option" such as $5,000 or $10,000 to practically assure that the tenant will exercise the purchase option.

DIFFERENT PURPOSES OF THE LONG-TERM LEASE-OPTION

The purposes of the long-term lease-option are entirely different from the short-term lease-option. A long-term lease-option should be used, in my opinion, only if the existing mortgage(s) on a property have a legally enforceable due on sale clause and if the buyer wants to retain the advantages of the old financing. In many states the land contract, also called a contract of sale, agreement of sale, uniform sales contract, contract for deed, or other similar names, will accomplish the same purpose. All these finance devices leave the title in the seller's name to thwart the lender from calling the loan upon transfer of title.

I have been using long-term lease-options since 1970 and have never yet had a lender try to accelerate. Some mortgage forms give the lender the right to enforce the due on sale clause if a lease-option is created, but I have never heard of a lender trying to do so and am not aware of any court decisions upholding the lender's claimed right to do so. As a practical matter, the lender would have great difficulty proving a lease-option exists unless the buyer-tenant records the lease-option. Some buyer-tenants record a memorandum of the long-term lease-option, but I would not recommend doing so.

If the tenant is living on the property, he is there to give notice to anyone of his ownership rights. Even if the seller was crooked and tried to sell the property twice, the rights of the lease-option buyer would predate the second buyer's, and the second buyer would take subject to the first buyer's rights. In my opinion, a long-term lease-option should be recorded only if the buyer-tenant is not occupying the property. Consultation with a real estate attorney is suggested for more information on this recording vs. nonrecording issue.

The best way to illustrate a long-term lease-option is to go through an actual transaction. Each long-term lease-option will differ, primarily because the existing financing is always unique. A real estate attorney should draw up the lease-option, but a regular purchase offer can be made when the "buyer" offers to buy the property on a lease-option. Such a purchase offer would contain words such as "This purchase offer contingent upon buyer and seller approving the final draft of the lease-option to be written by Larry Lawyer, Esq."

Here is an actual long-term lease-option, with only the names and address changed to protect the privacy of the parties.

LEASE WITH OPTION TO PURCHASE

This lease with option to purchase is between SAM SELLER, hereafter called Lessor, and BOB BUYER, hereafter called Lessee.

1. Description of Premises

Lessor agrees to lease to Lessee and Lessee hires from Lessor, as herein provided, the premises located at 1234 Easy Street, a single-family house, including any fixtures, window and floor coverings, built-in appliances, draperies including hardware, shades, blinds, window and door screens, awnings, outdoor plants, trees, and other permanently attached items now on the premises, in the County of Washington, State of California, City of Prosperity, and more particularly described as follows:

(The legal description should be inserted here.)

BEING also known as Assessor's Parcel number 123–456–7890.

2. Term

The term of this lease shall be for thirty (30) years beginning January 1, 1981 and ending December 31, 2010. Possession of premises is to be given to Lessee on January 1, 1981.

3. Consideration for Granting This Lease

Lessee agrees to pay to Lessor the sum of $5,000 as consideration for granting this lease with option to purchase.

4. Rent

The monthly rent payments shall be made payable to Sam Seller, P.O. Box 111, Retirement City, California 99999 or to such person or at such place to be designated by Lessor in the future. Such rent payments are to be paid by the first day of each month, with a ten (10) day grace period.

Lessee to pay a late charge of ten (10) percent if the monthly rent is not received by the tenth day of each month. Failure of Lessee to make any rent payment within thirty (30) days of due date, including any late charge, shall terminate this lease and purchase option.

Lessor shall be paid as rent the sum of the following monthly payments:

a. The principal balance of the existing promissory note and deed of trust to Greedy Federal Savings and Loan Association recorded February 2, 1976 in Book 999, at Page 21, Official Records of the County of Washington, payable as follows:

Date: January 1, 1981
Principal Balance: $53,425.01
Interest Rate: 9.5 percent
Payable: $463.00 per month

b. Balance of the purchase price shall be Lessee's promissory note to Lessor secured by this agreement; said note attached as Exhibit A:

Date: January 1, 1981
Principal Balance: $71,574.99
Interest Rate: 12 percent
Payable: $715.75 per month (interest only) or more. The interest rate on this note can be adjusted by Lessor on January 2, 1986, 1991, 1996, 2001, and 2006 to the interest rate then being charged by Greedy Federal Savings and Loan Association, or its successor, for single-family home loans made on those dates.

5. Use of Premises

The premises are leased to Lessee for use as a residence and Lessee agrees to restrict its use to such purposes, and not to use or permit the use of the premises for any other purpose without first obtaining the written consent of Lessor.

6. No Use That Increases Insurance Risk

Lessee agrees not to use the premises in any manner, even in his use for the purposes for which the premises are leased, that will increase risks covered by insurance on the building where the premises are located, so as to increase the rate of insurance on the buildings where the premises are located, or to cause cancellation of any insurance policy covering the building. Lessee further agrees not to keep on the premises, or permit to be kept, used or sold thereon, anything prohibited by the policy of fire insurance covering the premises. Lessee agrees to comply with all requirements of the insurers applicable to the premises necessary to keep in force the fire and public liability insurance covering the premises and building at Lessee's expense.

7. Insurance

Lessor agrees to procure and maintain in force during the term of this lease fire, extended coverage, public liability, and any other insurance requested by Lessee, adequate to protect against fire damage not less than ONE HUNDRED THOUSAND DOLLARS ($100,000). Lessor to procure public liability insurance coverage in a minimum amount of ONE HUNDRED THOUSAND ($100,000) DOLLARS for each person insured, and THREE HUNDRED THOUSAND ($300,000) DOLLARS maximum for any one incident. Such insurance policies shall provide coverage for Lessor's and Lessee's contingent liability on such claims or losses. The policies shall be subject to Lessor's and Lessee's mutual inspection and approval. The insurance premium for such policies procured by Lessor are to be paid by Lessee within thirty (30) days after receipt of a statement therefor. If unpaid within such time, Lessor may procure such insurance, pay the premium therefor, and such premium shall be repair to Lessor as additional rent for the month following the date on which such premiums are paid. Failure to pay such insurance premiums is a default in this lease that will cause it to be terminated.

8. No Waste, Nuisance, or Unlawful Use

Lessee shall not commit, or allow to be committed, any waste on the premises, or nuisance, nor shall he use or allow the premises to be used for any unlawful purpose.

9. Repairs and Maintenance

Lessee shall maintain the premises and keep it in good repair at his own expense. Lessee shall make any alterations and changes that he deems advisable in the operation of the property providing such changes shall not decrease the inherent value of the premises. Lessee to pay for any such costs of repairs and maintenance.

10. Payment of Utilities, Property Taxes, and Operating Expenses

The property taxes for the current year ending June 30, 1981 and insurance acceptable to Lessee as specified above, rents, and other current expenses of the premises shall be prorated to January 1, 1981, the date of commencement of this lease. After transfer of possession to Lessee,

Lessee shall pay for all utilities, property and other taxes, and other operating expenses of the property including gas, water, garbage, and all necessary and customary expenses of operating the property.

11. Delivery, Acceptance, and Surrender of the Premises

Lessor represents that the premises are in fit condition for use as residential property. Lessee agrees to accept the premises upon possession as in a good state of repair and in sanitary condition. Lessee agrees to surrender the premises at the end of the lease term to the Lessor in substantially the same or better condition than when he took possession, except for damage by acts of God, unless Lessor shall have exercised the purchase option prior to termination of this lease.

Lessee agrees to take possession of the premises subject to any month-to-month thirty (30) day rental agreements to its residents that exist as of January 1, 1981.

Lessee agrees to accept the property in its current condition with no warranties or representations by Lessor both at time of accepting possession and at time of future exercise of the purchase option.

12. Nonliability of Lessor for Damages

Lessor shall not be liable for liability or damage claims for injury to persons, including Lessee or his agents or employees, or for property damage from any cause, related to Lessee's occupancy of the premises, including those arising out of damages or losses occurring on sidewalks or other areas adjacent to the leased premises, during the term of this lease. Lessee hereby covenants and agrees to indemnify Lessor and to save him harmless from all liability, loss, or other damage claims or obligations because of or arising out of such injuries or losses.

13. Lessee's Assignment, Sublease, or License for Occupation by Other Persons

Lessee agrees not to assign or sublease the premises leased, any part thereof, or any right or privilege connected therewith, without first obtaining Lessor's written consent, or to allow any other person, except Lessee's agents and employees, to occupy the premises or any part thereof, without first obtaining Lessor's written consent. However, this shall not be construed to prohibit Lessee from normal operation of the property, including renting or leasing the property for use as a residence. The term of such rentals shall not exceed one year, although such rentals may be renewed at the end of each year.

Lessee's unauthorized assignment, sublease, or license to occupy shall be void, and shall terminate the lease at Lessor's option.

14. Lease Breached by Lessee's Receivership, Assignment for Benefit of Creditors, Insolvency, or Bankruptcy

Appointment of a receiver to take possession of Lessee's assets (except a receiver appointed at Lessor's request as herein provided), Lessee's general assignment for benefit of creditors, or Lessee's insolvency or taking or suffering action under the Federal Bankruptcy Act is a breach of this lease which shall terminate it.

15. Lessor's Remedies Upon Lessee's Breach of This Lease

If Lessee breaches this lease, Lessor shall have the following remedies in addition to these other legal rights and remedies in such event:

a. *Reentry.* Lessor may reenter the premises immediately and terminate Lessee's occupancy of this premises.

b. *Termination.* After reentry, Lessor may terminate this lease by giving ten (10) days written notice of such termination to Lessee, the reason for such termination, and giving Lessee the opportunity to correct any breach of this lease specified in such notice of termination within twenty (20) days after notice to lessee. Reentry alone will not terminate this lease.

c. *Appointment of a Receiver.* After reentry, Lessor may procure the appointment of a receiver to take possession and collect rents and profits of Lessee's operation of the property. If necessary, the receiver may continue to operate the property without compensating Lessee therefor. Proceedings for appointment of a receiver by Lessor, or the appointment of a receiver and conducting by him of Lessee's operations, shall not terminate this lease unless Lessor has given Lessee written notice of such termination as provided herein.

d. *Rights.* Upon termination of this lease for breach of any of its conditions and terms the Lessee shall relinquish all rights, privileges, and financial considerations including the equity buildup, appreciation in market value of the property, and moneys spent for improvements. Lessee agrees to vacate the premises upon such breach and termination of this lease.

16. Arbitration of Disputes

Lessor and Lessee agree that any disputes under this lease, unless resolved by the parties, shall be arbitrated in accordance with the arbitration laws of the state of California, as supplemented by the rules then obtaining of the American Arbitration Association. Judgment on the arbitration award rendered may be entered in any court having jurisdiction of the parties.

17. Manner of Giving Notice

Notices given pursuant to the provisions of this lease or necessary to carry out its provisions shall be in writing and delivered by first class mail with return receipt to the person to whom the notice is to be given. For such purposes, Lessor's current mailing address is P.O. Box 111, Retirement City, California 99999 and Lessee's current mailing address is 1234 Easy Street, Prosperity City, California 88888.

18. Lease and Purchase Option Applicable to Successors

This lease and its terms, covenants, and conditions apply to and are binding on the heirs, successors, executors, administrators, and assigns of the parties thereto.

19. Time of Essence

Time is of the essence to this agreement. Dates and time limits specified in this agreement may not be waived without the written consent of both parties.

20. Effect of Eminent Domain Proceedings

Eminent domain proceedings resulting in the condemnation of part of the premises leased herein that leave the remaining portion usable by Lessee for purposes of operating the property will not terminate this lease. The effect of such condemnation will be to leave this lease in effect as to the remainder of the premises. All compensation awarded in the eminent domain proceeding as a result of such condemnation shall belong to Lessee.

Lessor hereby assigns and transfers to Lessee any claim he may have to compensation for damages as a result of such condemnation. In the event that eminent domain proceedings result in condemnation of the premises so it cannot be operated as residential property, Lessee shall be entitled to any compensation awarded and the provisions of paragraph twenty-one (21) below shall become operative as an exercise of the option to purchase. Any disputes in such case are to be decided by arbitration as specified above.

21. Option to Purchase the Premises

Lessor grants to Lessee an option to buy the leased premises at any time Lessee may elect before December 31, 2010, provided Lessee shall have performed the terms of this lease and made all payments required hereby to that time of exercise of such purchase option. In the event of the exercise of this option, Lessor agrees to convey said property to Lessee by grant deed free and clear of all encumbrances except property taxes and assessments that under this lease are to be paid by Lessee.

Lessor hereby agrees not to further encumber the leased premises. Any encumbrances now existing against the property created by or on the account of Lessor may, however, remain until time of exercise of this purchase option. Lessor agrees to protect and defend Lessee and the property against foreclosure or loss by reason of any encumbrances created by or through the Lessor and now existing against the property.

The obligations of Lessee under the lease shall cease after the exercise of this option and completion of said transfer of title to Lessee or his designate.

Whenever Lessee shall desire to exercise this purchase option before its expiration, Lessee shall give Lessor written notice thereof. Lessor will within thirty (30) days after receipt of such notice deliver to Lessee a preliminary title search report by the Talented Title Company of Prosperity City, California. Defects in title, if any, shown by such report shall be remedied by Lessor within thirty (30) days after notice to him of such defects and he shall deliver to Lessee at the time of closing of escrow an unconditional grant deed to the property.

The purchase shall, in any event, be completed by conveyance of the property and payment of the outstanding purchase obligations within thirty (30) days from the delivery by Lessee of notice of intent to exercise this option. If said notice is not given by Lessee before December 31, 2010, then this purchase option shall be null and void. The consideration for granting this purchase option shall be the FIVE THOUSAND DOLLARS ($5,000.00) specified in paragraph three (3).

22. Exercise of the Purchase Option

To exercise the purchase option referred to in paragraph twenty-one (21), in addition to giving notice to Lessor of intent to exercise this option as stated above, Lessee must also:

a. Arrange to pay, assume, or take title "subject to" the encumbrance to Greedy Federal Savings and Loan Association, referred to in paragraph four A (4a), and either (1) pay the promissory note referred to in paragraph four B (4b) to Lessor or (2) secure that promissory note to Lessor referred to in paragraph four B (4b) by a second deed of trust against the property.

1. In the event Lessee exercises the purchase option and is unable to assume the existing loan from Greedy Federal Savings and Loan Association and is required to obtain financing elsewhere, then Lessee shall obtain financing to pay off the then existing balance of the existing first loan to Greedy Federal Savings and Loan Association, together with any prepayment penalty and other charges, and the balance of the purchase price owed under the promissory note to Lessor.

2. Should the proceeds of such new loan be insufficient to pay off the full remaining balance owed to Lessor, Lessor then agrees to accept a promissory note in the form of the note attached and marked Exhibit A and secured by a second deed of trust in the standard form for said balance, said note and deed of trust to be payable to Lessor on the same terms as the original promissory note referred to in paragraph four B (4b), with the unpaid balance due December 31, 2010.

b. Pay the title insurance and normal escrow and transfer costs for acquisition of property in the County of Washington, City of Prosperity.

22. Acceleration Clause

Lessee acknowledges being advised that the deed of trust to Greedy Federal Savings and Loan Association contains a provision for acceleration of the indebtedness in the event of a sale or transfer of the property. If purchase of this property is consummated, or if and when there is deemed to be or have been a purchase, then Lessee shall assume and agree to pay any charges or prepayment penalties to Greedy Federal Savings and Loan Association. In such event, both Lessor and Lessee agree to carry this purchase option agreement into effect.

23. Tax Consequences of This Lease Agreement

It is the intent of the Lessor and Lessee to eventually consummate a sale of the leased premises to the Lessee. Therefore, for income tax purposes, this transaction shall be treated by Lessor and Lessee as if the Lessor had sold the property to the Lessee as of January 1, 1981. The Lessee shall be entitled to all normal income tax duties and benefits of real estate ownership, including depreciation of the property improvements and deduction of operating expenses and interest paid on the loan obligations to the Lessor and to Greedy Federal Savings and Loan Association, as allowed by the Internal Revenue Code. Lessor shall treat payments received under this agreement as if a deferred payment installment sale of the property has occurred, as provided for by the Internal Revenue Code.

24. Recordation of Option to Purchase

A memorandum of the option to purchase the premises may be recorded by Lessee in the Official Records of the County of Washington at any time. Lessor agrees to sign such memorandum before a Notary Public at any reasonable time when requested by Lessee.

25. Modification

This lease and option to purchase may be modified only by a written agreement signed by both parties.

26. Acceptance

This lease with option to purchase shall be deemed to have been accepted by both Lessor and Lessee when:

a. A signed copy is delivered by Lessor to Lessee and Lessee signs and returns that original copy to Lessor, and

b. Lessee pays to Lessor FIVE THOUSAND DOLLARS ($5,000.00) consideration for the purchase option referred to in paragraph twenty-one (21).

c. Lessee pays to Lessor the following additional amounts:

1. Rent of ONE THOUSAND ONE HUNDRED SEVENTY-EIGHT AND 75/100 ($1,178.75) DOLLARS for the month of January, 1981, plus

2. Prorated fire insurance and public liability insurance premium of $195.39 ($211.00 annual premium less credit of $15.61 at .578¢ per day for 27 days; policy expires December 3, 1981; Lessee acknowledges receipt of a copy of this insurance policy).

3. Less any security deposits or other credits due to the current tenants of the property.

4. Total of ONE THOUSAND THREE HUNDRED SEVENTY-FOUR AND 14/100 ($1,374.14) DOLLARS.

This offer by Lessor to Lessee shall remain valid until acceptance by Lessee but not later than December 21, 1980. Upon acceptance by Lessee, Lessor agrees to pay to ABC Realty a commission of FOUR THOUSAND DOLLARS ($4,000).

This offer to lease is made December 5, 1980.

ACCEPTED: SAM SELLER
_____

                                   BOB BUYER
_____

NOTARY PUBLIC ACKNOWLEDGMENT

This long-term lease-option form is presented for illustration purposes only. It should not be used for actual transactions without consultation with a real estate attorney who can either adapt it to the particular circumstances of the sale or draft another lease-option form that meets the needs of the parties. There are no standard long-term lease-option forms, so the services of a real estate attorney are essential for each such transaction.

The reason for using a thirty-year term is that such a lease, which includes a purchase option, is acceptable to the IRS as the equivalent of a sale. IRS Revenue Ruling 60–4, now superseded by Revenue Ruling 72–85, leads to this result. There is a long chain of tax cases holding that for income tax purposes, where the lessee is treated like an owner, a sale will be recognized. See *Oesterreich* v. *IRS*, 226 F.2d 798, and IRC Regulation 1.1031 (a)-1-C.

For emphasis, it is worth repeating that the primary reason for using a long-term lease-option is to avoid a lender enforcing a "due on sale clause." If this condition is not present, a long-term lease-option is of little value to the buyer and seller.

One final footnote. Most mortgage lenders learn of a title transfer when they receive a new fire insurance policy that shows a new insured's name. The long-term lease-option overcomes this problem because the fire insurance policy remains in the name of the lessor so the lender will not learn of the transaction from the insurance agent. In states where a due on sale clause in a mortgage is legally enforceable, the long-term lease-option makes it virtually impossible for the mortgage lender to learn of the sale. Thus the buyer retains the benefit of the old low interest rate mortgage.

QUESTIONS AND ANSWERS

Q. You often say a wrap-around mortgage is better than a second mortgage. I don't understand why. If I sell my house, which has a VA mortgage of about $38,000 at 8 percent interest, for $100,000 with a $10,000 down payment, would I be better off with a $90,000 wrap-around mortgage or a $52,000 second mortgage?—*Adrian M.*

A. You will be better off with a wrap-around mortgage. Suppose you charge 10 percent interest on the $90,000 wrap-around mortgage. That is about $9,000 annual interest. But you will have to keep up the VA loan payments (using part of the money your borrower pays you). Your interest cost on $38,000 at 8 percent will be about $3,040, leaving you net annual interest earnings of about $5,960. On the $52,000 you will have "at risk," this is a return of 11.46 percent.

You could earn the same return on a $52,000 second mortgage by charging 11.46 percent interest. But that is usurious in some states and is less acceptable to most buyers than would be a wrap-around mortgage with a 10 percent interest rate.

Before using a wrap-around mortgage, however, check with your attorney as to the maximum interest rate which can be charged in the state where your property is located.

WHY WRAP-AROUND MORTGAGES ARE SO GOOD

Q. Please explain more details about wrap-around mortgages. (1) Why would a seller or buyer want one? (2) Where can they be obtained? —*Margo M.*

A. Suppose you sell your home for $50,000, and it has an existing FHA

$25,000 first mortgage at 7 percent interest. The buyer offers you $10,000 cash down payment, asks you to carry a $15,000 second mortgage at 9 percent interest, and agrees to assume the existing $25,000 FHA mortgage, which remains undisturbed. You would earn about $1,350 annual interest (9 percent of $15,000).

But a $40,000 wrap-around mortgage at 9 percent interest would be better for you. You would take in about $3,600 interest, pay out about $1,750 interest on the old mortgage, and keep about $1,850 interest ($3,600 minus $1,750). That is a 12.33 percent yield on your $15,000 "at risk" loan.

(1) Such a loan maximizes the seller's total yield and still lets him qualify for installment sale tax benefits (installment sale details are in Chapter 8). Wrap-around all-inclusive mortgages are good for buyers too, since the interest rate is usually below conventional mortgage interest rates.

(2) Property sellers are the most common sources of wrap-around mortgages. But some banks, finance companies, and individual lenders now make "hard money" wrap-around mortgage loans too. Shop around among local lenders in your community to see which lenders make wrap-around mortgage loans.

HOME LEASE-OPTION DIFFERS FROM LEASE-PURCHASE

Q. Some time ago you said your favorite creative finance method is the lease-option. I recently contacted a real estate agent about buying a home, and she suggested a "lease-purchase plan." Is this different from a lease-option?—*Ginny S.*

A. Yes. A lease-purchase means the buyer temporarily leases the home now but agrees to purchase it later, presumably when mortgages are more readily available than today. The tenant-buyer is obligated to complete the purchase. If he does not, he loses his deposit and may incur a penalty too.

But a lease-option gives the buyer the option of deciding if he wants to buy the property before the option expiration date. The lease-option is good for both the tenant and the landlord-seller.

Tenant advantages of a lease-option include (1) full or partial credit toward the purchase price for rent paid, (2) opportunity to try the home before buying, (3) no obligation to the landlord-seller if the purchase option is not exercised, (4) knowing the sales price and terms in advance, and (5) having a big incentive to save up the down payment to use to exercise the purchase option.

Lease-option advantages for the seller include (1) practically being assured of a sale, since few people walk away from a large rent credit toward the purchase price, (2) rental income to pay mortgage and other payments, (3) tax advantages, (4) lease-option tenant usually takes good care of the property, and (5) option consideration is not taxable until tenant either exercises the option or lets it expire.

DO NOT FORGET LEASE-OPTION HOME-BUYING TECHNIQUE

Q. We must buy a home soon before my wife and I wind up in a mental hospital. At present we live with our two children, ages four and two, in a two-bedroom apartment where we are about to go crazy. But with the difficulty of getting a home loan, we wonder if we can buy a home at all. I earn about $21,000 per year, including overtime. My wife works Saturdays and Sundays at a supermarket where she earns about $5,000 per year. One agent found us an ideal house on which we could have easily afforded the mortgage payments. But the lender said we would have to have $38,000 annual income to qualify for a loan. Please help us. —*Craig M.*

A. You and thousands of other prospective home buyers are having the same problem of qualifying for a mortgage in today's market. The truth is, and lenders will not tell you this, they do not want to make new mortgage loans today. So they have raised the interest rates so high few people can qualify. From a public relations viewpoint, this is better than telling loan applicants the lender is out of money.

If you want to buy a home today, you will have to buy without getting a new mortgage. It is not really so hard. My favorite technique is the lease-option where you lease a house for twelve or twenty-four months with an option to buy during the lease term at a price agreed upon today. By then, mortgage financing should be more affordable. But in case it is not, be sure the lease-option provides for alternative seller financing.

Other home finance possibilities for you include (1) making a down payment, taking over payments on the existing mortgage, and getting the seller to take back a second mortgage for any balance, and (b) getting the seller to finance the sale on a wrap-around (all-inclusive) mortgage. Work with a good real estate agent who understands that creative finance is the key to successful home buying today.

LEASE-OPTION PERFECT FOR HOME BUYERS WITH $1,500

Q. We are a young couple, both college graduates, with total annual income of about $23,000. It's so low because we are teachers. We have saved close to $1,500 but are very discouraged by every real estate agent we talk to about buying a home. They claim we need 10 percent to 20 percent cash down payment to qualify for mortgage money. How should we proceed?—*Robert and Susan F.*

A. I have rented many homes to young couples in situations like yours. The lease-option is perfect for honest, employed, reliable people like you.

Look in the newspaper want ads under "houses for rent." Make appointments to visit those which interest you. When you find one you like, ask the landlord if he would consider a lease with option to buy. Many will.

Offer to put up your $1,500 as "consideration for the option."

Try to structure the lease-option so all or part of your lease rent payments are credited toward the purchase price. Owners of dumpy, run-down houses are especially good candidates for lease-options.

However, do not include me in that category, as my rental houses are in top condition. Ask my tenant-buyers. By the way, you will rarely find a lease-option available through real estate agents because the agent does not get his commission until the purchase option is exercised, usually in twelve to twenty-four months. Realty agents like to be paid now.

READER TELLS HOW TO BEAT
MORTGAGE "DUE ON SALE CLAUSE"

Q. Our house has been for sale several months with no buyer. The old mortgage is not assumable because it has a "due on sale clause." Since the lender wants a stiff assumption fee and wants to raise the interest rate for a buyer, the house hasn't sold. But I found a real estate lawyer who told me how to get my house sold. He drew up an option contract, and the buyer recorded a "memorandum" of this option. The buyer paid $20,000 "consideration for the option" (which was the down payment). He must make regular monthly payments to me to keep the option in force. I use part of this money to keep up the payments on the old mortgage. The rest goes to pay off what the buyer owes me, gradually reducing the buyer's option purchase price. It's like a wrap-around mortgage. Since there has been no title transfer, the lender can't enforce the due on sale clause and is stuck with its old 9 percent mortgage. My lawyer says the IRS recognizes this as a sale for tax purposes. Just thought you'd want to know there's a way to beat the nasty lenders.—*Elmer G.*

A. The "due on sale clause" issue is a very controversial one with lenders, especially federal savings and loan associations. A valid "due on sale clause" allows a mortgage lender to "call" a loan when the property is sold.

Many states, either through court decisions or new laws, prohibit the infamous "due on sale clauses" that curtail property sales, as you found out. But federal S&Ls feel they are not governed by state laws since, they argue, rules of the Federal Home Loan Bank Board allow "due on sale clauses." This issue of federal preemption of state due on sale clause laws is unsettled and may wind up in the U.S. Supreme Court.

However, there is one possible flaw in your lawyer's option idea. From the buyer's viewpoint, how does he know he will receive good title? It is possible to buy title insurance on options, but this does not assure your buyer that the title will remain good until he exercises his purchase option and obtains the deed from you. This is a "gray area" of real estate law so a real estate attorney should be consulted.

8.

How to Maximize
Your Profits
at Resale Time

Smart investors not only make good profits while owning property, but they maximize their profits at resale time. This resale profit maximization starts at the time of purchase. By purchasing only property which is well-located, in sound condition, and with good financing, the investor then is in a position to gain the maximum potential from the property.

Unfortunately, many home buyers and investors in other properties buy the wrong way. Profit maximization begins the day the property is bought.

Assuming the property is in a reasonable location and in sound physical condition, the other key to getting the most from the property is its financing. The last few chapters have discussed various finance methods which can meet your needs when buying a property. When financing your acquisition, always ask the key question *"How can I best finance this property to buy it now and to eventually resell it in the future with a maximum profit?"*

To illustrate, think of all the retirees who sold their homes up north, received a bundle of cash from the sale, and bought a retirement home in the south or west. Most of those people paid all cash. But when they want to resell today, perhaps because of illness or changed family circumstances, they are finding that it is hard to resell for all cash. The reason is the potential buyers, today's new retirees, are having trouble selling their old homes for cash. But if those homes had been financed with assumable mortgages, they would be easy to resell today (although the seller would probably have to help out by carrying a second mortgage).

In other words, when you buy a property, finance it so it can be sold easily. This means *mortgage it to the hilt* at the time of purchase. The bigger the mortgage, the easier it will be to resell that property in the future.

Even if you can afford to pay all cash, or make a big cash down payment, DON'T! Like every good rule, however, this one has an exception. The only time to pay all cash or make a big cash down payment is if that cash will gain you a substantial discount off fair market value. A "substantial discount" means at least 20 percent below fair market value.

Just as financing is the key when buying property, it is the key to success when selling property too. But there is more to maximizing resale profits than just offering good financing. When getting ready to sell a property, there are two additional considerations: (1) the physical aspects and (2) the income tax aspects. Both are important. Smart investors consider both when they decide to dispose of a property they no longer want to own.

Although the next section deals with selling your principal residence, most of the comments also apply to the sale of investment property too. Further suggestions for maximizing resale profits of investment properties are in the installment sale section, toward the end of the chapter.

THE "RED RIBBON DEAL"

Selling your home, whether it is a single-family house, a condominium or cooperative apartment or townhouse, or perhaps a houseboat or mobile home, can be a very rewarding and profitable experience. Or, it can be financial disaster.

To earn the greatest net profit from your property sale, *after taxes,* requires taking a series of steps, one at a time. The sales process is really quite simple. But do not risk selling your property until you fully understand every step of the sales procedure.

Selling your property, especially your home, is one of the greatest profit opportunities you will ever have—DON'T MESS IT UP! One mistake can easily cost thousands of dollars in low profit or taxes paid unnecessarily. It is far cheaper to pay fees for expert advice than to make a mistake that costs far more.

Here are the easy steps to maximizing your profit and minimizing the tax when selling your residence.

GET YOUR HOME IN TOP PHYSICAL CONDITION

To get top dollar for any home, it must be C-L-E-A-N! That means really clean. If necessary, paint it inside and outside. *Paint is the cheapest and most profitable improvement you can make.* Be especially certain the entrance has been recently painted and all outside trim is in top condition.

Clean the yard, basement, and garage thoroughly. A neat, clean home brings full market value, but similar dirty homes repel buyers from making any purchase offer. You may be accustomed to the dirt, dog smells, cooking odors, and other personality traits of your home, but potential buyers are not. It is the rare buyer who can overlook sloppy housekeeping, poor maintenance, and dirt. Those buyers who will buy such a house expect to buy at a rock bottom price. If you are buying, and can find a messy property which the seller will not get into top condition before sale, that is your opportunity to buy for a bargain price because you will have little or no competition from other buyers.

So *do not even think of putting your residence up for sale until you have cleaned and fixed it up*. Your home may not be the Taj Mahal, but it can be as neat and clean as if it were. Spending $1,000 or $2,000 on cleaning and painting can return many times that small cost in the form of a higher sales price.

INCOME TAX SAVINGS FOR FIX-UP COSTS

If you are buying a replacement principal residence, many expenses to fix-up your old home, which normally have no tax consequence, take on tax aspects. Examples of such fix-up costs include painting, cleaning, and repairing.

Such expenses, to be subtracted from your home's gross sales price, must be incurred within ninety days before the date of signing the sales agreement, and they must be paid for within thirty days after the close of the sale.

The net tax result will be no tax saving if you are buying a qualifying, more-expensive replacement principal residence (because all your tax is deferred anyway), but it will be a greater tax deferral if you are buying a less-expensive replacement. When buying a less-expensive replacement principal residence, the sale profit from your old home is only taxed up to the difference in the two prices. The fix-up costs reduce this difference.

To illustrate, suppose you sell your old home for $100,000 with $2,000 of fix-up costs, and buy a replacement for $80,000. Normally, your profit would be taxed up to the $20,000 price difference. But because you spent $2,000 on fix-up costs, only $18,000 of your sale profit will be taxed.

This fix-up rule only applies to costs of preparing your home for sale. Items of a major capital improvement nature, such as installing a new air conditioner, new built-in appliances, or a new roof, should be capitalized and added to the cost basis of your residence. Be sure to save the bills for both capital improvements and home sale fix-up costs.

Money spent fixing up your home for sale is money well spent. But of course do not go overboard and overimprove your house for its neighborhood. For example, installation of a swimming pool in a neighborhood of working-class tract subdivision homes probably will not increase the home's market value by the cost of the new pool.

PRICE YOUR HOME CORRECTLY

After your home is in top physical condition and ready for sale, then it is time to determine its market value. "Market value" is defined as the price a willing buyer agrees to pay to a willing seller, neither being under pressure to buy or sell, with the property given exposure to the marketplace for a reasonable period of time.

Nothing is worse than for a home seller to overprice his residence. After all, if the local real estate agents and their potential buyers find out it is overpriced, they will avoid the house like the plague. The reason is they figure the seller is not serious about selling, so why waste time?

Buyers often will not even make offers at an overpriced home's true market value because there are too many other homes available for sale, so why beg a seller to sell an overpriced home for its true value? But smart buyers do make purchase offers on overpriced homes, after the houses have been on the market for sale a long time. By then, other buyers and their agents have lost interest in the overpriced house, and the seller is often so desperate he will accept a below-market purchase offer.

The market value of a home depends on recent sales prices (and terms) of similar residences in the immediate neighborhood. Home prices are *not* based on (1) how much the seller thinks his home is worth, (2) what he needs to get for it to make a good profit, (3) how much he has invested in the house, or (4) how much he needs to pay off his debts.

For example, although your three-bedroom home is different from the three-bedroom home next door in appearance, floor plan, and physical condition, if the house next door sold for $75,000 last month, yours is probably worth about $75,000 too, with price adjustments up or down for any major differences in features and condition.

By comparing recent sales prices of several homes in your neighborhood, you will soon arrive at a good approximation of your home's fair market value. Not to be overlooked, of course, is the effect of mortgage financing terms available. If "easy financing" is available, buyers will often pay more than if the seller is demanding 100 percent cash.

HOW TO FIND COMPARABLE PROPERTY SALES PRICES

Real estate sales agents, through their local board of realtors or multiple listing service, usually have easy access to comparable home sale prices. When you talk with several realty agents about possibly listing your home for sale with them, find out what the agent estimates your home will sell for *and why*. The top agents will prepare written "competitive market analysis" forms for you. These forms show recent sales prices of similar nearby homes, as well as current asking prices of other homes for sale now (your competition).

Before listing your home for sale with any agent, however, check with at least three active local agents before deciding on your asking price. Set your price too high, and you discourage potential buyers (and more importantly, their agents who have *other* buyers). Set your price too low, and you have lost a big part of your profit. If you set your price too high, to test the market, it often takes a big price reduction to rekindle any interest in the property, since it has been "shopped around" too long.

It is OK to set your asking price 3 percent to 5 percent above what you expect to accept for the residence, but do not set it so far above market value that you price yourself out of the local market. Once you do that, you are wasting valuable time that costs you (and your agent) money. If you really want to sell, and you have overpriced your home, you will eventually have to reduce your price to fair market value, or below. Why not save time, money, and hassle by pricing your home right from the start?

TO MAKE THE BIGGEST PROFIT, OFFER THE BEST TERMS

If an automobile dealer tells his prospective auto buyers who walk into his showroom "You'll have to pay all cash or arrange your own financing to buy any car we sell here," he would soon be out of business. Whether we like it or not, credit is a way of life in the U.S. for almost every car buyer. CREDIT IS EVEN MORE A WAY OF LIFE FOR VIRTUALLY EVERY HOME BUYER. When was the last time you heard of a buyer paying all cash for a house? It rarely happens.

Circumstances may require that you receive 100 percent cash when you sell your residence. If so, that usually means your buyer has to put up a cash down payment of at least 20 percent of the home's sale price. The balance is often paid with an 80 percent conventional mortgage from a bank, S&L, or mortgage broker. Or the buyer may want a low down payment FHA or VA mortgage (govermment-backed mortgages are discussed later). Another possibility is a PMI (private mortgage insurance) mortgage for 90 percent or 95 percent of the home's sale price.

The better the "built-in financing," the better the home seller's chances of selling his home for top dollar. You suddenly increase the number of potential buyers who can afford to buy your home if you will agree, at the time of listing the home for sale, to help finance the sale. The greater the seller's participation in the sale financing, the greater the number of potential buyers for that home.

However, at the time a new VA, FHA, or PMI is made to sell a home, there can be no secondary financing. But when the home is resold in the future and the second buyer purchases "subject to" an existing VA or FHA mortgage, second mortgages are allowed.

So be flexible about taking back a first or second mortgage to make your home appeal to the largest number of potential buyers. In fact, if you want to really get your home sold quickly when you list it, include on the listing the exact financing you will accept, such as 10 percent down payment, buyer to assume existing mortgage, and seller will carry back a second mortgage for the balance of the sales price (then spell out the terms you want on that second mortgage).

Suppose two similar homes are for sale in the same neighborhood on these terms:

No. 1. THREE-BEDROOM HOME
$95,000—All cash to seller

No. 2. THREE-BEDROOM HOME
$100,000—Financing Available
$15,000—Cash Down Payment (15%)
$75,000—1st Mortgage, 12%, 29 years
$10,000—2nd Mortgage, 10%, 10 years
$772—1st Mortgage monthly payment
$100—2nd Mortgage monthly payment
$872—Total monthly mortgage payments

Which home will have the most potential buyers? Which terms would you, as a buyer, prefer? Which house is likely to sell first? Assuming both sellers have the same cost and sell for their full asking price, which seller will earn the largest total profit? In addition to earning $5,000 more profit on his sales price, which seller will earn $1,000 in annual interest income on the second mortgage he carried back?

House No. 2, of course. By now you probably have the general idea that to get the best possible sales price when selling your residence, it is very important to (1) offer it in top condition, (2) at the right asking price, and (3) on the best possible sales terms.

But do not go overboard by offering terms that are too good, such as *no* down payment. Be sure the buyer has sufficient equity in the residence so he will not be tempted to walk away from it if he loses his job or becomes sick and unable to work.

No down payment purchases make it too easy for the buyer to abandon the house if he cannot make the monthly payments or if it suddenly needs expensive repairs. Let the FHA and VA mortgage loan programs take care of the high risk buyers. You cannot afford to. Every home seller, before he will consider taking back all or part of the financing on a first or second mortgage, deed of trust, or land contract, should insist on a cash down payment of at least 10 percent of the sales price, plus a credit history check on the buyer.

However, like every good rule, *there is an exception.* If a buyer offers you a small cash down payment (and you do not need more cash), that can be safe for the seller *if* the buyer will give adequate security. To illustrate, suppose a buyer offers you a 5 percent down payment with you to finance the sale on a first or second mortgage. Normally, that is dangerous for you, the seller, because the buyer has so little equity. But if the buyer secures his promissory note to you with a first or second mortgage on the property you sell him *plus* a first or second mortgage on other property he owns, then you have got a safe loan. If the buyer defaults, then you can foreclose on both the property you sold him and also on the second property he gave you as security. But be sure you receive title insurance on both properties for your first and second mortgage. Title insurance is the only safe protection to be sure the buyer really owns the second property he is offering as security.

BEWARE OF 110 PERCENT FINANCING

Occasionally home sellers who are willing to help finance the sale are confronted by offers that look like this. Suppose your home is for sale at $100,000. A buyer offers you full $100,000 price, contingent upon his getting a new first mortgage for $75,000 from a S&L. His offer further provides you will receive a second mortgage on the house for $35,000. This means that of the $75,000 cash from the new first mortgage, the buyer gets $10,000! In other words, when the smoke clears you will get $65,000 cash (from the new first mortgage) plus a $35,000 second mortgage. The buyer gets $10,000 cash.

This is dangerous for the seller. It is good for the sharp buyer because he walks away from the purchase with $10,000 cash. If he is a crook, he may keep walking and never make any payments either to you on your second mortgage or to the first mortgage lender.

The reason this is so risky for the seller is if the buyer defaults, the original seller forecloses on his second mortgage and will probably get the property back (there are not likely to be many bidders at the foreclosure sale of a second mortgage for 100 percent of the property's market value). But when you get the house back, you will owe the first mortgage lender $75,000, of which you only received $65,000.

However, this can be turned into a perfectly safe transaction for the seller, and the buyer still gets his 110 percent financing. By securing that second mortgage with both the property being sold and other property the buyer already owns, the second mortgage holder (seller) has more than adequate security if the buyer defaults. But be sure the buyer has plenty of equity in the second property and that title insurance is obtained on the second lien on it.

This 110 percent finance scheme is being used nationwide by shrewd buyers who take advantage of naïve sellers. If you know how to handle such an offer, you can benefit from it. In fact, you may want to go out and buy property this way. But to protect the seller, be sure there is adequate equity security in two or more properties for the amount of the second mortgage to the seller.

OFFER THE BEST SALE TERMS
FOR BOTH THE BUYER AND SELLER

Most home buyers (and buyers of investment property too) want to buy with the lowest possible cash down payment (if they can comfortably afford the resulting monthly mortgage payments). In fact, it is downright smart to buy with the smallest down payment possible. Reasons include (1) mortgage repayment in cheaper, inflated dollars worth less than today, (2) maximum income tax deduction for mortgage interest, (3) cash conservation for emergencies and other investments, and (4) easy resale if the property has a big assumable existing mortgage.

But from the seller's viewpoint, if the buyer cannot afford a 10 percent or 15 percent cash down payment, that buyer might not be a good risk if the seller is considering helping finance the sale. The FHA, VA, and PMI loan programs are available for these low down payment, high risk buyers.

But unless you have no other way to finance the sale of your home, try to avoid selling to a buyer who wants to get a FHA or VA mortgage. Reasons include (1) the seller usually must pay "loan points" (one point equals one percent of the amount borrowed) for the buyer to get a new FHA or VA home loan because FHA and VA will not allow their buyers to pay the loan fee, (2) FHA and VA appraisals are often lower than those of conventional lenders, (3) FHA and VA appraisers often require minor repairs to be made before they will approve the loan, (4) red tape bureaucratic delays frequently prolong the closing time for FHA and VA home sales to sixty or ninety days, sometimes longer, and (5) second mortgages are not allowed with new FHA and VA mortgages, thus reducing your profit potential for earning extra income from interest on an installment sale.

Fortunately, it is usually possible to match the most desirable sales terms from both the buyer's and seller's viewpoints to minimize the seller's tax on the sale, thus maximizing his profit. When structuring the sale terms, consider the tax aspects closely. There are four major tax breaks to consider when planning the sale of your personal residence.

1. The "Over-55 Rule" $125,000 Home Sale Tax Exemption
As discussed in Chapter 3, the "over-55 rule" benefits many home sellers

who are fifty-five or older. If you meet the easy requirements, then you have little or no tax to be concerned about when planning the sale of your residence. To review the three requirements of this rule, they are (1) one or more co-owners must be fifty-five or older on the title transfer date, (2) the seller must have owned and lived in the principal residence three of the last five years before its sale, and (3) the seller cannot have used this tax exemption before (any unused portion of the $125,000 profit tax exemption cannot be saved for future use).

EXAMPLE: Larry and Mary, husband and wife, paid $13,500 for their house many years ago. They sell it for $75,000 so they can enter a life-care retirement home. If either Larry or Mary is at least age fifty-five on the title transfer date and that spouse holds a title interest in the home, the entire $61,500 profit ($75,000 minus $13,500) is tax-free if they lived in the house as their principal residence any three of the last five years before the sale. But the unused $39,500 of their $125,000 possible tax exemption cannot be saved for future use.

2. The Principal Residence Replacement Rule

In Chapter 3, this tax deferral rule was thoroughly explained. But it bears repeating that this rule is available to taxpayers of any age who (1) sell their principal residence and (2) buy a replacement principal residence within eighteen months before or after the sale (an additional six months is allowed if a new home is constructed).

However, this tax break results in 100 percent profit tax deferral only if a more expensive replacement is bought. If the replacement costs less, then the profit is taxable up to the difference in the prices of the two residences.

EXAMPLE: Howard, age sixty, sells his principal residence for $95,000 and buys a condominium in Florida for $120,000. Although he qualifies for the "over-55 rule," he should save it for future use since his profit tax is deferred anyway using the replacement residence rule.

EXAMPLE: Evan and Ellen, ages fifty-six and fifty-four, sell their principal residence for $90,000, earning a $40,000 profit. They buy a $75,000 condominium. Since their replacement costs $15,000 less than the sale price of their old residence, $15,000 of their $40,000 profit is potentially taxable. But if they meet the requirements of the "over-55 rule," they can use their $100,000 exemption to avoid paying tax on this $15,000 profit.

By the way, purchase of life-care in a retirement home does *not* qualify as a principal residence replacement under the "replacement residence rule" of Internal Revenue Code section 1034, discussed next.

3. The Installment Sale Tax Deferral Method

If the sale qualifies for neither the "over-55 rule" nor the "residence replacement rule," then an installment sale should be considered. Most property sellers who use installment sales (available on any sale, whether the property is your principal residence or owned as an investment or for use in your trade or business) do so (1) to minimize their profit tax by spreading out the payments received from the buyer (and the tax on those payments) into future years, (2) to maximize their profit from interest income and from a higher sales price due to a lower cash down payment required from the buyer, and (3) to provide for future income security with a first or second mortgage, deed of trust, or land contract on their former property.

> EXAMPLE: Ann, age fifty, decides to sell her home for $100,000. Her cost was $44,000. Thus her profit will be $56,000 ($100,000 minus $44,000). She owns the home free and clear (this is not an installment sale requirement, however). A buyer offers Ann a $15,000 cash down payment on an installment sale. Ann agrees to take back the $85,000 mortgage at 12 percent interest for 25 years. Each month she will receive $874.58 from the buyer. The interest portion of each payment will be taxed as ordinary income. Of the principal part of each payment, 56 percent ($56,000 divided by $100,000) is taxed as long-term capital gain at the lowest tax rates available. The other 44 percent ($44,000 divided by $100,000) is tax-free return of Ann's initial $44,000 cost basis in the home. Over the next twenty-five years, Ann will receive a total of $262,374 in payments, of which $177,374 is interest and $85,000 is principal. It is like getting two profits from the sale of one house.

HOW THE NEW INSTALLMENT SALES LAW
CAN INCREASE YOUR REALTY PROFITS

One of the few major accomplishments of the 96th Congress was passage of the 1980 Installment Sales Revision Act. This new law opened new opportunities to real estate profits. But it also created some new pitfalls to avoid.

Property sellers with large profits are always anxious to eliminate or at least minimize their income tax on their profit. If the property and the seller both qualify for the "residence replacement rule" of Internal Revenue Code Section 1034 or the "over-55 rule" $100,000 home sale tax exemption of Internal Revenue Code Section 121 (both rules apply *only* to the sale of the taxpayer's principal residence), then profit tax can be either completely eliminated or deferred.

But many property sales do not qualify for these two tax breaks. Even those sales that do qualify can be structured to use the installment sale principles to maximize the seller's total profit. Installment sales can be used on *any* property sale. Not only do installment sales defer the seller's profit tax payment, but they also usually lower the total tax too. This is done by avoiding a boost of the taxpayer into a high tax bracket in the year of the property sale, as would occur if he receives all his profit in the sale year.

WHAT IS AN INSTALLMENT SALE?

An installment sale is any real or personal property sale where the buyer's payment of the sales price is not fully received in the tax year of the sale. Until 1980, the definition of an installment sale also required that not over 30 percent of the gross sales price be received by the seller in the year of sale and payments must be made by the buyer to the seller in two or more tax years. Both of these limiting rules were repealed by the 1980 Installment Sales Revision Act.

In other words, an installment sale is simply a sale where the buyer's payments to the seller are deferred over a period of time. The seller pays his profit tax as he receives those payments, rather than paying the entire tax in the year of the property sale.

WHY USE AN INSTALLMENT SALE?

There are many reasons for structuring a property sale as an installment sale. Some of the major reasons include:

1. *Facilitate the sale and improve the sales price and terms*. If the seller assists the property buyer in obtaining easy financing, the buyer will be willing to pay a higher purchase price or offer more generous terms to the seller.

The usual security for the buyer's installment debt to the seller is a mortgage, deed of trust, land contract (called a contract for deed in some states), or a long-term lease-option. In tight mortgage markets, an installment sale may be the only practical way to get a property sold because seller financing may be all that is available.

2. *Deferral of profit tax over the years in which the buyer pays for the property*. Since the seller waits for the buyer's deferred payments, it is only sensible for the seller to postpone tax payment until the buyer's payments are received. The 1980 Installment Sales Revision Act encourages this tax result by making all deferred payment sales *automatically* installment sales with deferred tax payment.

3. *An installment sale can defer tax payments into future tax years when the seller expects to be in a lower tax bracket.*

EXAMPLE: Lucy will retire next year from her job. Her taxable income then will drop by about 50 percent. But she has an excellent offer today to sell her four-family apartment house. The buyer may not be interested next year. By using an installment sale, Lucy can finalize the sale now, get either no or a small cash down payment this year, and begin getting installment payments next year. The interest income on the buyer's unpaid balance to Lucy will supplement her retirement pension and social security. Although interest income is taxed as ordinary income, Lucy's profit portion of each installment sale principal payment received will be taxed at the lower long-term capital gain tax rates if she owned the property over twelve months before selling.

4. *Deferral of a capital gain into a future tax year can offset an expected loss from other sales, such as sale of common stock at a loss.*

5. *Avoidance of a boost into a high tax bracket in the year of a property sale maximizes profit by saving tax dollars.* By spreading out the buyer's payments over several years, the taxpayer can avoid being thrown into a high tax bracket in the year of sale. For example, if a taxpayer is normally in a 20 percent tax bracket, if he makes a property sale of his farm for all cash, he could easily be thrown into a 40 percent or 50 percent tax bracket. An installment sale can avoid this bad result by spreading out the buyer's payments over several tax years.

6. *Safe, secured interest income increases the seller's annual earnings and makes them more predictable.* Retirees especially like installment sales because the interest income, secured by a mortgage, deed of trust, land contract, or long-term lease-option on the property sold adds to their retirement income. Although this interest income is taxed as ordinary income, since most retirees are in low tax brackets, the tax bite on the interest is not of major importance to them.

The general rule is that a deferred payment or installment sale of real or personal property defers the tax on the seller's profit until the money is received from the buyer. Each payment received has three parts: (1) interest on the buyer's unpaid balance (taxed as ordinary income), (2) nontaxable return of the seller's capital investment in the property, and (3) taxable profit (taxed as long term capital gain if the property was owned over twelve months before sale).

Interest must be charged on installment sales. From time to time the IRS adjusts the minimum interest rate required. If it were not for this interest requirement, property sellers would raise the price (since most profits are taxed at the lower long-term capital gains rates) and lower the interest (taxed as ordinary income). Congress is considering new legislation on this topic, so watch for changes in the minimum interest rate which must be charged on installment sales.

After July 1, 1981, the IRS will not impute interest to installment payments received by a property seller if at least 9 percent interest is specified in the installment sale obligation of the buyer. The IRS can impute interest at 10 percent if a rate lower than 9 percent is contained in the installment contract.

NEW RULES FOR INSTALLMENT SALES

The 1980 Installment Sales Revision Act made several important installment sale rule changes. Here is a summary of the major changes.

1. *Elimination of the 30 percent year of sale maximum payment.* The old installment sale rules disqualified many taxpayers from deferring their profit tax over the years of receiving the buyer's payments. A slight miscalculation could cause income tax disaster by making the full profit tax due in the year of sale if over 30 percent of the gross sales price was received in the sale year.

The simple new rule says tax is owed on the sale profit in the tax year it is received by the seller. Each principal payment the seller receives is split in the normal way between tax-free return of capital investment and taxable profit (long-term gain if the property was owned over twelve months before its sale).

But a word of caution is in order. If the property seller refinanced the mortgage before selling, and if that mortgage exceeds the seller's adjusted cost basis (book value) for the property sold, the amount of excess mortgage counts as a payment received in the year of sale.

To illustrate, suppose you sell your property for $100,000 with $10,000 cash down payment. If your adjusted cost basis is $25,000, the buyer assumes or takes title "subject to" your old $40,000 refinanced first mortgage, and the buyer gives you a second mortgage for the $50,000 balance of the sales price, your $15,000 "excess mortgage" over adjusted cost basis ($40,000 minus $15,000) is partly taxable in the year of the sale.

The reason the excess mortgage amount is taxable when a property is sold is an excess mortgage balance over the property's adjusted cost basis is the same as if the seller had received that amount as part of the cash down payment. In fact, the seller did receive that excess mortgage money in cash at the time he refinanced the mortgage. This excess mortgage taxable result is the same as under the old installment sale law.

Elimination of the 30 percent year of sale maximum payment limit applies to installment sales made after January 1, 1980.

2. *Two payment rule abolished.* Another major change was elimination of the old minimum two payment installment sale rule. The old law required at least two installment payments in two separate income tax years. Now it is possible to sell a property for no down payment in the sale year and still qualify for installment sale benefits.

For example, suppose a property seller has had a very good income year. In November he receives an excellent offer to sell his property. But if he sells this year, it will boost him into a sky-high income tax bracket. Frankly, he does not need any more income this year. So he makes an installment sale with the payment for the property due in January of next year.

This provision is retroactive to installment sales made after January 1, 1980.

3. *Automatic installment sale election.* As mentioned earlier, the new law requires taxpayers to use installment sale tax deferral benefits unless they elect not to do so. This election is now automatic for installment sales made after October 19, 1980.

Occasionally a property seller wants to pay his entire profit tax in the year of the property sale, even though he will not receive all his payments from the buyer until future years. Such a taxpayer must now "unelect" his automatic installment sale election.

4. *Special rules for sales to relatives and controlled corporations.* One of the most complicated provisions of the 1980 Installment Sales Revision Act involves property sales to relatives and closely controlled corporations. Oversimplified, the new law says the original seller will owe tax on any resale profit if the installment sale buyer resells the property within two years after the original installment sale. But this only applies to persons related to the original seller if they resell within two years.

The purpose of this new provision is to control intrafamily property sales which are motivated by tax purposes. Such sales made after May 14, 1980, are affected. If the profitable resale is made within two years after the original sale, before installment sale payments to the original seller are completed, the resale profit is taxed to the original seller.

But there are numerous exceptions to this two-year resale "relate back" rule. One applies if there is no tax motivation for the sale. Another applies to sale of marketable securities, trust funds, and mutual fund shares. Still another applies if the second sale was after the death of either the original installment sale seller or the related purchaser, or if the second sale was due to an involuntary conversion.

For purposes of this rule, "related purchasers" are defined as spouse, child, grandchild, or parent (brother and sister are NOT on the list), controlled corporations, partnerships, and trusts and estates.

5. *"Like-kind" tax-deferred exchanges can now be installment sales too.* The installment sale law now says a trade of a "like-kind" property in an Internal Revenue Code Section 1031 tax-deferred exchange (discussed in Chapter 9) will not be treated as a payment when it is received with an installment obligation. In other words, installment sale benefits can now be combined with a tax-deferred exchange.

To illustrate, suppose you trade your property with a $400,000 basis for "like-kind" property worth $200,000, plus an installment note for $700,000, plus $100,000 cash paid in the year of trade. In other words, you are trading down and receiving "boot" (boot is personal property, rather than real property). Under the old law, the contract price is $1,000,000 ($200,000 + $700,000 + $100,000) with a $600,000 gross profit ($1,000,000 minus $400,000 basis). This is a 60 percent ratio of $600,000 profit divided by $1,000,000. The old law would require taxation on 60 percent of $300,000 ($100,000 cash plus the $200,000 value of the "like-kind" property received) which is $180,000.

But the new law excludes value of the "like-kind" real property received even though it is a "down trade." The contract price is now $800,000 ($700,000 + $100,000) with a $600,000 gross profit ($1,000,000 minus $400,000). The gross profit ratio now is 75 percent ($600,000 divided by $800,000) so the reportable gain in the year of sale is 75 percent of $100,000 cash payment received, or $75,000. Gain reportable in future tax years is 75 percent of the $700,000 installment note, which is $525,000. Total gain on the sale is $600,000, the same as under the old law.

This exchange applies to sales closed after October 19, 1980.

6. *Open-end contingency sales now qualify for installment sales.* Open-end property sales, where either price or terms of the sale remain to be determined after the sale closing, now can qualify for installment sale benefits. This portion of the new law applies to sales closed after October 19, 1980.

This new provision, however, will eliminate use of the "cost recovery method" whereby a taxpayer first recovered his cost basis in the property before he incurred any tax liability on the contingency sale. Now payments received are taxed on a pro rata basis, using the maximum sales price to determine the contract price and gross profit ratio in the normal installment sale manner (described later).

However, if the maximum sale price is later reduced in a future tax year, such as when a performance mortgage's rental income from the property does not meet expectations, then installment sale figures must be recomputed. Congress left it up to the IRS to issue regulations implementing this complicated part of the new law.

WHICH PAYMENTS ARE TAXABLE IN AN INSTALLMENT SALE?

1. *Buyer's down payment.* Part of the buyer's cash down payment represents profit to the seller and will be taxable. A portion is tax-free return of capital investment. The taxability ratio is determined according to the method discussed later in this chapter. Also taxable would be the profit portion of any noncash down payment made by the buyer, such as transferring to the property seller common stocks, bonds, personal

property (such as a car or boat), or any other payment made to a third party on behalf of the seller (such as buyer's payment of seller's debt to a finance company).

However, payments made by the buyer on a debt secured by an existing lien (such as a mortgage or deed of trust) on the property are not taxable to the seller (except an excess mortgage, of course).

2. *Buyer's principal payments to seller in year of sale.* Any principal payments made by the buyer to the seller on the installment obligation in the year of sale are partly taxable according to the taxability ratio.

EXAMPLE: Craig sold his land for $100,000 and received a $40,000 cash down payment from the buyer. But in the year of sale the buyer also paid $2,000 of principal on the installment sale second mortgage Craig carried back to finance the sale. The $42,000 total received by Craig in the year of sale is partly taxable to him as profit.

3. *Excess mortgage over seller's basis (book value).* If the existing first mortgage (plus a second, third, etc., mortgage) that the buyer assumes or takes title "subject to" exceeds the seller's adjusted cost basis in the property, the excess mortgage amount becomes partly taxable to the seller in the year of sale.

4. *Option payments.* If the buyer paid consideration for an option to buy the property, in the tax year the purchase option is exercised the option money becomes partly taxable to the seller.

5. *Rental payments.* Similarly, if the buyer made prior rent payments that are credited toward the purchase price, the rent paid becomes partly taxable unless the seller already reported that rental income on his prior year income tax returns. This might occur, for example, when a tenant has a lease with option to buy the property.

SPECIAL INSTALLMENT SALE PROBLEMS AND HOW TO HANDLE THEM

1. *Buyer's debt to the seller.* The buyer's obligation to the seller, usually secured by a first, second, or third mortgage, trust deed, or land contract on the property, is *not* taxable in the year of sale. It does not matter whether or not the buyer's obligation is secured or unsecured. The buyer's obligation becomes taxable to the seller only when the buyer actually pays the seller on that debt obligation.

2. *Existing obligations secured by the property sold.* Any existing mortgage or trust deed obligations already secured by the property sold are *not* taxable to the seller in the year of the sale, even though the buyer makes payments on those obligations to a third-party lender. It does not matter whether the buyer takes title "subject to" or assumes those liens. The only exception, of course, is an "excess mortgage" where the mortgage balance exceeds the seller's adjusted cost basis for the property.

Such excess mortgage amount is taxable to the seller in the first year of an installment sale.

> EXAMPLE: Don sold his land for $70,000. The buyer made a $10,000 cash down payment and assumed Don's existing $30,000 first mortgage. Don took back a $30,000 second mortgage from the buyer. The land cost Don $25,000. This is his book value or adjusted costs basis. The $5,000 excess mortgage over Don's $25,000 adjusted cost basis represents partially taxable profit in the year of the sale. In other words, Don pays profit tax on the profit portion of the $10,000 cash down payment plus the $5,000 excess mortgage exceeding his basis.

3. *Proceeds of seller's sale of buyer's obligation.* After the sale is closed, the seller may find he needs cash. To raise cash, he may sell his mortgage, trust deed, or land contract received from the buyer. The cash received from the sale of the note and security is a separate transaction from the property sale. But part of the proceeds will be taxable as if payments were made on the buyer's promissory note.

> EXAMPLE: Lenny sold his home for $100,000. The buyer paid $10,000 cash down payment. Lenny took back a $60,000 first mortgage for 25 years and a $30,000 second mortgage. Later, Lenny sold his second mortgage for $22,000 cash. The $22,000 received from the sale of the second mortgage is partly taxable as capital gain profit. The rest is nontaxable return of capital investment.

4. *Buyer's payments on existing loans.* The payments the buyer makes toward the principal reduction on any existing loans secured by the property before the sale (which were assumed or taken "subject to" by the buyer) are *not* taxable to the seller.

5. *Seller's refinancing of existing loans before the sale.* If the seller refinanced an old loan or put on a new mortgage before selling the property, the money raised from the refinance is *not* taxable unless a portion is an excess mortgage (discussed earlier).

> EXAMPLE: Benny desires an installment sale of his apartment house that has an adjusted cost basis of $32,000. His old mortgage is paid down to $15,000. Before the installment sale, Benny refinances for $32,000 and then sells the apartments on an installment sale for a $100,000 adjusted sales price. Since the refinanced mortgage does not exceed Benny's adjusted cost basis, he does not owe any tax on the $17,000 cash proceeds ($32,000 minus $15,000) from the mortgage refinance. But if the refinanced mortgage exceeded Benny's adjusted cost basis (book value), then he would owe capital gains tax on the profit portion of that excess mortgage.

HOW TO CALCULATE TAXABILITY OF
INSTALLMENT SALE PAYMENTS RECEIVED

Whether received in the year of sale or in a later tax year, a percentage of each principal dollar received by the seller from the buyer toward payment of the principal balance on the installment sale debt is taxable profit.

Interest received is taxed as ordinary income, of course. The remainder of each dollar of principal received is nontaxable return of capital investment.

NET GAIN (profit) is the "adjusted sales price" (gross sales price minus sales expenses such as realty sales commission and transfer costs) minus the "adjusted cost basis" (purchase price plus capital improvements added during ownership, minus any depreciation and casualty losses deducted during ownership).

CONTRACT PRICE is the gross sales price minus any existing liens or mortgages taken over by the buyer (whether he assumes or takes "subject to"), plus the excess (if any) of any existing mortgages over the property's adjusted cost basis to the seller.

$$\frac{\text{NET GAIN}}{\text{CONTRACT PRICE}} = \text{Percent of each principal dollar which is taxable}$$

EXAMPLE:

Gross sales price	$100,000
Existing mortgages, trust deeds, or liens	$40,000
Seller's adjusted cost basis	$50,000

CONTRACT PRICE:

Gross Sales Price	$100,000
Minus: Existing Mortgages, Trust Deeds, etc.	$ − 40,000
	$60,000
Plus: Excess mtg. over adjusted cost basis	$ + 0
Contract Price	$60,000

NET GAIN

Gross Sales Price	$100,000
Minus: Selling expenses	$ − 6,000
Adjusted Sales Price	$94,000
Minus: Adjusted cost basis	$ − 50,000
Net Gain (Profit)	$44,000

$$\frac{\text{NET GAIN}}{\text{CONTRACT PRICE}} = \frac{\$44,000}{\$60,000} = 73.3 \text{ percent}$$ of each principal dollar received is taxable long-term capital gain profit

When a property sale is made with tax-deferred installment sale payments, the seller's questions then become "How much of each payment I receive is taxable?" and "How much is tax-free return of my capital investment?"

Of course, before these questions can be answered, the interest portion of each payment received must be subtracted to get the amount of principal received. Interest is taxed as ordinary income. As the loan is amortized, this interest portion of each payment will decline, and the principal portion will increase.

As mentioned earlier, interest must be charged on installment sales. The IRS can impute interest if the taxpayer-seller failed to charge the buyer a reasonable interest rate. This minimum changes from time to time. As of this writing if at least 9 percent interest is not charged on the unpaid installment sale balance, the IRS can impute interest at 10 percent.

HOW TO MAXIMIZE SALE PROFITS WITH
AN INSTALLMENT SALE

Suppose you sell your property for $100,000 on an installment sale with a $15,000 cash down payment from the buyer, and you take back an $85,000 installment sale mortgage at 10 percent interest from the buyer for a 30-year term. The monthly payments will be $745.95. Over the 30-year mortgage term, total payments will be $268,542, including the $85,000 principal. The happy result is you, the seller, double the amount you receive from the property by taking back an installment sale mortgage. The extra profit comes in the form of the interest income earned on the buyer's unpaid balance owed to you.

But in these days of high inflation rates, the installment sale seller should protect himself by providing for periodic interest rate adjustments every three or five years. This will guard the installment sale seller against hyperinflation. Provision in the promissory note and the mortgage for interest rate adjustment to the national average mortgage index rate every three or five years is fair to both the seller and the buyer.

COMPREHENSIVE EXAMPLE OF AN INSTALLMENT SALE

Since all deferred payment real estate sales now qualify for installment sale tax deferral benefits, it is important for property sellers and real estate agents to understand how to compute the taxable and tax-free portions of each principal payment received (after the interest portion of each payment is first subtracted.) These computations apply only to the principal, *not* to the interest part of each payment received.

Gross sales price	$100,000
Buyer's cash down payment	20,000
Existing mortgages or trust deeds	30,000
Installment sale second mortgage or trust deed to seller	50,000
Sales expenses (realty commission and transfer costs)	7,000
Seller's adjusted cost basis (depreciated book value)	60,000

Calculation of taxability of principal payments:

A—NET GAIN:

Gross sales price	100,000
Minus: Sales expenses	$ − 7,000
Adjusted sales price	93,000
Minus: Adjusted cost basis *(depreciated book value)*	− 60,000
Net gain (profit)	$33,000

B—CONTRACT PRICE:

Gross sales price	$100,000
Minus: Existing mortgage or trust deed	− 30,000
Payments made or to be made by buyer	$70,000
Plus: Excess of mortgages over adjusted cost basis	+0
Contract price	$70,000

TAXABLE PERCENTAGE OF EACH PRINCIPAL PAYMENT RECEIVED:

$$\frac{\text{NET GAIN}}{\text{CONTRACT PRICE}} = \frac{\$33,000}{\$70,000} = 47.1 \text{ percent}$$

The result is 47.1 percent of each principal payment received by the seller, including the buyer's cash down payment of $20,000, is taxable (as long-term capital gain if the property was owned over 12 months before the sale). Installment payment long-term capital gains received after October 31, 1978 (the effective date of the 1978 Tax Act) are taxed at the new, lower long-term capital gains rates (basically, 40 percent of the long-term capital gain is taxable, 60 percent is tax-free).

4. Income Averaging

Regardless of the tax method you qualify for when selling your property, if your taxable income jumps drastically in any one tax year, consider income averaging. Taxpayers using installment sales or receiving other long-term capital gains can qualify for income averaging.

Real estate profits, whether ordinary income (if the property was owned less than twelve months before sale) or long term capital gain (if the property was owned over twelve months before sale) can use income averaging to cut their income tax on the sale profit. If your taxable income, including long-term capital gains, exceeds by 20 percent your average taxable income for the last four years, it will usually pay to use income averaging.

Although the income averaging computations can be long and difficult, the tax savings are worth the extra effort to be sure you pay the lowest possible tax. An experienced tax adviser's services are essential for this complicated tax calculation. It is especially advisable to use a tax preparer with access to a computer tax program to assure accurate calculations. The tax savings of income averaging can often be very dramatic.

SUMMARY

All of the above methods of maximizing your profit from the sale of your home or other real estate can be used alone or in combination with other tax breaks, if you qualify. For example, you can combine the "over-55 rule" and the "residence replacement rule" when selling your large old house and purchasing a less expensive condominium replacement principal residence.

The purpose of this chapter is to highlight how to maximize sale profit at the time of disposing of property. The next chapter, probably the most profitable in the book, explains how to use tax-deferred exchanges to legally avoid tax payment on investment properties. It is another technique for maximizing your benefits from owning real estate.

QUESTIONS AND ANSWERS

Q. Our home has been for sale several months. The agent has presented us with two purchase offers, but both provided for us to carry back a large second mortgage for the buyers. We couldn't do that since we need $40,000 cash for another house we have already contracted to buy. Our existing VA mortgage is assumable. How can we get a cash sale? —*Lannie O.*

A. Few all-cash home sales are being made today. It is much easier to make a sale with seller financing. Even though mortgage interest rates have dropped a little, it is still difficult for most potential home buyers to qualify for a new mortgage.

Although you did not give the price of your home, if it is below $125,000, you might consider advertising it with GI financing. You would have to pay the loan fee for the buyer's new VA home loan, but it would give you an all-cash sale.

To get your home sold, you have got to make it a "red ribbon deal." That means make your home an attractive package, both physically and financially, for the buyer. Here is another idea to consider.

Suppose your home is worth $100,000. Have your agent advertise it as follows: (1) seller to obtain a new refinanced first mortgage for $75,000, (2) buyer to pay $15,000 cash down payment, and (3) seller to take back a $10,000 second mortgage. Of course, be sure the new first mortgage is not due upon sale. The cash from the mortgage refinancing, plus the buyer's down payment, will probably give you the $40,000 cash you need.

You may be able to use that small second mortgage as part of your down payment on the house you are buying. If necessary, you can probably sell it at a discount to raise more cash. To get your home sold, work with a creative real estate agent who understands innovative finance because that is how homes are sold today.

HOW SELLER FINANCING RELATES TO INSTALLMENT SALES

Q. Recently you mentioned "installment sale tax benefits." Please give more details.—*Palmer MacD.*

A. Installment sale tax deferral can be a major benefit of selling property. The big advantage is the seller's profit is spread out over future tax years, thus avoiding a boost into a high tax bracket in the year of sale.

Other installment sale advantages include (1) easy, quick sale (since no outside financing need be obtained by the property buyer), (2) top dollar sales price due to the built-in financing offered to the buyer, and (3) excellent, safe income for the seller at a high interest rate, secured by a first, second, or third mortgage on the property being sold.

To qualify for installment sale tax deferral benefits, the seller can accept any amount of payment in the year of sale. The old 30 percent limitation has been abolished.

Only the profit portion of the buyer's down payment, his principal payments on the installment sale note to the seller, and any "excess mortgage" over the seller's adjusted cost basis (due to refinancing) get taxed in the year of sale. For further details, consult your tax adviser.

HOW TO COMBINE WRAP-AROUND MORTGAGE
WITH INSTALLMENT SALE

Q. I am considering selling a house where I used to live. It is now rented to tenants. Its mortgage is an assumable loan from a bank. My idea is to sell on an installment sale to spread out the profit tax and give me some extra interest income. But after reading your article about wrap-around mortgage benefits, I'm wondering if it would be possible for me to use both an installment sale and a wrap-around mortgage?—*Hugh E.*

A. Yes, installment sales and wrap-around mortgages make a great combination.

For example, suppose you sell the house for $100,000 with a $15,000 cash down payment. If your first mortgage is $40,000 at 8 percent interest, you might take back an $85,000 wrap-around mortgage at 12 percent (assuming that does not exceed the usury limit in the state where the house is located). You will earn 12 percent on the top $45,000 "at risk" plus the 4 percent differential on the underlying $40,000 first mortgage, which remains undisturbed. This totals about $7,000 annual interest ($5,400 plus $1,600) for a yield of 15.5 percent.

Using a wrap-around mortgage, the buyer makes one monthly payment to you. You then use part of that payment to keep up payments on the old first mortgage, which remains undisturbed.

As you can see, a wrap-around mortgage is a "good deal" for the buyer. Where else can he borrow at 12 percent interest with no loan application or other red tape? And it is a good deal for you, the seller, too because you will earn high yield secured by a mortgage on your old house.

Thanks to the 1980 Installment Sale Revision Act, any deferred payment sale now qualifies for tax deferral. The tax will be automatically spread out over the years the buyer makes his wrap-around mortgage payments to you. Your tax adviser can explain further.

SHOULD SEVENTY-FOUR-YEAR-OLD HOME SELLER
FINANCE HOME SALE FOR THIRTY YEARS?

Q. I am selling my home and moving to a retirement home. I am seventy-four. A buyer offered to pay my full asking price, with a $10,000 down payment, if I will carry the mortgage on a 30-year term, payable at $1,640 per month. I want to accept, but my children say I am foolish to do so since I probably won't live thirty years. When I die, the payments will go to my children until the loan is paid off. If I should live thirty years, I'll have good income. What do you think?—*Olive P.*

A. I think you should listen to your children. The thirty-year amortization schedule is fine, but insist on a five- or ten-year "balloon payment" due date on that mortgage. When the balance comes due in five or ten years, you can either extend the loan or have the buyer pay off the balance. High inflation rates make long-term lending unsound. P. S. By financing the sale on deferred payments, you will make your home easy to sell and assure yourself of excellent retirement income. That is the right way to "package" your home for maximum sale profit.

"OVER-55 RULE" AND INSTALLMENT SALE
CAN BE COMBINED

Q. The cost of my home was $35,000 and it is worth at least $135,000 if I sell it today. I qualify for that "over-55 rule" $125,000 home sale tax exemption, so I have the potential of receiving the entire $135,000 tax-free. If I sell on an installment sale, in what order do I report the payments received? Can I wait until I receive the full $135,000 and then start reporting the interest to the IRS? Neither my CPA nor the local IRS people can answer my question.—*Lorenz N.*

A. Your situation shows how to combine use of the "over-55 rule" with the installment sale principle.

In the year you sell your principal residence, file IRS Form 2119 with your income tax returns. Use this form to elect use of the "over-55 rule" $125,000 home sale tax exemption. The result will be that your future payments received from the buyer will be free of capital gains tax if your sale profit does not exceed $125,000. If it does, you pay tax on the capital gain profit as you receive it from the buyer.

The IRS requires (as of this writing) at least 9 percent interest be charged on any unpaid installment sale balance. If you don't charge at least 9 percent interest on each payment, the IRS can impute interest at 10 percent.

The interest portion of each installment payment received is taxable as ordinary income. Interest is first deducted from each payment received. The balance is then credited to principal reduction. If your CPA was not aware of this, perhaps you need to find a new tax adviser.

DELAY HOME SALE TO MAXIMIZE TAX SAVINGS

Q. My wife's doctor urges us to move to Arizona for her health. The problem is neither of us is yet fifty-five, and if we sell our home now, we will have a big profit, probably about $85,000. I am fifty-four and my wife is fifty-two. But I don't think we can wait a year to sell. We would like to rent in Arizona for a year or two to see if we like living there. Any ideas for saving tax if we sell our home now?—*David C.*

A. Yes, do not sell now. To qualify for the "over-55 rule" $125,000 home sale tax exemption, at least one co-owner spouse must be fifty-five or older on the day of title transfer. In addition, the principal residence must have been owned and occupied at least three of the five years before sale. So you will maximize your net profit by waiting to sell your home until you are at least fifty-five.

But you can rent your present home for up to two years (assuming you have owned and lived in it the last three years) before closing the sale.

An especially good way to offer your home would be to have your agent advertise it on a "lease with option to buy." Tenants who have a purchase option usually take remarkably good care of the home. With a substantial "consideration for the option" of perhaps several thousand dollars, then you can consider the house practically sold. By waiting to close the sale until you are fifty-five, you will avoid paying tax on that $85,000 profit. Your tax adviser can explain further.

9.

How to Legally Pyramid Your Wealth Without Paying Income Taxes

In Chapter 4 the concept of tax avoidance by ownership of depreciable real estate was explained. If you own enough such properties, you can shelter all your income from taxation.

But most of us do not want to stand still, just owning our current real estate holdings. We would like to increase our real estate wealth, preferably without paying income taxes as we do so.

The good news is it is possible to pyramid your wealth in real estate from a small investment to as many properties as you would like to own—all without paying income tax as you do so.

HOW TAX-DEFERRED PROPERTY EXCHANGES CAN PYRAMID YOUR WEALTH

Real property has unique tax advantages most other investments do not have. Already explained were the "residence replacement rule" and the "over-55 rule" which apply to the sale of your principal residence. This chapter concentrates on the greatest wealth-building technique of all—the tax-deferred exchange.

Internal Revenue Code Section 1031(a) says no profit or loss is recognized (that means taxed) when one property *held for investment or for use in a trade or business* is exchanged for another "like-kind" property.

This unique tax rule applies to just about any property *except* your personal residence. For simplicity, *keep your personal residence out of any tax-deferred property exchange.* The reason is your personal residence is' "unlike property" because it is not held for investment or for use in your trade or business.

EXAMPLE *of a Tax-Deferred Exchange:* George owns rural vacant land worth $200,000. But it produces no income with which to pay the

218

property tax and mortgage payments. George's cost for this land was $150,000. Instead of selling his land and paying tax on his $50,000 profit, George makes a tax-deferred trade of it for a $400,000 apartment house. The tax on George's $50,000 profit is deferred indefinitely until he sells the apartment house since George is trading up and receiving no "boot" (unlike property such as cash or net mortgage relief). If George wishes, he can later trade the apartments for a larger "like-kind" property and continue his tax-deferred exchange pyramid chain endlessly. In this example, George (1) improved his cash flow and (2) had his full $50,000 equity to trade, without income tax erosion. It is almost always better to defer paying tax than to pay it now because tomorrow's dollar will be worth less than today's, due to inflation.

WHAT IS A "LIKE-KIND" REAL ESTATE EXCHANGE?

Property which is eligible for a tax-deferred exchange is any real property, fixtures, and leaseholds of at least thirty years, held for investment or for use in a trade or business. Although this definition excludes your personal residence, it does not exclude a house which you rent to tenants (because such a house is trade, business, or investment property).

Nonqualifying property is called "boot" which means "unlike property." Examples of boot include cash, promissory notes from third parties, personal property such as cars, boats, and trailers, property held primarily for sale (such as a builder's supply of new homes for sale), your personal residence, and net mortgage relief (when the mortgage on the property traded exceeds the mortgage on the property acquired). Boot received in a property exchange is taxable, up to the amount of the profit on the property being relinquished.

Therefore, a tax-deferred property exchange usually requires a property trade up from a smaller to a larger property. The "down trader" in such an exchange will usually pay tax on his profit, to the extent "boot" is received. But, as mentioned in Chapter 8, tax on this boot can now qualify for installment sale tax benefits.

WHY TRADE INSTEAD OF SELLING?

Many real estate owners desire to sell their investment property and use their proceeds to acquire a larger investment property. But a sale, followed by a purchase of other investment property, means the profit on the property sold will be taxed. Paying profit tax on such a sale, followed by a purchase, erodes the net equity available for acquisition of the larger property.

It is not normally possible to sell one investment property, use the proceeds to buy another such property and avoid paying profit tax. However, if you plan ahead, you can come pretty close by use of the new

"Starker" and "Biggs" delayed-exchange techniques, discussed later.

However, if both properties are your principal residences, you can sell your old home and buy a more expensive replacement within eighteen months before or after the sale (take up to twenty-four months after the sale if you build a new residence) and defer paying the property tax. This "residence replacement rule" was discussed in Chapter 3.

The primary reason for use of a tax-deferred exchange is tax deferral. But another major reason is the ability to pyramid wealth, without paying profit taxes, from a small nest egg into substantial holdings. Two well-known investors who have done this are William Nickerson, author of *How I Turned $1,000 into $5 Million in Real Estate in My Spare Time* (Simon and Schuster, 1980) and Albert J. Lowry, author of *How You Can Become Financially Independent by Investing in Real Estate* (Simon and Schuster, 1977).

SIX MAJOR REASONS
FOR USING TAX-DEFERRED EXCHANGES

There are at least six major reasons why it is important to understand tax-deferred exchanges. Although tax avoidance is a major motivation, there are others too. Some are nonfinancial reasons.

AVOIDANCE OF TAX EROSION

By deferring paying of tax on his sale profit, an investor using a tax-deferred exchange has more cash available with which to acquire a larger investment property. Depending upon the investor's income tax bracket, tax conserves 5.6 percent to 20 percent of his total profit. This is a big benefit for putting up with the slight inconvenience of making a tax-deferred exchange instead of a sale followed by purchase of a larger property.

AVOIDANCE OF RECAPTURE OF ACCELERATED DEPRECIATION

For income tax purposes, tax-deferred property exchanges are viewed as one continuous investment from the date the first property was acquired. For this reason, there is no need to be concerned about the twelve-month holding period for long-term capital gains taxation. Similarly, since there is no "sale," any accelerated depreciation deducted that exceeds the straight line depreciation rate (normally "recaptured" and taxed if there is a sale) is not taxed as ordinary income as it would be if a sale took place.

However, the depreciation recapture rules of Internal Revenue Code Section 1250 apply to an exchange unless the value of the property received by the taxpayer equals or exceeds the value attributable to the depreciable realty given up on the exchange. To illustrate, if you traded your depreciable building for raw nondepreciable land, recapture could occur.

DISPOSAL OF OTHERWISE UNSALABLE PROPERTY

Taxpayers can often trade a property that is unsalable, except at a loss to the owner, for one that is either more easily salable or more profitable to retain. This result is possible since price tags are often not used when making property trades. The owners of the two parcels suddenly avoid the need to "save face" when the dollar amounts become insignificant.

SOLUTION TO TIGHT MONEY MORTGAGE FINANCE PROBLEMS

When property buyers do not have cash, and mortgages are not easily available, an exchange of equity in an already-owned property can substitute for cash. Cash or a mortgage taken back by one of the traders can be added to balance the equities in the exchange.

INCREASED DEPRECIABLE BASIS

An exchange can increase the up trader's basis for depreciation deductions, such as a trade of land with a rental house on it for a commercial office building offering substantial improvements to depreciate. The basis of the larger property acquired in the trade will usually be the up trader's book value for the old property plus the value of any additional encumbrances (mortgages) on the acquired property. Perhaps a simpler way of computing basis for the up trader on his acquired property is to subtract from its trade value (usually the same as market value) the amount of the untaxed profit on the property relinquished in the trade up.

TAX-DEFERRED EQUITY PYRAMIDING

Tax-deferred exchanges offer the only method of pyramiding one's investment into larger holdings without paying profit tax along the way. For the down trader, an exchange can be a way to dispose of property without being boosted into a high tax bracket in the year of sale.

The down trade can be combined with an installment sale to spread out the tax over several years and to increase the down trader's profit from the interest earnings on the unpaid balance owed to the down trader on the larger building acquired by the up trader.

Another aspect of equity pyramiding involves consolidating several properties into one large property. Many investors, for example, start out by acquiring one or two investment properties per year. Eventually all these little properties become a management headache. So the investor can combine them all into a trade and exchange for a large investment building that is efficient to manage.

Still another angle to equity pyramiding involves fixing up run-down property, thereby increasing its market value by more than the cost of the improvements, and then trading up to a larger "fix up" property. This is the principle that Nickerson and Lowry advocate in their formula of fortune building.

REQUIREMENTS FOR TAX-DEFERRED EXCHANGES

To comply with the simple requirements of Internal Revenue Code Section 1031 is quite easy. In the last few years these rules have become easier to meet by virtue of liberal court decisions, including the well-known Starker cases and the new Briggs ruling.

TRADING UP TO A LARGER PROPERTY

Exchanges are tax-deferred only for the party trading up from a smaller to a larger property if no boot is received by the up trader. To qualify, it must be a direct trade or a delayed "Starker" or "Biggs" exchange. The up trader cannot first sell his property and then use the proceeds to buy a larger property without owing tax on his sale profit (unless a Starker-type delayed exchange is documented).

Frequently, however, the "seller" of the larger property in the trade does not want to keep the smaller building. After the exchange is completed, the party receiving the smaller property in the exchange can sell it to a third-party cash buyer in a "cash out sale." This will not affect the up trader's tax deferral. Such an exchange is called a "three-way" or "cash out" trade.

EVEN EXCHANGES

Sometimes two taxpayers will make an even exchange of one property for another, with no cash or mortgages used to balance the equities. This is done most frequently by businesses seeking property more suitable for their business needs. Or it may be done by individuals seeking property of a different type.

EXAMPLE: Tom owns a lot that is zoned for apartments. Mark, a contractor, has just completed a fourplex apartment house that Tom would like to own. Mark would like to own Tom's lot on which he can build another apartment house for profit. Mark's equity in the apartment house (because it has a large mortgage on it) equals Tom's free and clear equity in the lot. So an even exchange can be made. However, Mark is the down trader and he will owe profit tax on his boot (net mortgage relief) received. As a builder, this does not bother Mark because he expected to pay tax on his profit. A down trader such as Mark should be aware of this profit taxation problem whenever boot is received in an exchange.

DOWN TRADES DISPOSE OF PROPERTY EQUITY

Each tax-deferred property exchange usually involves an up trader (who defers paying tax on his profit since he receives no boot) and a down trader (who owes tax on his profit since he receives boot). Boot (unlike property), of course, is taxable.

But trading down can be an excellent way to liquidate holdings which may otherwise be too large to sell. Another advantage of trading down is it can be a great way to dispose of property very profitably, pay tax on that profit, and defer the rest of the tax by liquidating gradually instead of all in one tax year.

> EXAMPLE: Mary wishes to retire and be free to travel if she can sell her $600,000 apartment house. Her depreciated book value is only $100,000, which is approximately the value of the nondepreciable land. In other words, Mary has run out of depreciation deductions. If Mary sells for cash, however (assuming a cash buyer can be found), she will owe tax on a $500,000 long-term capital gain.
>
> Len owns a parking lot, free and clear, worth $300,000, which is leased to a trucking company. He wants to acquire income property that will give him tax shelter from depreciation tax loss (but with positive cash flow).
>
> Mary agrees to accept Len's parking lot $300,000 equity in trade on her apartment house. Len gives Mary a mortgage on the apartment house for the $300,000 balance. Since this is a trade down for Mary, she will owe tax on the boot (the $300,000 mortgage) received. But Mary's tax on this boot profit will be taxed as an installment sale as she receives the payments from Len in future years. Mary accomplishes her desire of gradual liquidation and freedom from property management so she can travel. Len acquires the depreciable building he wants so both traders are happy.

The same result could have been attained whether or not these properties had mortgages on them before the trade. If Mary should need tax-free cash before Len pays off the $300,000 mortgage, she can probably hypothecate her mortgage at her bank and borrow on the security of that mortgage. Or Mary could mortgage the parking lot, tax-free, if she prefers since loan proceeds are not taxable.

HOW TO CALCULATE BASIS
FOR THE PROPERTY ACQUIRED IN A TRADE

Basis from a property traded in a tax-deferred exchange carries over to the property acquired in the trade, with several important adjustments. These adjustments to basis are made only if boot is received or gain is recognized (basis is reduced by boot received and increased by gain recognized, that is, taxed, in the exchange).

ADD:

A—Original purchase price or basis, including any mortgage, land contract, or trust deed to finance the original purchase

B—Capital improvements made during the ownership period

C—Boot or other property paid to acquire the property traded up to

D—Special assessments paid (e.g. sidewalks, sewers, streets)

E—Recognized (taxed) gain on which tax was paid

MINUS:

A—Boot received (cash or other "unlike" property) in the trade

B—Any mortgage or trust deed remaining after the trade (net mortgage relief)

C—Depreciation deducted during ownership on the property traded

D—Any casualty loss deducted from basis during the ownership period

RESULT:

Basis for the property acquired in the exchange

But a much easier way to arrive at the basis of the property received in an up trade is to subtract from its market value the amount of deferred gain traded as down payment. This is then the up trader's basis for the property acquired in the exchange.

EXAMPLE: Robert's basis in a rental house is $33,000. It is worth $45,000 market value. Subtracting a realtor's commission of $2,000, he has $10,000 net profit. Robert trades this rental house for a $100,000 apartment building. Robert's new basis in the apartment house will be $100,000 minus his $10,000 deferred gain, which is $90,000.

To avoid receiving taxable boot, usually cash or net mortgage relief, in an exchange, the taxpayer trading up should refrain from refinancing the larger property as part of the exchange. Any refinancing should wait until after the exchange is completed. Or its "seller" can refinance before the trade if he needs cash. If the refinance is part of the exchange, the mortgage on the property being traded may be classified as boot. By exchanging the two properties "subject to" their existing mortgages and not refinancing in the trade, this problem is avoided.

A SUCCESSFUL FOUR-WAY TAX-DEFERRED EXCHANGE

As explained earlier, the primary motivation for tax-deferred exchanges is to defer profit tax on the smaller property being traded up for the larger one. But another major motivation for an exchange can be to dispose of difficult-to-sell property which the owner no longer wants. Here is an actual trade which satisfied the property needs of four traders.

OWNER #1 (George) wanted to retire. He owned an apartment house worth $415,000. For two years he tried to find a buyer for it. He was even willing to accept a 10 percent cash down payment and take back a large secondary mortgage for the balance. But due to the location in a low-income area, buyers with $41,500 chose to invest in better neighborhoods.

OWNER #2 (Alice) had $20,000 cash, plus $40,000 free and clear equity in a vacant city lot which cost her money for property taxes, weed clearing, and trash removal. The lot produced no income and was difficult to sell because of its location in a low-income neighborhood. Alice wanted income.

So she offered to trade her $60,000 ($20,000 cash plus $40,000 lot equity) "down payment" for George's $415,000 apartment house. Owner #1, George, accepted the exchange offer, subject to a "cash out sale" of the lot for $40,000 cash. For Alice this will be a tax-deferred exchange up. For George, it will be a down trade, and he will owe tax on the $60,000 cash boot he eventually received in the exchange and subsequent cash out sale. George will have an installment sale on the remainder of his profit as Owner #2, Alice, pays off the mortgage to him on the $415,000 apartment house.

OWNER #3 (Vic) wants to buy the vacant lot which is zoned for light industry. Vic wants to build a small industrial building for his growing kitchen cabinet manufacturing business. But Vic has no cash with which to buy the lot. However, he does have about $45,000 equity in a six-unit apartment house in a city about fifty miles away.

Vic offers to trade his equity in the six-unit apartment house for the lot. George accepts, contingent upon cash out sale of the six apartments to produce not less than $40,000 cash after paying the realty agent's commission. A cooperating realty broker in the distant city is given the listing, and within a month, he decides to personally buy the six apartments for $40,000 cash down payment.

RESULTS. All four parties are happy (and so are the realty agents who split over $25,000 of sales commissions). Owner #1, George, got rid of his apartment house so he could retire. Owner #2, Alice, got rid of her vacant lot and obtained an income-producing property. Owner #3, Vic, acquired a lot on which to construct his manufacturing building. Owner #4, the realty broker, acquired a six-unit apartment house that he later profitably resold.

As a sidelight, Alice was a seventy-three-year-old widow acquiring her first apartment house. Three years later she sold the large apartment building for $550,000 for $20,000 cash down payment on an installment sale which produces for her (or her heirs) about $1,600 monthly net income for the next twenty years.

DELAYED TAX-DEFERRED PROPERTY EXCHANGES—STARKER AND BIGGS CASES

In April, 1975, Judge Gus J. Solomon of the Oregon Federal District Court rendered his landmark Starker I decision (75–1 USTC 87142). That decision held that a tax-deferred exchange occurs even if the up trader does not yet own the second property to be acquired in the trade. This case adds to Revenue Ruling 75–291 which approves nonrecognition (nontaxation) of loss or gain even if the property to be acquired in the up trade is specifically bought for the purpose of exchanging it. The holding of Starker I, in other words, was that trading of the properties in a tax-deferred exchange need not take place simultaneously.

In Starker I, Bruce and Elizabeth Starker received a purchase offer for their Oregon timber land from Crown-Zellerbach and Longview Fibre Company. The Starkers agreed to the transaction, but they directed the buyers to hold the money in trust until the Starkers could locate a second property for Crown-Zellerbach and Longview to buy and then trade to the Starkers to complete the tax-deferred exchange.

Crown-Zellerbach and Longview were directed by the Starkers to buy eight parcels between 1968 and 1972. The IRS disallowed this transaction as a tax-deferred exchange. But Judge Solomon ruled it qualified for tax deferral under IRC 1031. The IRS, after originally filing an appeal, dropped the appeal for some unexplained reason.

But in May 1977, serious doubt was cast on the precedent value of Starker I. Judge Solomon rendered a contrary opinion in Starker II, involving Bruce's father, T. J. Starker (77–2 USTC 87675, 432 Fed. Supp. 864). But Judge Solomon's ruling in Starker II was reversed on appeal by the U.S. Court of Appeals for the Ninth Circuit (602 F.2d 1341). In Starker II, the appeals court approved the result of Starker I and allowed T. J. Starker to rely on it as precedent.

The facts of Starker II are important to understanding the new "delayed-exchange" concept. In 1967 T. J. Starker received an offer from Crown-Zellerbach Corporation to buy his 1,843 acres of Oregon timberland. Because Starker did not want to sell, but C-Z needed his land, C-Z agreed to find Starker other suitable properties and to trade these at a later date for the timberland that they immediately acquired. C-Z promised to hold the $1,502,500 timberland money in trust until Starker could find properties for C-Z to buy and then trade to Starker to complete the tax-deferred exchange. In addition, C-Z agreed to add a 6 percent annual "growth factor" to the value. By 1969 when Starker located all the properties, his credit had grown to $1,577,387.91.

In the Starker II decision, Judge Goodwin of the Court of Appeals for the Ninth Circuit ruled this "delayed exchange" qualified as a tax-deferred exchange under Internal Revenue Code Section 1031. But he said the 6 percent growth factor was taxable as interest in the year received.

However, Goodwin ruled this was not a tax-deferred trade as to two properties acquired by C-Z at Starker's direction, since he ordered them conveyed to his daughter, Jean Roth, instead of to Starker. But Goodwin ruled that tax-deferral applied to the other ten properties acquired by C-Z and then conveyed to Starker to complete the exchange.

STARKER OPENS NEW TRADING OPPORTUNITIES

Although the Starker cases open new trading opportunities, certain cautions apply. Of course, a real estate attorney should always be used to draft the documents that follow guidelines outlined in the Starker cases.

1. The contract must boldly express the taxpayer's desire for a tax-deferred exchange, not to receive cash for the purchase of his property.
2. If an interest or "growth factor" is charged on the proceeds being held in a trust arrangement, that looks like a sale rather than an exchange.
3. If the up trader has a right to receive the cash paid for his property instead of finding other property to complete the exchange, then the IRS auditor would have strong grounds for denying a tax-deferred trade. Leaving the money in an escrow, where the up trader has a right to claim his money at any time, clearly will not qualify. Some type of trust arrangement is required so the money is beyond the up trader's reach. Although this was not necessary because Crown-Zellerbach could be trusted to keep the money in the Starker cases, most traders are not dealing with such high-caliber buyers.
4. The seller's contract rights should be nonassignable (to block the IRS argument the transaction was really a sale rather than an exchange).
5. Consult with an experienced real estate or tax attorney who has handled Starker-type exchanges previously.

The IRS has alerted its auditors to challenge Starker-type exchanges whenever possible. However, there is no IRS form for reporting property exchanges so their existence usually only becomes known if the taxpayer's return is audited. The telltale sign is the disappearnce of one property off the taxpayer's return and the appearance of a new property without the report of any long- or short-term capital gain transaction.

Starker "delayed" exchanges are a rapidly developing new area of tax-deferred exchange law that makes exchanges easier than ever. The philosophy behind Starker exchanges is (a) a buyer wants to acquire a property now, (b) he is offering a good price and terms, (c) if the seller does not immediately accept the purchase offer, the buyer may not wait until the seller can find another property for a direct tax-deferred exchange, (d) it is better to attempt a Starker "delayed" exchange than to pay tax on an outright sale.

Although the Starker decisions are technically binding on the IRS only in states in the Ninth Circuit (Alaska, Arizona, California, Hawaii, Idaho, Montana, Nevada, Oregon, and Washington), taxpayers in other states are using Starker-type exchanges too. But the IRS is not bound by the Starker concept except in the Ninth Circuit so taxpayers should be aware of this situation.

THE UNIQUE BIGGS CASE

In December 1980, the Court of Appeals for the Fifth Circuit (with authority in Alabama, Florida, Georgia, Louisiana, Mississippi, and Texas) ruled in the tax-deferred exchange case involving *Franklin B. Biggs* (632 F.2d 1171). Upholding the tax court's approval of a tax-deferred exchange, the appeals court further liberalized the exchange concept.

The facts in the Biggs case, greatly simplified, involved a Maryland tract of land that Biggs wanted to exchange for a Virginia parcel. Biggs had a buyer for the Maryland land, Mr. Powell. But Powell apparently either would not or could not acquire the Virginia land to trade to Biggs for the Maryland land. So Biggs loaned the Shore Title Company money to acquire the Virginia land, which was then traded to Biggs for his Maryland land. After the trade, the Maryland land was deeded to Powell (who then immediately resold the Maryland land at a substantial profit).

The issue was whether this qualified as a tax-deferred exchange because (a) Powell never had title to the Virginia land, and (b) Biggs supplied the cash with which the Virginia land was purchased by Shore Title so it could be traded to Biggs.

Frankly, the documentation was very sloppy in this case because the wording used terms of "sale" rather than "exchange." A few commentators feel this case means "anything goes" as long as it looks like an exchange after the smoke clears. But more rational commentators believe the Biggs case (a) means indirect deeding in an exchange is all right, (b) it must be clear that the exchanger at no time had a right to receive cash proceeds from the exchange, and (c) advance of funds by the exchanger to a fourth party to acquire the property to be acquired in the trade is all right.

At the least, the Biggs case strengthens the Starker concept of a delayed tax-deferred exchange. Simultaneous, direct deeding of the properties is clearly no longer required to qualify for a IRC 1031 tax-deferred trade.

Although Biggs was successful in deferring his profit tax, future exchangers are cautioned to use careful documentation prepared by a real estate or tax attorney to make sure an exchange can be proven, if necessary, to the IRS.

SUMMARY

Tax-deferred exchanges are the only way for owners of investment, trade, or business property to dispose of one property and acquire another such "like-kind" property without paying tax on their profit. Such trades have become more flexible since the Starker and Biggs court decisions, but the requirements of Internal Revenue Code Section 1031 must still be met. In this area of real estate transactions, assistance of an experienced real estate or tax attorney is essential to avoid adverse tax consequences.

QUESTIONS AND ANSWERS

Q. You've said the best way to avoid paying tax when disposing of investment property is to make a "tax-deferred exchange" for a larger such property. As we own a four-family apartment building with about $40,000 equity, how can we use such a trade to get a bigger apartment house without paying tax on our profit of about $25,000?—*Gwinn A.*

A. Virtually the only way to dispose of investment or business property without paying profit tax is to make a tax-deferred exchange as authorized by Internal Revenue Code Section 1031.

For example, suppose your apartment building is worth $100,000 and you owe $60,000 on the mortgage. Your equity is therefore $40,000. If you sell outright, you would pay tax on your $25,000 profit. But if you trade your $40,000 equity as down payment on a larger "like-kind" investment property, you defer the tax until the acquired property is sold without trading again.

As you can see, exchanging is an excellent way to pyramid a small equity into a fortune, all without any tax erosion along the way. However, you cannot take any "boot" out of the trade. Boot means "unlike property," such as cash or net mortgage relief.

If you trade for a larger property owned for investment or use in your trade or business (called an "up trade"), it should be tax-deferred for you. The down trader, however, will owe tax on all or part of his profit. Work with a good realty exchange specialist who can show you how to make your exchange work, usually by use of a three-way (three-party) trade where a third-party cash buyer purchases your property after you make the tax-deferred exchange.

HOW TO PYRAMID YOUR PROPERTY PROFIT
WITHOUT PAYING TAX

Q. We own some farmland for which we have received an excellent purchase offer. But the tax on our profit would be huge. I recall your saying it is possible to exchange properties without paying any tax. Please explain how that might work for us. We would like to acquire some property that would produce tax shelter and income, such as a small shopping center or maybe apartments.—*Bennie S.*

A. You are an excellent candidate for a tax-deferred "like-kind" property exchange. For example, suppose your farmland is worth $500,000. You can make a tax-deferred trade of it for any other property, except a personal residence, worth $500,000 or more if you do not take any "boot" out of the trade. Boot includes personal property such as cash or net mortgage relief.

Your exchange would work like this. You trade your farmland for, perhaps, a small shopping center of equal or greater value. But your farmland would be traded subject to the purchase offer you have for it. One minute after your tax-deferred exchange is completed, the other trader can sell your farmland for cash to the third-party buyer you already have lined up. It is called a three-way exchange because there are three parties involved.

By means of tax-deferred trades, you can pyramid your farmland equity into a fortune without having your profit eroded by income taxes. See your tax adviser for details.

HOW TO FIND REALTY AGENTS
WHO LIKE TO TRADE PROPERTIES

Q. I've enjoyed your explanations of tax-deferred exchanges. As I own a two-family rental house that I would like to trade, tax-deferred, for a larger income property, where can I find a realty agent who understands exchanging? I've talked to several, and they tell me exchanging isn't done here.—*Wendy T.*

A. Tax-deferred property trades are made in large and small towns throughout the country. Some realty agents are afraid of exchanges because they have not bothered to educate themselves about them. A sale is much easier, of course. But wise agents prefer exchanges because two commissions are involved.

One way to find local property exchange specialists is to phone your local board of realtors for a roster of their exchange club members. Another way is to contact real estate brokers who specialize in commercial properties; these firms usually have real estate exchange specialists.

NO TIME LIMIT ON STARKER EXCHANGE TIME LAG

Q. Your report on the new Starker "delayed-exchange" concept was very educational. What is the time limit from the day the first property is sold until the second property must be acquired to complete the tax-deferred Starker exchange?—*Betty W.*

A. There is no time limit. Basically, the Starker decision of the Court of Appeals for the Ninth Circuit held it is possible to defer profit tax when selling one property if the proceeds of that sale are held in a trust arrangement beyond the reach of the seller. The trustee can then be directed by that seller to buy a second property with that money and deliver the title to the up trader.

The Starker exchange time lag can be several years. But both properties must be held for investment or for use in a trade or business. Keep your personal residence out of such exchanges. Your tax adviser can explain further.

ATTORNEY WARNS OF STARKER TAX-DEFERRED TRADE PITFALLS

Q. You are to be commended for writing of the tax benefits of the new Starker "delayed" exchanges and for cautioning readers to always use a real estate attorney for such tax-deferred exchanges.

However, I think you have been remiss for not emphasizing two other aspects. One is that the IRS has indicated it will challenge Starker-type trades, even though the Court of Appeals for the Ninth Circuit has approved the technique. As you know, the IRS does not have to and often refuses to follow court rulings in future similar tax situations.

Second, I think it is important to emphasize that it is better for a taxpayer to try a "Starker exchange" and probably defer his profit tax than to make an ordinary property sale and surely pay the tax. As a real estate attorney, I have handled dozens of Starker-type exchanges, but I always caution my clients that the IRS may disallow the tax-deferral. By use of a trust arrangement to hold the cash sale proceeds until a second property can be found to complete the trade, I believe the tests established by the Starker decision are met.—*John H.*

A. Thank you for your suggestions with which I fully agree. Although the IRS did not appeal the Starker decision, future IRS challenges of such delayed trades can be expected.

For readers not familiar with a Starker tax-deferred exchange of property held for investment or business use, it is a way to avoid paying profit tax when selling one property and buying a more expensive replacement. This method does not apply to sale of the taxpayer's principal residence.

By use of a trust agreement to hold the sale proceeds until the second property is found to complete the exchange, a Starker trade can qualify for tax-deferral allowed by Internal Revenue Code Section 1031.

HOW TO BUILD YOUR PYRAMID OF TAX-DEFERRED REAL ESTATE PROFITS

Q. At a dinner last week, the man next to me said it is possible to "pyramid" real estate profits, tax-free, by trading up from a small property into larger ones. He tried to explain the concept to me, but I don't understand. You explain real estate so well; please explain realty pyramids to me.—*Sonnie M.*

A. Internal Revenue Code Section 1031 encourages tax-deferred, "like-kind" real estate exchanges. The basic idea is to trade your equity in a small property as down payment on a larger one. After the second property's equity grows, often due to improvements that increase value more than they cost, then the second property can be traded for a larger investment property. The profit tax can again be deferred. It is called pyramiding. There is no limit to the number of times this tax concept can be used in a chain of tax-deferred exchanges.

Advantages of tax-deferred property trades include no income tax erosion, increased tax deductions from depreciation of larger properties, and tax-deferred estate building.

To qualify for a "like-kind," tax-deferred exchange, both properties must be held for investment or for use in your trade or business. In other words, your personal residence and personal property cannot qualify. Trades are usually tax-deferred for the "up trader" if he receives no "boot," such as cash or net mortgage relief. Your tax adviser or realty exchange specialist can give you further details.

HOW CAN I TRADE MY HOME FOR APARTMENTS?

Q. You wrote that a tax-deferred exchange applies only to "like-kind" properties, such as apartments and commercial buildings. Is there any way I can trade the equity in my home, about $65,000, for income property? —*Corla S.*

A. Yes. Your personal residence is "unlike property," which cannot qualify for a tax-deferred exchange if you wish to acquire investment or business property.

But you can convert your home into "like-kind" property by (1) moving out and (2) renting it to tenants. The law does not specify how long you must rent it to tenants. Just to be safe, six to twelve months should be adequate. Then trade your home for the income property you want to acquire. If you trade up to more-expensive investment or business property, without receiving any taxable boot in the exchange, it will be a tax-deferred exchange for you.

10.

How Realty Brokers Can Help Accomplish Your Real Estate Goals

Real estate agents have the best job in the world—and they know it. They have the opportunity for unlimited earnings, freedom to work as hard or as little as they want, flexible working hours, and nonroutine work. But there are drawbacks too, such as peaks and valleys in their commission earnings (also called feast or famine), frequent evening and weekend working hours, and intense competition with other agents.

The quality of real estate agents has vastly improved in the last few years. Real estate sales attracts the finest people you will ever meet. But it also attracts some of the sleaziest characters too, probably because it is possible to earn a handsome income without working too hard. Real estate, due to its financial structure, opens doors to all types of "innovative finance," some of which is not completely honest.

In other words, do not put blind trust in a real estate agent. Make them back up their statements unless they are just expressing their opinions, such as "I think this is the best neighborhood in town." But if the agent says "This house is in perfect condition," that is a statement you should have in writing signed by the agent and the seller, just in case it is not true.

REAL ESTATE AGENTS ARE THE PROPERTY INVESTOR'S BEST FRIENDS

By virtue of their daily contacts, realty agents know who is buying and selling. The top agents keep files of buyers and sellers of specialized properties. It is not unusual for a good agent, when he learns of a new listing, to sell it within twenty-four hours to a buyer he knows will buy that type of property. A quick sale like that can save the seller hundreds, sometimes thousands of dollars, in carrying costs.

Buying through real estate agents costs the buyer no more than if he purchased direct from the seller. The reason is the market value of a property is determined from recent sales prices of similar nearby properties. Since the buyer is going to pay market value anyway, he might as well get all the extra services provided by a realty agent.

To understand better how to work with realty agents, let us view the situation from the perspective of a home seller. Later, tips on how buyers can effectively work with realty agents will be explained.

HOW TO SELL YOUR HOME WITH OR WITHOUT A REAL ESTATE AGENT

Selling your residence, whether it is a single-family home, condominium, mobile home, or even a houseboat is the greatest profit opportunity you will probably ever have. But home sellers must be careful not to make costly mistakes that can cut into their resale profit. Thousands of dollars can be lost when selling property if it is not done right.

GETTING YOUR HOME READY FOR SALE

When you go to your job each day, or when you go out for a special event such as a party or dinner, you prepare. You probably take a bath, brush your teeth, and put on clean clothes. Getting your home ready for sale is a similar process that also requires preparation. The goal is to present your home at its best. Just as an actor or actress wants to show his or her talent in a play or movie, your home should give its best appearance when you present it for sale to prospective buyers.

Painting and cleaning a home for sale is the cheapest, yet most profitable, step to take before putting your home on the market for sale. Get it in top condition. Perhaps even invite your mother-in-law or other supercritical person to inspect it and to make suggestions for fixing it up for sale.

Home buyers have remarkably little imagination. They often cannot visualize how desirable a home can look after it is painted and fixed up. That is why you, the seller, must make the home look its best to help the buyer visualize how desirable your home can be.

Even though the buyer may not like your choice of colors, and will probably repaint shortly after buying your home, having your home appear at its best will command top sales price and terms. A home that is in bad condition invites buyers to look for defects, thus hurting your negotiating power on sale price and terms. Many potential buyers will not even make purchase offers on a home that is in less than first class condition.

The idea is to make your home physically so attractive that its condition will not be objectionable to any buyer. *If you do not fix up your home before sale, it will appeal to only a very limited market of buyers.*

Those buyers are the bargain hunters—also known as the forty thieves!

They buy only at rock bottom prices. But if the home is dirty and in bad condition, these are the only buyers it will appeal to.

Within reason, correct all significant defects in your home before putting it up for sale. For example, new gutters make buyers confident of the home's structural integrity. But leaky gutters cast doubt on the building's entire condition by indicating the owner probably has not maintained the home very well.

BUT DON'T GO OVERBOARD! Overimprovement for the level of homes in the neighborhood will not pay off. To illustrate, adding a $20,000 swimming pool to a home in a working-class area of two-bedroom, one-bathroom homes in the $75,000 price range probably will not produce a high enough additional sales price to even pay for the pool's cost.

FIX-UP COST TAX BENEFITS

In Chapter 3, the "residence replacement rule" and the home sale fix-up cost myth were explained. Just for emphasis, it should be remembered that costs of fixing up your principal residence for sale, contrary to popular myth, never qualify as itemized income tax deductions. The only tax benefit for fix-up costs (home cleaning, painting, and repairing costs that normally have no income tax significance because they are personal living expenses) occurs when selling your old principal residence and buying a less-expensive replacement within eighteen months before or after the sale.

Home sale fix-up costs, as emphasized in Chapter 3, will never eliminate any profit tax. But they can postpone the time of tax payment if a less-expensive replacement principal residence is purchased. If a more-expensive replacement is bought, the tax is postponed anyway, with or without the fix-up cost expenses. Such fix-up expenses must (a) be incurred within ninety days before signing the home sale agreement (not the listing but the sales contract) and (b) be paid for within thirty days after the sale closing.

Of course, capital improvement costs, such as for a new furnace, new roof, or new wall-to-wall carpets, should be capitalized and added to your home's purchase price cost basis. Save the receipts forever!

HOW TO DETERMINE YOUR HOME'S FAIR MARKET VALUE

After your home is all spruced up, looking its best, and ready for sale, the issue becomes "How much is my home worth?"

The answer is determined from the local real estate market. Recent sales prices for similar homes in your neighborhood determine the price at which a willing buyer will buy your home, assuming you are under no urgent pressure to sell for less than its fair market value. Generally, homes need to be exposed to the marketplace for at least ninety days.

They should sell within this time at their true market value.

Home prices are based on fair market value, as determined by recent sales prices of comparable neighborhood homes. Your home's value is *not* based on (1) how much you think it is worth, (b) how much you need to get to make a good profit, (3) how much you have invested in the home, or (4) how much you need to get from the home to pay your other expenses.

For example, although the home next door to yours is different, if both your home and the one next door have three bedrooms, two bathrooms, and six rooms, and the one next door sold last month for $100,000, your home is probably worth about the same amount, with adjustments higher or lower for any significant differences in features or condition.

There are two excellent methods of determining your home's fair market value.

A. Professional Appraisal of Fair Market Value

An appraisal of a home's fair market value is an expert appraiser's opinion of its probable sales price, based on recent sales prices of similar neighborhood homes (or your home's replacement cost, minus depreciation, if it is of unusual design and there are no comparables available).

Professional appraisals cost from $100 to $200 for an average home and are especially recommended for home sellers considering selling without the professional services of a real estate agent. Local banks and savings associations can usually recommend experienced residential appraisers. Be sure to select an appraiser with home appraisal experience.

But remember that an appraisal is only an expert's opinion of your home's value, so be sure to hire an appraiser familiar with recent residential sales in your area. Be sure to tell the appraiser you want a thorough, written appraisal that you can show to prospective buyers and real estate agents.

B. Comparative Market Analysis

Another method of determining your home's market value is to invite several active local real estate agents to give you their listing presentation. Most realty agents will be happy to prepare a free written "comparative market analysis" showing recent neighborhood home sales prices, including the home's size, sale price, and terms. Of course, they hope to get your listing by doing this work for you. Any agent who does not prepare such a written analysis should probably be dismissed from your listing competition.

A comparative market analysis will show not only recent sales prices (not listing prices), but also current asking prices of unsold homes available for sale (your competition).

THE ASKING PRICE SETTING PROCEDURE

Setting the asking price for a home is critical. Set it too low, and you have lost part of what could have been profit. Set it too high, and your home will remain unsold for a long time. Costs of holding an unsold home add up quickly, especially if you have already bought another home and are making payments on two homes at the same time.

Home buyers are not dumb. They are hard to fool. That is because they know home values by comparative shopping. Many potential buyers have been looking for months and have inspected dozens of homes for sale. Some know more about market value of local homes than do realty agents who do not keep up with recent sales prices.

Although it is considered good practice to set your home's asking price a little above the price you expect to accept (to allow room for negotiation on terms), setting the price too high repels buyers who will not even inspect an overpriced home. Setting the asking price about 5 percent above the price you expect to accept will not normally discourage buyers from inspecting your home and making a purchase offer if they like it.

HOW TO DECIDE WHETHER OR NOT TO HIRE A REAL ESTATE AGENT TO MARKET YOUR HOME

Most home sellers are confronted with the question of whether or not to use a real estate agent to market their home. The main reason for not using an agent, of course, is to save the sales commission. On a typical home sale at $75,000, for example, the average 6 percent sales commission saving is $4,500. Or is it?

Nationwide, home mortgage lenders report an average of eleven mortgage loans made on sales arranged by realty agents for every mortgage on a "for sale by owner" (FSBO) home sale. There must be reasons why eleven out of twelve home sellers use real estate agents. Yet there are some home sellers who have no need to use a real estate agent to market their home. Consider the pros and cons of hiring an agent or not.

SETTING THE SALES PRICE

Even if you obtained a professional appraisal of your home's market value, it pays to double-check it. The appraiser may not have been fully aware of a rapidly appreciating or declining local market which even the best real estate agents, frankly, have difficulty anticipating.

Therefore, every home seller should invite at least three local realty agents to evaluate his home's value, using the "comparative market analysis" approach. Select agents whose "sold" signs or newspaper advertising in your area attracted your attention. Do not, however, be "snowed" by the fancy ads of some nationwide franchise organizations that, after all, depend on locally owned independent offices and the services of their local realty agents.

Invite these three or more agents to "bid" on listing your home. Tell them frankly you are undecided about listing your home with an agent. Explain that you want their opinion of your home's market value *and why!* Any agent who cannot or will not explain how your home's estimated sales price was computed should not be seriously considered further. That means disregarding any agent who does not give you a written market value analysis.

Ask about the marketing services each agent will offer if he or she gets your listing. Ask for references of at least three previous clients from each agent and check them out by phone. Ask the client references "Would you list your home for sale again with this agent?" Do not be afraid of young or new agents—sometimes they are very eager to succeed and will work twice as hard as a salesperson who has been very successful in realty sales and who now is taking life easy.

After interviewing at least three realty agents, and checking their client references, then decide (a) if you can handle the sale of your home without a realty agent, and (b) if you elect to list with an agent, list with the best (not necessarily the agent who estimates the highest sales price). Here are the factors to consider in making your decision whether or not to hire an agent:

A. Advertising

Are you prepared to write newspaper want ads about your home? How much will the advertising cost? Who will answer the phone? What information will be given out on the phone? What time will inspections be allowed? Will you have to take off work to accommodate a prospective buyer who wants to see your home? Will you hold weekend open houses? Are you familiar with Regulation Z (Truth in Lending) limitations on advertising finance terms, such as down payment, interest rate, mortgage amount, and other finance conditions? Are you going to have a lawn "for sale by owner" (FSBO) sign? How can you effectively compete with the many homes agents have in the multiple listing service since you have only one home to sell?

B. Financing

Are you familiar with current available mortgage finance terms? FHA? VA? State mortgage programs? Installment sale benefits? Purchase-money mortgage terms to be included in any seller financing? Land contract benefits and pitfalls? Existing mortgage payoff and prepayment penalty, if any? How large should the earnest money deposit be? Should the current mortgage be assumed or should the house be sold "subject to" its existing mortgage?

C. Can You Write a Legally Binding Contract?

Are you prepared to negotiate the sale price and terms in face-to-face negotiations with the buyer? Do you or other family members become upset easily, especially when involved in financial matters? Are you aware how many bargain-hunters prey on "for sale by owner" (FSBO) sellers? Can you draw up a legally binding sales contract? Do you have an attorney who has advised you on essential terms to include? Can you qualify your buyer to be sure he can really afford to buy your home and is not wasting your time?

D. Sale Terms and Conditions

Are you able to negotiate with a buyer regarding sales terms, such as financing, who pays title insurance, transfer tax, escrow fee, attorney fee, fire insurance premium, and other negotiable costs? What about property tax proration, move-in date, rental for hold-over occupancy, personal property items included and excluded, hidden defects in the home that buyer must be told about, and title transfer date?

E. Urgency

Is a rapid sale necessary to avoid paying for two homes at the same time, or due to an out-of-town job transfer?

F. Security

Can you screen out potential troublemakers and even thieves from the serious buyers? Can the home be shown at any time or only when you are not at work? How can you know if the person ringing the doorbell for an inspection is a serious buyer or a curiosity seeker?

G. Closing the Sale

Are you familiar with local title settlement closing procedures? Is an attorney necessary? Will the lender require title insurance? An abstract? Escrow? How will the documents be recorded, loan papers processed, old loans paid off, and liens cleared?

A FINAL WORD ON SELLING YOUR HOME ALONE

Lawyers have a motto: "He who is his own lawyer has a fool for a client." That same wisdom may apply to home sellers who try to sell their own home without professional marketing help from a real estate agent. One costly mistake can cost a home seller far more than the sales commission he thought he was saving by selling his own home.

HOW TO MARKET YOUR INVESTMENT PROPERTY

Selling a home is easy compared to marketing investment or business property. The reason is smart investors do not sell their property, they exchange it to avoid having to pay tax on their profit.

As emphasized in Chapter 9, tax-deferred exchanges are much easier to make than they previously were. No longer are direct, simultaneous exchanges required. Delayed "Starker exchanges" and "Biggs exchanges" are now available. But they require the assistance of a real estate or tax attorney who know how to document delayed exchanges. Such exchanges also require the services of a real estate agent who understands the mechanics of Starker and Biggs exchanges.

Frankly, finding these experts for the legal and marketing aspects of tax-deferred exchanges is not easy. Realty agents who handle residential sales are not qualified, in most cases, to handle tax-deferred exchanges, but they can often recommend exchange specialists who understand the procedures for both direct and delayed tax-deferred exchanges.

Locating a real estate or tax attorney to handle the documentation can be equally difficult because most attorneys have never heard of Starker or Biggs exchanges. One good method for finding such an attorney, in addition to asking for recommendations from realty agents and exchange specialists, is to check with local universities and community colleges offering real estate law or taxation courses. The instructor of those classes is usually a part-time instructor and a full-time real estate or tax attorney who thoroughly understands tax-deferred exchanges.

Real estate agents can accomplish miracles for property owners and buyers in the investment field. But investment or commercial specialists are a different breed from the typical residential salesperson. If you are involved with investment property, such as apartments, offices, and other commerical property, it is best to work with a specialist in that field because most residential sales agents are not qualified to handle commercial sales too.

QUESTIONS AND ANSWERS

BE CAREFUL OF REALTY AGENT'S OPINION STATEMENTS

Q. Were we swindled? We bought a house that the realty agent said was "in tip-top condition?" After we moved in, we found the cement foundation had a bad crack which cost us over $4,000 to have rebuilt. Do you think we should sue the agent for his misrepresentation?—*Eve C.*

A. See your attorney. Remarks by real estate agents, such as "This is the best house on the block" are usually just opinion statements that carry no legal liability. But if the agent misrepresents the house intentionally, then the agent is liable for resulting damage.

For example, if the agent says "This house has all copper pipes," and it doesn't, the agent is liable for damages. But if he says "I think the plumbing is in good condition," that is probably just an opinion statement which incurs no legal liability.

ARE LISTING CANCELLATION FEES NORMAL?

Q. We want to cancel the listing on our home as we've decided not to sell after all. Our agent says there is a $400 "cancellation fee" for his expenses and time. I recall several months ago you told another reader to just let her listing quietly expire when she changed her mind about selling. Do we have to pay the cancellation fee?—*Alan A.*

A. No. Some realty brokers charge listing cancellation fees to discourage sellers from changing their minds. But if you take my suggestion and quietly let your listing expire, you owe nothing to the listing agent.

Of course, if he brings you a purchase offer which exactly meets the listing terms and if you do not accept that offer, then you will owe the agent the full sales commission. But this is highly unlikely. Ask your attorney to explain further.

REALTY SALES COMMISSION SAVING CAN CAUSE NET LOSS

Q. As I was reading your article about the benefits of selling a home with a real estate agent's help, I thought of my former neighbor who felt she saved the realty commission by selling her home without any agent. Her attorney handled the whole transaction for a fee of about $700, she told me. Although I didn't say anything, I know my neighbor sold her home for at least $7,000 below the going rate for neighborhood homes at the time. Your explanation does an excellent job of laying out the pros and cons of selling one's home without any agent.—*Scottie M.*

A. Thank you for the compliment. People who sell their property without a realty agent, of course, save the real estate sales commission. But that saving often results in a net loss, as you emphasize, because they sell too cheaply. There are many other pitfalls of selling without professional marketing help, especially in today's unusual real estate sales market.

WHY SOME LAWYERS ARE KNOWN AS "DEAL KILLERS"

Q. Do you think we should have a lawyer advise us on the sale of our home? The realty agent who will be getting our listing strongly advises against also hiring a lawyer. We told her we wanted our lawyer to advise us. I had the feeling the agent was trying to keep us away from our lawyer's office. Do we need a lawyer?—*Ken L.*

A. Lawyers can perform valuable services in advising on the legal aspects of a property sale. But be sure your lawyer advises only on the law, not on the marketing aspects of the sale, or you will get into a hopeless conflict with your realty agent.

Unfortunately, unless a lawyer specializes in real estate law, he may not have kept up to date on changes in realty law and customs. Another problem is that some of my fellow lawyers give low priority to real estate sales transactions since the "big money" is in other fields such as personal injury and business law. Lastly, a few lawyers feel they must justify their fees, so they nit-pick and find minor objections which result in the sale not closing.

If you have a lawyer who understands real estate law, he or she can be of great assistance in a realty transaction. To test the lawyer on his real estate knowledge, ask for an explanation of how a "Starker exchange" and a "Biggs exchange" works. If the lawyer cannot explain those important cases to you in simple language in less than five minutes, find another lawyer.

HOW TO AVOID OVERPRICING
OR UNDERPRICING YOUR HOME FOR SALE

Q. We want to put our home up for sale. There is a nice real estate lady who stops by about once a month with a little real estate newsletter. We are thinking of giving her our listing. Last time I saw her I asked how much she thought our house was worth. She says she's sure she can get us at least $97,000. How can I be certain this price isn't too low?—*Sara I.*

A. The best way to avoid overpricing or underpricing your home is to invite at least three active local realty agents to give you their listing presentations. A major part of their explanation should be a written "comparative market analysis" prepared by each agent.

This form will show you in black and white the recent sales prices of similar nearby homes and the selling terms. Each agent will then help you add or subtract value, depending on your home's advantages and drawbacks, to arrive at an estimate of its current market value. Only by having at least three of these market analysis forms from different agents can you be sure each agent used the most recent and accurate sales price data.

Another approach is to hire a professional appraiser to estimate your home's current market value.

When you talk to the agents, be sure to ask for client references of previous sellers. Before listing with any agent, phone those previous sellers to ask "Would you list your home with that agent again?" and "Were you in any way unhappy with the agent's service?"

WILL RECESSION MEAN FALLING HOME PRICES?

Q. Do you think home sales prices will drop soon? I ask because we are considering selling our present home and buying a larger one for our growing family. If you think prices will drop, maybe we should sell now and wait until prices drop to buy a new home. In the meantime, we could rent.—*Kevin T.*

A. In the 1974–1975 recession, home prices did not drop in most communities. Due to continuing demand for homes, especially from the forty-two million new potential home buyers who will reach age thirty in the 1980s, plus the rapidly increasing numbers of single-person households, I do not expect any significant home sale price decreases now.

If mortgage interest rates drop a little, buyers will come out of the woodwork. This increasing demand, with a limited supply of homes for sale, especially in areas where home-building volume has dropped, should result in rising prices for homes.

To summarize, buy now before prices go higher. You should be able to get a good price for your home if you "package" it right with affordable financing for your buyer.

HOW TO FIND THE SECOND-BEST REALTY AGENT IN TOWN

Q. I want to sell my former home in the city where I used to live. As I only know one real estate agent there, I'm wondering the best way to go about the sale. My friend works for a tiny realty brokerage. I really don't have much confidence in her sales ability as she only works part-time. How should I select a real estate agent to sell my old home, which is now rented to a tenant?—*Wes M.*

A. Before you list your home for sale, ask your tenant if he would like to buy. He is your most logical buyer.

But if he does not want to buy, phone your agent friend. Ask her to inspect your house and give you a written "comparative market analysis" of its value. Then ask her for the names of the second- and third-best real estate salespeople in town.

Phone them and ask them to also give you a market analysis showing your home's value and why you should list it for sale with them. Ask all three agents for reference names of former sellers. Then phone those clients to inquire if they would list with their agent again.

Spending a few dollars on phone bills is a cheap way to select the best agent to sell your old home. By the way, do not be suckered by the agent who estimates the highest sales price. Select the agent with the best success record. All things being equal, steer away from part-time realty agents as they usually cannot give you first class service on your listing.

LISTINGS CREATE SPECIAL DUTIES FOR REALTY AGENTS

Q. About four months ago, we listed our home for sale with a real estate agent we thought was reputable. Since then we have hardly heard from her, except just before the listing was about to expire. Then she held two weekend open houses and advertised our home in the newspaper twice. We have been very disappointed. Through a friend we heard our agent discouraged several prospects from making offers on our home. We now realize our asking price is a little high, but we followed our agent's advice on this. What should we do to get our home sold?—*Vivian M.*

A. When you signed that listing with your real estate agent, special duties were created by that contract. Your agent undertook to use "due diligence" to find a buyer for your home. She also undertook to inform you of all "material facts" which develop during the listing term.

Material facts include purchase offers that prospective buyers wish to make. Ask your agent about those alleged offers. All offers, no matter how ridiculous, must be presented to sellers during the listing term. Failure to present all offers is a violation of the principal-agent listing contract and grounds to revoke the agent's license.

But a listing is a two-way contract. You, the seller, have a duty to keep your agent informed of all material facts that develop, such as change in the home's condition or your desire to reduce the asking price.

It is possible the agent overestimated your home's market value. Perhaps she was using old data of comparable sales prices of nearby similar homes. Or maybe the local market was rising, and she anticipated a further price rise which did not materialize.

While 99 percent of all real estate agents do a satisfactory job for their clients, it appears your agent is doing less than her best. When your listing expires, switch to a better agent. But check that agent's client references thoroughly. Before listing, ask the new agent's last three sellers if they would list their home for sale with that agent again.

READER SHOUTS PRAISES FOR MULTIPLE LISTINGS

Q. Why don't you ever mention all the benefits of multiple listings? We listed our home for sale last spring with a realty agent who has several offices. She said she doesn't like to use the multiple listing exchange because her firm has so many salespeople it sells most of its listings within the company. But our house didn't sell. When the listing expired we switched to another agent who works in a small office of only four salespeople. He put our exclusive listing into the multiple listing exchange, and within a week another agent from another realty company sold our home to his buyer. You ought to tell people about the benefits of using the multiple listings which didn't cost us anything extra.—*Grace M.*

A. Many times I have encouraged home sellers to insist their realty agent use the multiple listing service. The multiple listing exchange distributes listings to all member realty agents who may have buyers waiting to buy particular types of properties.

The reason a few realty agents are reluctant to use the multiple listing service is they earn a bigger share of the sales commission if the sale is made by two salespeople who work for the same firm. I believe this is not in the best interests of the seller because nonuse of multiple listings limits the seller's market exposure of the home, as you found out. Thanks for your letter telling of your good results from using the multiple listing service.

REALTY AGENTS MUST PRESENT
EVEN RIDICULOUS OFFERS

Q. You're always telling home buyers to "make an offer." That's what we've been trying to do as we badly want to buy a home. Two realty agents who showed us homes we wanted to buy have refused to write up the purchase offers we wanted to make. One said he knew the seller wouldn't accept our offer, as she had turned down a better one. The other agent said the seller had to have more cash than we were offering. Isn't there some law about this?—*Marcos M.*

A. Yes. Real estate agents represent the property seller. To carry out their agency relationship, all offers must be presented to the seller, no matter how ridiculous the offer may appear to that agent.

Just last week a real estate saleswoman told me of a ridiculous offer she presented to a home seller. The buyers, a young couple with very good jobs but little cash for a down payment, offered $1,000 down payment on a house priced just over $100,000. Their offer provided for seller financing with monthly payments of $2,000 per month (which the couple can afford). Guess what happened? The seller accepted. The realty agent agreed to take a promissory note, secured by a third mortgage on the house, for her sales commission payable at $200 per month.

If that agent had not written up and presented that offer, nothing would have happened. But the happy result was a house was sold, the buyers bought their first home, and the realty agent will have a steady commission income until her note is paid in full.

Insist your purchase offer be written and presented to the seller. If the agent refuses, report the incident to the state real estate commissioner who may revoke the agent's license for failure to properly represent the seller.

IS THE REALTY AGENT THE SELLER'S OR BUYER'S AGENT?

Q. In a recent article you said "most realty sales involve two salespersons, one representing the seller and one representing the buyer." I disagree. In the usual transaction, the real estate broker who takes the listing from the owner becomes the agent of the owner. This also applies to salespersons working for that broker as well as cooperating brokers and salespeople (who become subagents). Unfortunately, too many agents give the impression they represent the buyer when, in truth, they are the seller's agent and owe their primary loyalty to him.—*Paul M.*

A. You are absolutely correct. I did not intend to imply otherwise. Real estate brokers are agents of the property owner who lists the property for sale. The owner is the principal, and the broker is the agent. Cooperating brokers and their salespeople who have a buyer for the property, as you emphasize, are subagents for the seller.

The status of the buyer, however, is unclear. Some courts have held him to be a third-party beneficiary of the principal-agent listing contract. Others simply say the realty broker and any subagent owe the buyer the same duty of honesty and full disclosure that is owed to the seller.

Since this can lead to conflicts of interest, some realty brokers have a policy of never allowing the same salesperson to work on behalf of both buyer and seller in a transaction.

To summarize, the realty broker is the property seller's agent. Cooperating brokers and salespeople who may have a buyer for the property are subagents of the listing broker. But these subagents must be just as honest with the buyer as they must be with the seller.

SHOULD REALTY AGENTS SNOOP INTO HOME BUYER'S FINANCES?

Q. We've just started looking for a home to buy. Every realty agent we talk to starts out by asking "How much to you want to invest?" Our reply is "As little as possible." Then the agent usually says something like "How much do you earn?" or "How much can you afford for monthly mortgage payments?" Isn't this pretty snoopy? Or is this customary for realty agents to probe this personal information?—*Dave N.*

A. Those snoopy real estate agents are trying to save your time and theirs. In the "good old days," realty agents used to waste time showing prospects homes they could not afford to buy. Today, wise realty agents cut the preliminaries and get down to business fast.

Chances are you cannot afford to buy the type of home you really want. Agents probe your financial situation, so that you will be shown only houses you can afford to buy.

Be honest with your agent. Tell him or her what you earn and how much you have to invest in the down payment. If you are short of cash for a down payment, do not hide this fact from your agent. There are dozens of ways to buy a home with little or no cash. Not every home can be bought this way, of course, but smart agents know which listings are good candidates for low or no down payments.

A probing realty agent also wants to find out if you are eligible for special home finance programs such as VA, FHA, or special state and federal mortgage programs. Asking questions is the only way the agent can learn this information. Some agents may seem snoopy, but they are just trying to help.

GET REALTY AGENT'S PROMISES IN WRITING

Q. We recently bought a condominium apartment that we like very much. The location, size, and price are ideal. Our problem is the salesman promised us things like new kitchen appliances, new carpets, and fresh paint. As we were in a hurry to move in, he said these things would be arranged later. It has been seven months since we moved in, and the work hasn't been started. The salesman has moved away, but the seller is still around. He says he knows nothing about these promises. What can we do to get these promised improvements?—*Cornelia G.*

A. See your attorney. Misrepresentations are hard to prove without some written agreement. If the seller's salesman made promises, those promises may be binding on the seller if you can prove the details.

Were there any witnesses? If not, you may have a tough time convincing a judge or jury. Next time, get all promises in writing as if you expect to wind up in court. If you are well prepared, then everything usually turns out fine.

COOPERATION AMONG REALTY AGENTS MEANS MORE PROPERTY SALES

Q. I am a novice real estate saleswoman, as I've had my license only four months. When I signed up with my broker, he told me the firm belongs to the multiple listing exchange, which it does. Although I've already brought in three new listings, my broker won't let me put them in the multiple listings. He says we earn more money if the sale is made within the firm. He even refuses to cooperate with other agents who phone to inquire about our ads for these houses. I'm pretty discouraged as my listings haven't sold yet. Am I working for a crooked broker?
—*Agnes D.*

A. Cooperation among real estate brokers from different firms means maximum total earnings for everyone. In most towns the local multiple listing service distributes listings to member brokers to get the widest market exposure so the best price and terms can be attained for the seller.

It is shortsighted policy for a broker to refuse to cooperate with other local realty agents. Although some large firms have this policy, those brokers eventually find other local agents will not cooperate with them either. Although the broker and salespeople earn higher fees on "in-house sales," I feel a noncooperation policy results in lower sales volume than would be attainable by cooperating fully with other local realty agents. Perhaps you should consider switching to a broker who is more progressive about use of the multiple listing service.

HOW TO SELECT THE BEST REALTY AGENT
TO SELL YOUR PROPERTY

Q. We understand it is difficult to sell homes now, but we must sell ours in the next few months. What is the best procedure for selecting the best realty agent who can get our home sold without cutting the price? —*Mr. A. F.*

A. In today's market it is more important than ever before to select the best real estate agent to professionally market your home. Many of the inferior realty agents are being forced out of the market, due to lack of commission earnings, but the top agents will survive and prosper.

Never select a real estate agent on the basis of his commission rate or estimated sales price of your home alone. Choose the agent who will do the best job marketing your home on the terms you specify. Of course, base your asking price and terms on current market conditions in your area. The realty agent can help you make these decisions.

Before listing your home for sale, invite at least three active local agents to discuss the listing (separately of course). Ask your friends for recommendations or select them from names of agents who advertise often in the newspaper or who have "sold" signs on homes near yours. When you talk to these agents, ask about their commission rates, probable sales price of your home, and anything else you want to know.

Disregard any agent who does not prepare a written "competitive market analysis" showing how he arrived at the estimate of your home's probable sales price. Before listing with any agent, phone his client references, then select the agent you feel will do the best job.

WILL CUT-RATE REAL ESTATE BROKERS SURVIVE?

Q. I am a new real estate broker. My office has just been open about four months and it isn't breaking even yet. I am considering switching to cut-rate and charging only a 4 percent sales commission. Our area had a cut-rate broker, but he only lasted about ten months before he closed. Do you think cut-rate real estate brokers will survive the current mortgage credit crunch?—*John B.*

A. Cut-rate realty brokers, who charge less than the 6 percent or 7 percent customary sales commissions, are prospering in some towns and starving in others.

As you know, real estate sales commissions are fully negotiable between the seller and agent. In the past, realty brokers were reluctant to cut their commission schedule, but some brokers are now doing so, especially on the higher-priced properties.

The biggest problem for cut-rate brokers is the lack of cooperation with other local brokers who may have buyers for their listings. Cooperating brokers have been reluctant to show listings of the cut-rate brokers because each agent then earns such a small sales commission.

If your commission is 4 percent of the sales price, for example, you would earn only 2 percent and the cooperating broker would earn 2 percent. It is almost impossible to pay expenses with such a small commission.

However, if you represent both the buyer and seller, then you can probably survive on a 4 percent commission if you have a high enough sales volume. Perhaps you should provide in your listings for a 4 percent commission if you represent both buyer and seller but a 6 percent commission if a cooperating broker represents the buyer. At least 50 percent of all residential sales involve two cooperating brokers, so you cannot afford to overlook them if you want to succeed.

WHY AN OPEN LISTING IS NO WAY TO SELL A HOME

Q. My husband's boss, who is quite knowledgeable about real estate, suggested we sell our home on an "open listing" with several real estate brokers. So we prepared a little flyer about the house's features, property taxes, insurance, and mortgage details. This was mailed to about twenty local realty brokers. The result has been lots of activity from these brokers, not so much to get our home sold but to get an exclusive listing from us. What should I do to get the brokers to sell my house instead of pestering me for an exclusive listing?—*Anne M.*

A. Your first mistake was to send that open listing flyer to the twenty brokers. A better approach would have been to list your home exclusively with one agent who would then cooperate with other local brokers, usually through the local multiple listing exchange, who may have a buyer.

An open listing is really no listing at all. That is because if you find a buyer for the house, the brokers earn nothing. The result is most good realty brokers work on open listings only on rainy days when they have nothing better to do.

Rarely will brokers advertise or spend much time trying to sell open listings, as you found out. The reason is open listings are a race between you and the brokers to find a buyer. Since the brokers lack control over your property, they prefer to work on selling their exclusive listing properties.

TO GET YOUR PROPERTY SOLD,
WRAP IT IN AN ATTRACTIVE PACKAGE

Q. Our home has been listed for sale several months in a town that has too many homes for sale. I blame this problem on the home builders who built too many homes, many of which are unsold. We have an excellent realty agent who tells us to be patient. She says there are about five homes listed for sale for every home which sells. What can we do to get our home sold as we've already bought another?—*Sue Ann C.*

A. To sell your home for top dollar, in good or bad times, wrap it in an attractive package. First, look at your home's physical condition. Be sure it is in top condition. Look at it critically to see if it needs painting, cleaning, or repairing. If so, get the work done.

Next, look at your home's financing package. If you are expecting an all-cash sale, you will be waiting a long time in today's market. To get your home sold, offer special finance terms, such as taking back a second mortgage at a reasonable interest rate for at least three to five years.

There are plenty of buyers for "red ribbon deals," like this, that combine an attractive home with affordable financing. Make your home stand out from the crowd of listed homes for sale.

For example, price your home at its full market value, maybe even a little higher. But offer to carry back a second mortgage at 10 percent interest. I guarantee that will get attention in today's market. It is much cheaper for you to cut the interest rate a little on that second mortgage than it is to have an unsold home.

WHY HOME SALE PRICES WILL NOT FALL

Q. I am a real estate saleswoman. Lately many of my prospective buyers have said they think home sale prices will drop soon. So they are holding back selling their old homes and buying larger ones. Do you think home sale prices will drop if we have a recession?—*Janet A.*

A. No. The volume of homes sales, of course, has dropped in 1980 and 1981 from previous years, due to the high cost of mortgage money. Few buyers can qualify for new mortgages at today's high interest rates. In some communities, the median home sales price has dropped too. But do not be fooled. What is happening is the less-expensive homes are selling in greater volume than are the more-expensive ones, thus dropping the median sales price.

Although we are definitely in a "buyer's market" as of this writing, since there are more homes for sale than buyers looking for homes to buy, prices are generally not dropping. But they are rising more slowly than they did in 1979.

Except in communities where there is an oversupply of new homes for sale, sellers are holding firm on prices. But they are becoming very flexible on sales terms, thus creating some terrific bargains for buyers.

Owning a home or other good property is not a speculative investment like gold, silver, or common stocks where the value fluctuates beyond the owner's control. If a real estate owner cannot get the price he wants, he just waits until he can. Have you ever heard of a realty owner selling for less than he paid for a property? It rarely happens in real estate, but it happens every day to owners of gold, silver, bonds, and common stocks.

In other words, the great benefit of real estate investing is the property owner controls the destiny of his property. Tell your buyers to buy now before mortgage interest rates drop substantially. When that happens, buyers will be out in droves and home sale prices will rapidly escalate because there will be a shortage of new and resale homes for sale.

11.

How Real Estate
Can Give You
Lifetime Income

The last chapter of a book is supposed to tie everything together. Well, this chapter will not let you down. But it will do more. Since you got this far in the book, you are now saying to yourself either (1) this real estate investing is hard work, and it is not for me, or (2) real estate is the best investment I have heard of, and I can hardly wait to get started.

Lazy people will have made the first choice. For them, investing in passive investments is probably best. While the risk is much greater in such investments, little work is required. The rewards can be spectacular, such as picking a common stock which goes up in value, but the losses can be disasterous because the passive investor has no control over what happens to his investment. That is why the New York Stock Exchange is known as the world's largest casino. It is a pure gamble. Of course, it is possible to lessen the risk by careful study before making passive investments, but all the research in the world will not assure a profit. Just talk to the bond investors who now have huge losses. The only way they can come out ahead is to hold their bonds to maturity, but those dollars they then collect will have depreciated in purchasing power by 5 percent to 15 percent *per year*. If you own a twenty-year bond, at maturity it will pay off in full, but those dollars will be virtually worthless.

But if you have concluded that real estate offers the best investment opportunities, you have made the right choice. However, I hasten to point out that real estate is not the perfect investment. There is none, so stop searching.

THE BIGGEST DISADVANTAGE
OF REAL ESTATE INVESTING

Management time is the biggest drawback of investing in real property. Real estate is not a passive investment. If you invest in real estate (with the possible exception of raw, vacant land), it requires management time to (1) locate the right property to buy, (2) negotiate with the seller for its purchase, (3) find tenants to pay the rent, (4) collect the rents, (5) handle necessary repairs and improvements, and (6) prepare your income tax returns to maximize your tax shelter benefits from the property.

Somehow, around April 15 each year, that last time-consuming requirement does not seem bothersome at all because it is always a pleasure to see how many income tax dollars do not have to be paid to Uncle Sam because of my property ownership. Although someone has to pay income taxes, let it be another person. Congress wrote the tax laws to encourage real estate investment because this policy results in more housing, commercial prosperity, and individual reward. Of course, the tax benefits of investing in real estate are a major incentive, but property should never be bought for the tax gimmicks alone.

THE BIGGEST ADVANTAGE OF REAL ESTATE INVESTING

Time is the biggest drawback of real estate investing. But the biggest advantage is its inherent, basic value if it is (1) well-located and (2) of basically sound construction. That is why good real estate does not lose value. In fact, in recent years most good properties have appreciated in market value at least at the pace of the inflation rate and usually faster.

While that is nice to know, and it means good real estate is a safe place to invest as an all-cash buyer, real estate is even more profitable for the highly leveraged buyer. To illustrate, suppose you buy a $100,000 property with $10,000 cash down payment. If that property appreciates in market value at an inflation rate of about 12 percent (1 percent per month), a year from now that property will be worth $112,000. But as a percentage return on your $10,000 investment, that $12,000 value increase is 120 percent. Not many alternative investments offer this leverage advantage available in real estate.

Even if the property only appreciates in value 5 percent in the next year, that $5,000 return on the $10,000 investment is a 50 percent profit. How many other investments do you know of offering such high returns to keep pace with inflation?

The nice thing about real estate is if you buy depreciable income property, such as apartments, rental houses, or commercial income property, the rent from the tenants usually pays the carrying costs while you make these profits. If the purchase is properly structured, there will be little or no negative cash flow. Larger properties produce substantial cash flow. Even if there is a negative cash flow in the early years of ownership, as rents increase with inflation, after a few years the negative cash flow is usually wiped out by rising rents.

THE SECOND-BIGGEST ADVANTAGE
OF REAL ESTATE INVESTING

Inherent basic land value is real estate's greatest advantage. In other words, its usefulness will not be wiped out overnight (as can happen with stocks, bonds, commodities, and other investments).

But the second-greatest advantage of real estate investing is it can provide lifetime income for the owner. The variations of how good real estate can provide income to the owner are limitless.

Many owners who have owned income property for a long time live off the net rental income. Although it is difficult in most communities to buy property today with a high net income, the longer you own the property the greater its net income usually becomes. While the owner waits for the rent income to increase with inflation, he enjoys the income tax savings from the depreciable property's tax shelter. Another way of saying this is, buy all the income property you can when you are young, so you can live off its income when you are old.

Another way rental property can provide income to its owner is by periodic refinancing. As the market value of your property holdings rises, refinance the mortgage every few years. I have one property that I have refinanced three times. That cash produced from refinancing is tax-free to be spent with no strings attached by Uncle Sam. Hopefully, if the refinance cash is not needed for living expenses, it will be invested in more good-income property.

Still another method of income production from real estate occurs when the owner decides it is time to dispose of a property, pay Uncle Sam his long-term capital gain tax on the profit, and cash monthly installment sale checks from the buyer. Many retirees do this. When they retire from their jobs, they sell their properties, carry the financing for the buyer on an installment sale mortgage, and enjoy the income from those monthly checks.

Recall Alice in the chapter on tax-deferred exchanges. She sold her apartment house because she grew tired of its management. Now she receives a nice monthly check from the buyer. Her only work is endorsing that check and depositing it in her bank account. If the buyer should fail to make the payments, Alice can foreclose and either (a) get paid off in cash by the buyer at the foreclosure sale or (b) get the property back to resell it for another profit.

To summarize, real estate offers the best of all worlds. During ownership, investment property can offer (a) tax shelter, (b) net income cash flow, (c) tax-free refinance cash, and (d) inflation hedge protection as the property appreciates in market value. When the owner eventually decides to dispose of the property, this can be done on an installment sale to minimize resale profit tax and to provide retirement income.

A footnote, however, is in order. If the owner does not sell his investment property during his lifetime, when he dies, there is no capital gain tax on what would have been profit if the property was sold before the owner's death. To illustrate, suppose you own property with an adjusted cost basis of $100,000. If its market value on the date of your death is $300,000, the $200,000 difference between market value and adjusted cost basis escapes capital gain tax. Of course, the $300,000 value will be included in your estate for federal estate tax and state inheritance tax purposes.

But if you had sold that property the day before your death, then the $200,000 capital gain profit would be taxable on your last income tax return. So even death offers tax shelter from profit taxes, but it is a rather extreme and irreversible way to get out of paying capital gains taxes. By the way, if you have been making tax-deferred exchanges in a chain of trades, all those deferred taxes are forgiven at death too. The same applies to any deferred profit taxes using the "residence replacement rule" on the sale and replacement of your residences.

Thanks to the magic of our tax laws, it is not only possible to legally avoid paying income taxes during the real estate owner's lifetime, but that same property's "profits" escape capital gains tax on accumulated profits at the time of death. So whether the owner dies while still owning real estate, or if he sells it and lives off the installment sale income, good real estate investments provide the best tax advantages of any investment.

QUESTIONS AND ANSWERS

IS TODAY A GOOD TIME TO INVEST IN VACANT LAND?

Q. I know of some terrific bargains in land for sale about a mile away from a just completed subdivision tract of homes. When home construction starts up again when mortgage interest rates come down, this land will be ideal for a builder to buy. I can get it for only $45,000 down payment. Do you think now is a good time to buy it?—*Ramos M.*

A. No. Even professional home builders do not want to own land ahead of the time they can build homes on it. Holding land is very costly for property taxes, mortgage interest, and other carrying costs. Just to break even, the land value must appreciate at least 25 percent each year (inflation eats up purchasing power currently at 12 percent per year, mortgage interest will cost at least 10–12 percent, property taxes are 1–3 percent of market value, realty agent's sales commission is 5–10 percent, and miscellaneous costs run 1–? percent per year).

Unless you are very wealthy, I doubt you have the "staying power" to hold the land for several years.

Professional builders, rather than buy land, now purchase options to buy it. Options are far cheaper, often just 1 percent to 3 percent of the purchase price, depending on the length of the option term. The option holder controls the land, even though he has only a small amount of option money at stake. Rather than buying that land, get an option on it so you will not lose much if things do not go as you expect. Many fortunes have been made speculating in land, but far more have been lost. You should be a winner, not a loser, so do not get tied up in land speculation that produces no tax shelter and no immediate ownership benefits.

SHOULD FORMER HOME BE SOLD OR RENTED?

Q. We recently bought a new home. Fortunately, the builder had a mortgage commitment at a low interest rate. Our question involves the wisdom of selling or renting our old home. Some friends say we should sell it, but others say we should keep it for the tax advantages. What do you suggest?—*Bruce H.*

A. The more real estate you own, the better protected you are against inflation. Keep your old home. Today is not an especially good time to sell a house unless you must, due to the high cost of mortgage money.

By keeping your old home, you will also gain some tax advantages. You will be able to depreciate the lower of (a) your basis for the house (excluding the value of the nondepreciable land) or (b) its market value on the date of conversion to rental status.

The result of this noncash depreciation deduction should be to shelter all of the rent income and some of your other orindary income, such as job salary, from income taxes.

Another advantage of keeping your old home is that when you eventually retire, you can sell the house on an installment sale to provide extra retirement income. Or if you have children to send to college, you can sell the house and use the payments to pay your children's college tuition. In the meantime, you will enjoy your old home's tax shelter for some of your ordinary income.

HOW TO CREATE YOUR REAL ESTATE MONEY MACHINE

Q. I recently read a book about real estate that suggested that people buy one rental property per year for investment. The author said that after a few years, the property would go up in market value due to inflation and the mortgage could be refinanced to produce tax-free cash to buy more properties. This sounds too good to be true. If it is true, would it be possible to keep doing this and then retire by selling one or two properties each year and take back the mortgage financing to provide retirement income?—*Becker M.*

A. Yes. I suspect you are referring to Robert G. Allen's terrific book *Nothing Down* (Simon and Schuster, 1980). It is true that money produced by refinancing is tax free. The plan is a sound one.

It is like creating your own "money machine" each time you buy an investment property. That property not only should produce tax-sheltered income for the owner, but when it is refinanced, the money produced is tax-free.

Of course, when investment property is eventually sold, Uncle Sam is waiting to collect his capital gain tax. But an installment sale can be used to spread out this tax bite over future years, thus avoiding a boost into a high income tax bracket in the year of sale and also providing safe retirement income.

The hard part, however, is buying your first investment property and then keeping on buying one more property each year. But when you see all the income tax advantages on April 15 as you pay little or no income tax, that should provide sufficient motivation to keep buying more properties.

TEN-YEAR TAX-FREE REALTY TRUST
PAYS CHILDREN'S COLLEGE TUITION

Q. My lawyer suggests I set up a "ten-year trust" to pay for my children's college tuition costs. He says the money I contribute to the trust can go to buy good real estate, with the net income accumulating tax-free. Is this a good idea?—*George T.*

A. Yes. Such a trust, called a "Clifford Trust," must be for at least ten years plus one day.

You can transfer either property now owned or newly acquired property to the trust. The net income is reinvested in the trust. At the end of the trust period, the assets can be used to fund your children's college expenses.

Such a trust will not cost you any after-tax dollars. If paid out before your child is twenty-one, the accumulated trust assets are tax-free. You still retain the normal dependency income tax deductions for your children while the trust assets are growing, tax-free, in market value. It sounds like you have got a smart attorney who understands tax planning. Real estate can be the vehicle to help you achieve your goals with the ten-year trust for your children.

INHERITED PROPERTY NOT TAXABLE TO HEIRS

Q. My late uncle left me a duplex worth about $100,000. Will I have to pay tax on it?—*Tom R.*

A. You may owe state inheritance tax, but this is usually paid by the estate's executor before you receive the property. However, you will not owe any capital gains tax.

Even though your late uncle probably had a lower book value for the duplex, your basis will be its $100,000 market value on the date of your uncle's death. If you sell it for $110,000, for example, only your $10,000 profit will be taxed (as a long-term capital gain, by the way).

But there is no capital gain tax to pay on the difference between the duplex's market value on the date of your uncle's death and his book value for the property. If he had sold the duplex the day before he died, he would have owed capital gain tax. But upon his death, all capital gain tax liability is forgiven. Your tax adviser can explain further.

HOW TO CASH IN YOUR CHIPS

Q. Over the last ten years my ex-wife and I have bought four rental houses in which we now have about $200,000 total equity. We want to "tap out" and use the proceeds for semiretirement. What is the best game plan to maximize the dollars available after selling these houses while minimizing our tax bite? I'm in a 44 percent income tax bracket and my ex-wife is in a 20 percent tax bracket.—*Mr. C. K.*

A. Installment sales would be ideal for you. The security is a first or second mortgage on the property sold.

Advantages to you and your ex-wife include (1) high-interest income on the buyer's unpaid balance, (2) safe investment secured by a second mortgage on the houses, (3) spreading out your profit tax into future years when your retirement income will be low, and (4) easy quick sale for top dollar due to the built-in financing. Ask your tax adviser to further explain installment sale tax advantages.

HOW PROPERTY INVESTMENTS CAN CREATE
LIFETIME INCOME

Q. At present I invest the maximum in a Keogh Retirement Plan. But considering the taxes I will owe when I withdraw that money after retirement, I figure I'm barely keeping up with inflation. Would I be better off investing my money in good real estate, such as land, instead? Then when I retire, I could sell off the land for my retirement income and take back mortgages.—*Edwina R.*

A. While your basic idea is sound, it needs some refinement. The major advantage of Keogh and IRS retirement programs is the money contributed is tax-exempt until you withdraw it. Another advantage is the compounding of interest if the money is well invested.

While real estate can match the interest compounding benefits, due to the advantages of realty leverage, the money you invest in real estate will not be tax-deferred unless you find a Keogh Plan trustee who will invest in land for you. Many will not.

Another aspect of your plan that needs thought is your idea of investing in vacant land. While land can be an excellent investment, it often does not go up in value fast enough to cover its carrying costs and inflationary loss of the dollar's purchasing power. Good income property often does much better.

Before you switch retirement plan strategies, talk to an estate planning attorney or other specialist. While real estate can provide secure retirement income, its acquisition must be carefully planned for maximum benefits. There is a right and wrong way to use real estate for your retirement planning. It does not appear you have found the right way yet.

HOW REAL ESTATE CAN PROVIDE
YOUR RETIREMENT SECURITY

Q. We look forward to your newspaper articles, especially the questions about investment properties. For the last twelve years my husband and I have bought at least one property per year. At first it was a struggle to save for the down payment. But now we just refinance one or two of the properties to give us cash to buy another. In September, my husband will retire at age fifty-five, thanks mostly to the security our investment properties give us. We plan to keep refinancing our properties, perhaps selling one occasionally on an installment sale mortgage. Keep telling your readers that investing in good income properties is the best way to beat inflation. Another big advantage is we haven't had to pay any income taxes for many years thanks to the tax shelter of the depreciation deductions.—*Gertrude J.*

A. Thank you for sharing your success story. It will convince more people of the merits of real estate investing than I can. Real estate is definitely the most tax-favored investment available, probably because so many member of Congress invest in real estate.

Your letter pointed out three primary reasons why investors buy real estate: (1) for a hedge against inflation, (2) income tax shelter for ordinary income, such as job salary, and (3) retirement security. Of course, there are other advantages too, such as leverage benefits, tax-free refinancing cash, long-term capital gains upon resale, and safety of investment. No other investment offers all the advantages of real estate.

FOR FURTHER READING

There are many excellent real estate books which should be read for further information on the various advantages of real estate investing. New real estate books are being published constantly so watch for new offerings. For further reading, here is a list of the best real estate books currently available at larger libraries and bookstores. Real estate is a field where investors and salespeople never stop learning better methods of investing in and selling property.

1. *Nothing Down,* by Robert G. Allen (Simon and Schuster, 1980), a classic book explaining creative finance methods for acquiring property with little cash.
2. *Tax Factors in Real Estate Operations,* sixth edition, by Paul E. Anderson (Prentice-Hall, 1980), a very thorough guide to the tax aspects of real estate investing, written by an attorney who emphasizes how realty investors can take advantage of tax laws.
3. *Double Your Money in Real Estate Every Two Years,* by Dave Glubetich (Impact Publishing, 1980), an outline of how to create profits in real estate by investing in single-family rental houses. This book is the sequel to Glubetich's earlier classic on how to invest in single-family rental houses, *The Monopoly Game* (Impact Publishing), now in its fourth edition.
4. *How I Turned $1,000 into Five Million in Real Estate,* by William Nickerson (Simon and Schuster, 1980), a revision of the classic textbook on how to pyramid profits in real estate by buying run-down property, improving it to increase its market value, and exchanging for larger property. The unfortunate aspect of this new edition is it was not completely updated from earlier editions, and it uses outdated information which is no longer accurate for today's investors. But the book is still a classic real estate guidebook.
5. *How You Can Become Financially Independent by Investing in Real Estate,* by Albert J. Lowry (Simon and Schuster, 1977), follows in the footsteps of Nickerson's basic book. This best-seller (which needs to be updated) adds new information to Nickerson's principles and is well worth reading.
6. *Landlording,* third edition, by Leigh Robinson (Express Publishing, 1980), a practical, humorous guide to property management by a pro who emphasizes the profit aspects of managing for maximum return from income realty.
7. *Real Estate Law,* by Charles J. Jacobus and Donald R. Levi (Reston Publishing Company, 1980), a nationwide survey of basics of real estate law which every realty investor should understand.

Index

Index

stock market vs., 1–2, 9–10, 252
real estate counselors, 23
real estate sales license, 118–119
realty agents, 233–251
    classified ads of, 105–106, 108
    commissions of, 147, 237, 248–249
    dealing with, 106, 112, 119, 197–198
    lease-options disliked by, 175, 192
    multiple listings books of, 107–108
    selection of, 106–107, 237–238, 248
    switch sheets of, 106
    tax-deferred exchanges and, 230
realty lenders. *See also* financing;
        mortgages
    balance sheets for, 124–125
    characteristics of, 121–122
    credit vs. equity, 123, 128
    income statement for, 125
    S&Ls as, 130
    sellers as, 129–130
    shopping for, 122, 133, 172
    standards of, 128–129
    types of, 129–133
"red ribbon deals," 117, 195, 214, 250
refinancing, 10, 19, 127, 148
REITs (Real Estate Investment
        Trusts), 127
rent
    as income, 18, 20, 149, 176
    paying of, vs. home ownership, 35
REO (real estate owned) property,
        144–145
residence replacement rule, 55–57, 58,
        64–65, 66–67, 68, 72, 202
retirement, planning for, 19–20, 94,
        116, 194
Roosevelt, Theodore, 2

S

safety, as investment factor, 5–8
sale-leasebacks, 139

S&Ls (savings and loan associations),
        130, 152, 171
sandwich leases, 145
savings accounts, 6–7, 8, 9, 10, 22
Savings Bonds, U.S., 6, 10
schools, 117
"Section 1031 exchanges," 14–15
security, defined, 128
sellers. *See* property sellers
senior citizens. *See* "over-55 rule"
    investments for, 22, 23
    life estate financing for, 143–144
    $125,000 home sale tax exemption
        for, 33
"shopper," defined, 133
Solomon, Gus J., 226
speculators, characteristics of, 75–76
Starker exchanges, 14, 222, 226–227,
        231–232, 240
"stepped-up basis," 58
success, key factors of, 3
supply and demand, as factor in real
        estate profits, 7–8, 21

T

Tax Act (1978), 53, 54, 69
Tax Act (1981). *See* Economic Recovery Tax Act (1981)
tax benefits. *See also* deductions, income tax; tax-deferred exchanges
    explained, 24–35
    of home ownership, 36–73
    as key to successful investing, 3
    as yield component, 9
tax credits
    defined, 79
    for energy conservation, 50–51
tax-deferred exchanges, 14–15, 146,
        207–208, 218–232, 240
    anti-churning rules for, 88–89
    basis calculations for, 223–224
    benefits of, 220–222

ABOUT THE AUTHOR

Robert Bruss writes the nationally syndicated "Real Estate Mailbag" question and answer newspaper column, the "Real Estate Notebook" newspaper feature on real estate trends, "Real Estate Law and You" articles about new court decisions affecting real estate, and "Real Estate Book Review" features. The Chicago Tribune–New York News Syndicate distributes these features to several hundred newspapers.

Originally from Minneapolis, Minnesota, Bruss graduated from Northwestern University's School of Business Administration in Evanston, Illinois, in 1962. He received his J.D. law degree from the University of California's Hastings College of the Law in San Francisco in 1967. He was admitted to the California Bar the same year. In 1968, he received his California real estate broker's license.

Bruss has been and is involved in ownership of investment properties, primarily houses, apartments, and commercial buildings. He gained much of his practical how-to-do-it real estate sales and management insight as investment manager with Grubb & Ellis Company in San Francisco. Grubb & Ellis Company is one of California's largest statewide real estate brokerages. Bruss also teaches real estate practice and real estate law courses at the College of San Mateo and for the continuing education division of the University of Southern California. He also serves as a director of the National Association of Real Estate Editors.